The Presidents and the Public

The Presidents
and the Public

Washington, D.C.

Congressional Quarterly Inc.

Congressional Quarterly Inc., an editorial research service and publishing company, serves clients in the fields of news, education, business, and government. It combines Congressional Quarterly's specific coverage of Congress, government, and politics with the more general subject range of an affiliated service, Editorial Research Reports.

Congressional Quarterly publishes the *Congressional Quarterly Weekly Report* and a variety of books, including college political science textbooks under the CQ Press imprint and public affairs paperbacks on developing issues and events. CQ also publishes information directories and reference books on the federal government, national elections, and politics, including the *Guide to the Presidency*, the *Guide to Congress*, the *Guide to the U.S. Supreme Court*, the *Guide to U.S. Elections*, *Politics in America*, and *Congress A to Z: CQ's Ready Reference Encyclopedia*. The *CQ Almanac*, a compendium of legislation for one session of Congress, is published each year. *Congress and the Nation*, a record of government for a presidential term, is published every four years.

CQ publishes *The Congressional Monitor*, a daily report on current and future activities of congressional committees, and several newsletters including *Congressional Insight*, a weekly analysis of congressional action, and *Campaign Practices Reports*, a semimonthly update on campaign laws.

An electronic online information system, Washington Alert, provides immediate access to CQ's databases of legislative action, votes, schedules, profiles, and analyses.

JK
518
.P7488
1990

Copyright © 1990 Congressional Quarterly Inc.
1414 22nd Street N.W., Washington, D.C. 20037

Printed in the United States of America

Library of Congress Cataloging-in-Publication Data
Presidents and the public.
    p.   cm.
    Summary: An examination of the President's relationship with the public, from public opinion cycles to news media to interest groups.
    ISBN 0-87187-573-X : $15.95
    1. Presidents--United States--Public opinion. 2. Public opinion--United States. 3. Press and politics--United States. 4. Pressure groups--United States. [1. Presidents--Public opinion. 2. Public opinion. 3. Press and politics. 4. Pressure groups.]
    I. Congressional Quarterly, inc.
JK518.P7488   1990
353.03'5--dc20   90-31001
                                                      CIP
                                                      AC

Authors: Harold F. Bass, Jr.; Dom Bonafede; Charles C. Euchner
Editors: Margaret Seawell Benjaminson, Michael Nelson,
   John L. Moore
Production Editor: Jamie R. Holland
Indexer: Patricia R. Ruggiero
Cover Designer: Jack Auldridge

Contents

The Presidents and the Public

It has long been recognized that presidential success rests largely on favorable public opinion. "Public sentiment is everything," Abraham Lincoln declared. "With public sentiment nothing can fail, without it nothing can succeed." [1]

The precursor of the modern president was Theodore Roosevelt, who expanded the role of the chief executive to include that of chief legislator and leader of public opinion. He converted the presidency into a "bully pulpit" from which he spoke out against industrial trusts and in behalf of conservationist causes. He was the first president fully to appreciate the value of public communications in enlisting the electorate's support for his programs and policies. TR (he was the first president identified by his initials) maintained that "publicity, publicity, publicity" was the most effective way to keep government responsive to the will of the people.

For the most part, as exemplified in the presidency of John F. Kennedy, the success and popularity of presidents is determined not just by legislation won and lost but also by their ability to set a political tone and direction, to instill trust and confidence, to offer a vision of the future, and to create a national consensus. As political scientist Richard E. Neustadt has stated, the power of the presidency is in the power to persuade.[2] That they must do through the various channels of communication available to them if they hope to influence Congress, retain control of their party, and win reelection. Summarizing the relationship between the president and the public, media specialist Doris A. Graber concluded that "the president's relations with the public are important to him in three major contexts: they affect his personal political survival; they are crucial to his ability to do his job well; and they are important for establishing his historical image." [3]

In dealing with the public, presidents have many advantages and resources: the deference accorded the office; the historical aura and stately trappings of the institution; an overshadowing political presence; a huge corps of aides who advise chief executives, plan their schedules, and handle public relations; and recognition that the Constitution states "the executive Power shall be vested in *a* President of the United States of America." These advantages set the president apart in the eyes of the public, yet none of them guarantees public support, without which a president cannot govern effectively.

The presidency forms the cornerstone of the U.S. political structure and is the most conspicuous symbol of the nation. The dependency of the office on public appeal was recognized by Woodrow Wilson, who, before becoming president, underscored the bigger-than-life presence of the president in national affairs: "Let him once win the admiration and confidence of the country, and no other single force can withstand him, no combination of forces will easily overpower him. His position takes the imagination of the country. He is the representative of no constituency, but of the whole people. When he speaks in his true character, he speaks for no special interest. If he rightly interpret the national thought and boldly insist upon it, he is irresistible; and the country never feels the zest for action so much as when its president is of such insight and calibre." [4]

A comparison of the British parliamentary system with the American system provides a clearer understanding of the American presidency and of its need for public support. In the British system the prime minister and the cabinet, collectively responsible for government decisions, rise and fall together. In the U.S. system, however, final authority in the executive branch is vested in one person. Furthermore, the American president is neither served by an extensive party organization nor tied institutionally to the national legislative body.

The eminent British writer C. P. Snow emphasized the differences between the American and British systems in a series of novels grouped under the title *Strangers and Brothers.* Snow pointed out that the British system produces "brothers" at the top of government who have served in their respective parties for years and have gained extensive experience in national administration. In contrast, newly elected presidents frequently appoint to high positions people they barely know. The administration may well be led by people who are strangers to one another and who have little experience with the federal bureaucracy or the complexities of managing a central government. The president alone is the cohesive element and as such is dependent on public support to make the system work.

The Public's Need for Presidential Leadership

Lacking a monarchy with its resplendent reminders of history and traditions, the American people look to the

By Dom Bonafede

president as the unifying symbol of the country. Presidential scholar Clinton Rossiter noted that "the president is the American people's one authentic trumpet, and he has no higher duty than to give a clear and certain sound." [5]

The imprint of the presidency is graphically etched on the American psyche. Historical time is measured by presidential clockwork: Americans speak of "the Jacksonian era," "the Hoover depression," "FDR's New Deal," "Lyndon Johnson's Great Society." When a crisis threatens the nation's security and welfare, Americans look to and rally around the president. The White House itself—said by Thomas Jefferson to be "big enough for two emperors, one Pope and the Grand Lama"—is revered as a national shrine.

Political scientist Robert S. Hirschfield has written, "The office is truly a mirror of our national life, reflecting accurately the events that have made our history, the men we have chosen, for better or worse, to deal with those events, and our own willingness to entrust them with enormous authority over the nation's destiny." [6]

The emotional attachment of Americans to their presidents is evident when a president dies in office. The psychic impact of the death is reflected in the increase in public esteem and affection for the fallen president. This phenomenon is especially evident in the martyrdom of Lincoln and Kennedy and the nationwide mourning at the death of Franklin Roosevelt near the close of World War II.

As the chief representative of the most venerable democracy in history, the president looms as a sort of mythic superhero. Yet, ironically, the American presidency is riddled with anomalies and contradictions. The holder of the office is variously perceived as having too much power or too little power, as being too strong or too weak. The office has a physical presence, embodied in the White House and the legions of aides who surround the president; yet it has an almost spiritual aura as well.

In *The State of the Presidency* political scientist Thomas E. Cronin wrote, "Our expectations of, and demands on, the office are frequently so paradoxical as to invite two-faced behavior by our presidents." [7] Americans want their presidents to be compassionate, but tough enough to deal with the country's foes, as did John Kennedy in the 1962 Cuban missile crisis. Presidents should be religious, but not wear their piety on their sleeve, as some observers felt Jimmy Carter did. The country wants inspirational leaders, but not those who promise more than they can deliver, as did Lyndon Johnson in the Vietnam War. And Americans generally want an ordinary person who will give a seemingly extraordinary performance, as did Harry S Truman.

Virtually every move the president makes and every word uttered is transmitted to the public, especially in an age of mass communications. An archivist records to the second the president's comings and goings; the identity of visitors to the White House and the length of their stay; the papers read, documents signed, meetings attended, and speeches delivered. Even the president's choice of food at meals, hour of rising and retiring, and moments of relaxation alone or with family are chronicled for the public and posterity. No person is so public and yet so alone in carrying out official decision-making responsibilities, all of which adds to the mystique that envelops the presidency.

Political scientist Grant McConnell has proposed that the mystique of the presidency is part of what endows the office with informal, unstated power. Despite the intense scrutiny and criticism the president endures, "the aura of grandeur remains . . . no exposure of pettiness or human fallibility can destroy it. Indeed, the attention that hangs upon his every word and all the criticisms are signs that the president combines the symbolic role of chief of state with the substantive one of head of government. Every expectation proclaims that he is a man of power, and at every point the expectation is itself a source of power." [8]

Perhaps no president combined mystique, power, and public appeal more effecively than FDR. As one scholar wrote: "Voters knew that his legs were crippled by polio, but it seemed impossible that one who sounded so vigorous could be seriously handicapped. Careful, defensive management of the 'visual' helps to explain why. The White House discouraged the publication of photographs showing FDR from the waist down—and few such photographs appeared in print. Roosevelt's patrician artifices—the pince-nez and the cigarette holder—helped to make him look supremely self-confident. In our pictures of Roosevelt, we see a man so sure of himself that his vitality bursts out of the frame. The props help: that so-called fighting jaw, the angle of the cigarette holder, the rumpled hat. Roosevelt was our modern presidential salesman, the man who knew how to flatter and cajole."

Packaging and Selling Presidents and Policies

The advent of television, refinements in the "packaging" of candidates and the marketing of issues, the scientific canvassing of public opinion, and the sophisticated use of mass communications have radically changed electoral politics and the politics of governing.

To win election, lead the nation, deal with Congress, and negotiate with foreign governments, presidents must be able to strike a popular chord and gain the endorsement of the electorate. Their principal means of winning public support is through the mass media (chiefly network television and the national press) and other means of communication, including formal speeches, official proclamations, televised news conferences, press releases, nonattributable backgrounders, statements by designated spokespersons, domestic and foreign travel, and private talks with members of Congress, journalists, special interest advocates, financiers, and world leaders. Presidents learn this lesson long before entering the White House, for favorable public opinion is as important in winning an election as it is in governing the nation.

Selling the Candidate

The day after his defeat in the 1984 presidential election, Walter Mondale, the Democratic candidate, commented on the pervasive influence of the news media—particularly television—on campaign politics:

> Modern politics requires television. I think you know I've never really warmed up to television; in fairness to television, it's never really warmed up to me. . . . I like to look someone in the eye. . . . I don't believe it's possible any more to run for president without the capacity to build confidence and communications every night. [9]

As Mondale's remarks suggest, the changes in mass communications have radically altered the way politics is conducted. Candidates are tutored on how to deal with the media; their appearances are timed for maximum media exposure; and their speeches are written with the media in mind—for a thirty- or sixty-second "bite" that television producers can easily fit in their newscasts.

Almost all national candidates have media consultants who, along with the pollsters, professional campaign strategists, political advertising producers, and direct-mail specialists, make up the new political elite.

Author Theodore White observed in 1972, "Television *is* the political process: it's the playing field of politics. Today, the action is in the studio, not in the back rooms." [10] The influence of television has shifted emphasis from substance to style, and issues often are turned into slogans. Whereas television once covered news, news is now produced for television. An indistinguishable line exists between reality and imagery.

Modern presidential campaigns, therefore, center on "media events"—elaborately choreographed public appearances. The purpose of the careful planning and strategic scheduling behind such events is to draw press attention to the candidate for transmission to the voting public. Often, the size of the press contingent at a campaign affair and the stature of the news organizations they represent is more important than the number of people in the audience.

To a great extent, the press itself is recognized as a constituency. Solely for the benefit of the news media, campaign officials set up "press opportunities" in which reporters can talk with the candidates and photographers can take pictures. "Walking tours" are scheduled during which the candidate, followed by reporters, photographers, and television crews, visits potential supporters. Campaign staff also regularly set up press conferences, select interviews, and background briefings. Sometimes, brief, informal interviews are arranged between the press and the candidate on the campaign plane, in a hotel room, even in the candidate's rented limousine.

To political candidates, mass media coverage entails both "free" coverage provided by news organizations and "paid" coverage—television and radio commercials—supplied and paid for by them or their supporting campaign organizations. Although candidates attempt to manipulate free coverage, they cannot directly control it. For viewers, free coverage is more credible than paid commercials.

Another reason for presidential candidates to seek media exposure is the high cost of campaigning, particularly in an era when a thirty-second campaign commercial on prime-time network television may cost $150,000. It is a basic principle of politics that the candidate who garners media attention has a better chance of receiving public acceptance and raising campaign funds.

The Citizens' Research Foundation, a private group that studies campaign financing, reported that spending on national, state, and local political campaigns reached a record high of almost $2 billion in the presidential election year of 1988. Of that total, an estimated $500 million was spent by presidential candidates. It is generally acknowledged that from 50 to 75 percent of most candidates' campaign budgets is spent on political advertising, the vast proportion on television.

Selling the President

The first president to use public opinion surveys as they are known today was Franklin Roosevelt. From time to time Hadley Cantril, a Princeton University professor sometimes referred to as "the father of polling," and George Gallup conducted surveys for FDR. But not until the 1960s, when John Kennedy retained Louis Harris, did polls became an accepted tool of the White House to gain outside perspectives on presidential actions and to learn the concerns of the public.

In his book *The Selling of the President,* an inside account of Richard Nixon's 1968 presidential campaign, Joe McGinniss disclosed the critical role of professional media advisers and the way politics are shaped by contrived imagery, manipulation of the news media, and exploitative campaign advertising—in sum, how candidates often try to deceive voters with illusions. McGinniss noted that Eisenhower had used the New York advertising firm of Batton, Barton, Durstine and Osborn while in the White House and in his reelection campaign. Eisenhower also relied on actor Robert Montgomery to advise him on how to use the new medium of television.

McGinniss quoted Leonard Hall, the national Republican chairman in 1956, saying, "You sell your candidates and your programs the way a business sells its products." McGinniss concluded, "It is not surprising then that politicians and advertising men should have discovered one another. And, once they recognized that the citizen did not so much vote for a candidate as make a psychological purchase of him, not surprising that they began to work together. The voter, as reluctant to face political reality as any other kind, was hardly an unwilling victim." [11]

Jimmy Carter was the first president to include his pollster, Patrick H. Caddell, as a regular member of the White House staff—a sign in itself of the rising importance of public opinion surveys in the presidential decision-making process. Gerald Rafshoon, an Atlanta advertising executive and member of Carter's band of loyal Georgian aides, was teamed with Caddell, and together they provided public opinion research and marketing services for the president's policies. By this time it was recognized that "selling the president" was no longer so simple as promoting brand-name soap; rather, it involved computer science, socioeconomic data, and psychological analyses to plumb the motivational and behavioral aspects of public attitudes. Subsequently, Richard B. Wirthlin, a California-based public opinion specialist, performed a similar function for Ronald Reagan. Thus the president's pollster became an accepted part of the White House staff.

Presidents do not, however, blindly follow the findings of their pollsters or of those outside the White House. Caddell reported that Carter often questioned the polls; instead of being led by them, he used poll results to govern in keeping with his own convictions and instincts. Also, Reagan continued to push for U.S. aid to the contra rebels in Nicaragua despite public opinion polls that showed the majority of Americans to be against such help. In such instances, presidents can portray themselves courageously adhering to their principles rather than abandoning them to the caprices of public opinion or the demands of special interests.

A National Theater

The camera's eye focuses on the stately double doors. There is a long moment of silence. Suddenly, as if by magic, the two panels open and the president of the United States appears, standing tall and impeccably tailored. He is smiling slightly, and exuding confidence. As the camera pans in on him he strides briskly down the long East Wing corridor. With jaunty self-assurance, he hops on the platform and, flanked by the U.S. and presidential flags, looks into the face of America. It is the opening of one of Ronald Reagan's news conferences—a simple yet highly polished scene, minutely scripted and carefully orchestrated by his media advisers. What he says afterwards may well be of secondary importance; for in television, as Richard Nixon once noted regretfully, it often seems that it is looks that count.

The presidency is a form of national theater in which the chief executive is the most visible and important actor on the American stage. Presidents have recognized this since the Republic's beginning.

George Washington once a week held an afternoon reception, a "levee," at which he met with members of the public. Aware of the importance of the president's appearance, Washington saw to it that when he went riding, his horse's "hoofs were meticuloulsy blacked, its mouth washed out, its teeth picked and cleaned, its hide curried to a satin sheen."

Several years after Washington's death, John Adams offered an assessment of the first president's proclivity for the dramatic: "If he was not the greatest President he was the best Actor of the Presidency we have ever had. His Address to the States when he left the Army; his solemn Leave taken of Congress . . . his Farewell Address to the People when he resigned his Presidency. These were all in a strain of Shakespearean and Garrickal excellence in Dramatic Exhibitions." [12]

Almost a century and a half later Herbert Hoover, commenting on the same theme, sadly observed in his *Memoirs,* "I was convinced that efficient, honest administration of the vast machine of the Federal government would appeal to all citizens. I have since learned that efficient government does not interest the people as much as dramatics." [13]

As Hoover realized, modern presidents often must couch their ideas and proposals in melodrama to attract public attention and win support.

Looking to Peoria

Nixon's domestic policy adviser, John Ehrlichman, popularized the phrase "Will it play in Peoria?" The question, a common criterion at the highest levels of government, is asked to determine whether people throughout the United States—beyond Washington's political community—will endorse a particular presidential decision or administration policy proposal. Within that context, Peoria is a metaphor for "Middle America."

Before leaving on June 2, 1982, for a series of consultations with Western European leaders, President Reagan commented, "I know that what we've been doing doesn't read well in the *Washington Post* or the *New York Times,* but believe me, it reads well in Peoria." In so saying, Reagan was underscoring his support among the many Americans uninfluenced by Washington's intense political climate and Eastern establishment press.

Probably more than anyone else, politicians and government officials are cognizant of the relationship between public opinion and public policy. They know that the perceptions that most people have of events and public figures are filtered through the press and that much of the power

of the press lies in its selectivity—which stories make the news and how much emphasis is given to them. Recognition of the news media's influence on public opinion, in turn, often determines how the decision makers propose and promote presidential initiatives.

In a book on his White House years, John Ehrlichman provides a case in point:

> I would estimate that Richard Nixon spent half of his working time on the nonsubstantive aspects of the presidency, and probably 40 percent of that half dealing with the problems of communication. I have watched Nixon spend a morning designing Walter Cronkite's lead story for that evening and then send Ron Ziegler, Henry Kissinger or me out to a press briefing to deliver it in such a way that Cronkite couldn't ignore it. [14]

By all accounts, most contemporary presidents have operated in the same fashion.

Going Public

According to political scientist Samuel Kernell, "the frequency with which presidents in the past half century have communicated directly with the American public shows that the more recent the president, the more often he goes public." [15] Kernell contends that new communications technology and modes of transportation have enabled contemporary presidents to adopt an innovative strategy of going public to solicit popular support, thus substantially replacing political bargaining as a means to achieve their objectives.

He notes that since the early 1960s presidents have steadily increased their prime-time TV exposure. In 1981 Ronald Reagan delivered eight major televised addresses, setting a first-year record for any president.

Between the 1940s and the late 1980s, the annual number of minor public addresses by presidents increased fivefold. Foreign and domestic presidential travel also increased significantly, often solely in search of favorable publicity.

One of the compensations that presidents enjoy when fighting for their policies and programs or seeking reelection is constant media exposure. They are the prime news subject in the country, and they receive worldwide media coverage. No political rival can match the president as a publicity attraction. Also at the president's disposal is a vast publicity machine with a reach that encircles the globe.

The president has access to a fleet of the most modern aircraft and the services of U.S. Army Signal Corps specialists. The White House is equipped with its own television and radio broadcast facilities. A large staff of communications and public relations experts choreograph activities to ensure that the chief executive looks presidential. White House photographers are almost always present to record moments large and small in the president's daily routine. A highly structured White House press office deals with the constant demands of the news media. Speechwriters draft and polish the president's messages.

Today, it is acknowledged that continual publicity is a critical aspect of presidential politics. As former journalist and White House aide Douglass Cater observed, publicity is as essential to the orderly functioning of modern American government "as the power to levy taxes and pass laws." [16]

Patterns of Public Opinion toward Presidents

President James A. Garfield complained that he was "the last person in the world to know what the people really want and think." Today, with the development of the mass media and the refinement of opinion survey techniques, it is unlikely that a president would utter the same complaint.

David B. Truman, an American government scholar, defines public opinion as "the expression of an attitude on an issue or proposition." There are, however, a number of publics, divided, for example, by race, religion, cultural background, political affiliation, social beliefs, occupational pursuits, and financial income. To enhance their leverage and promote their interests, they may band together into organizations, such as the American Bankers Association, Veterans of Foreign Wars, U.S. Chamber of Commerce, or National Wildlife Federation.

Public opinion, however, can change dramatically over time or through a revised perspective on an issue. The American public had been staunchly opposed, for example, to the recognition of Communist China; but Nixon's celebrated trip to the People's Republic in 1972 led to a policy of accommodation, and many Americans, following the president's leadership, reversed their position.

Because presidents are constantly in the public eye, they are particularly vulnerable to the subtle and sometimes tempestuous shifts in the winds of popular sentiment. No matter what they do, their public standing fluctuates erratically since they seldom can fully satisfy the expectations their supporters had when they entered office. Even as President Reagan achieved consistently high popularity ratings, many of his followers on the far right expressed displeasure because they felt he had not gone far enough in following the conservative credo.

Occasionally, the public turns on a president even when the White House is not fully the cause of what went wrong. As a case in point, President Carter bore the brunt of public displeasure in 1979 when OPEC (Organization of Petroleum Exporting Countries) policies led to a hike in U.S. gasoline prices. Yet the public is just as likely to rally around the president during periods of national peril, even those that administration policies may have created. For example, Americans supported President Kennedy in the 1961 Bay of Pigs fiasco when U.S.-backed Cuban exile forces failed in an effort to invade the island and overthrow Fidel Castro.

Minute scrutiny by the national news media further intensifies the ebb and flow of presidential public opinion. Harry Truman, who disdained presidential pandering to public opinion surveys and was subject to wild swings in popularity, said the experience was "like riding a tiger."

Public Opinion Cycles

Students of government almost universally agree that presidents begin their tenure in office with a high level of popular support and a willingness, even an eagerness, by the public to accord them a full measure of trust and goodwill. A subliminal sense exists that the public and the president are joined in the hope that the new administration can bring peace and prosperity to the nation. This period of good feeling, roughly the first few months of a presidency, is referred to as the "honeymoon."

Although there are risks of misreading the events of an administration's early days, the period does offer a convenient opportunity to take the measure of the new president and project what may be expected throughout the term. During that brief spell, presidential character begins to form, working habits are set, and the changing of the guard is nearly completed. Following FDR's first one hundred days, Walter Lippmann wrote, "We became again an organized nation confident of our power to provide for our own security and to control our destiny." [17]

The fickleness of public opinion toward a president is reflected in President Gerald R. Ford's experience. The euphoric spirit in which his administration began was promptly deflated by his pardon of Nixon and offer of conditional amnesty for Vietnam draft evaders and war deserters. He also incurred criticism because he appeared unwilling—or unable—to get out from under the shadow of his predecessor, particularly in his insistence on keeping Nixon holdovers on the White House staff and his reluctance to reorganize the cabinet. After one hundred days, the Ford White House still lacked its own distinctive character, other than that of a benign stewardship—a trait that plagued his entire presidency.

Reagan's early days were widely perceived as a personal success, marked by the release of the American hostages from Iran at the same time that he was taking the oath of office. A "second honeymoon" followed the assassination attempt on March 30, 1981. There was, however, less effusion in many quarters over Reagan's supply-side economic plan and the retraction of his pledge to balance the budget by 1983. Moreover, each of his introductory overtures in foreign affairs prompted controversy—the elevation of the El Salvador conflict to a test of U.S.-Soviet relations, the lifting of the Soviet grain embargo, and the proposed sale of AWACS (Airborne Warning and Control System) surveillance planes to Saudi Arabia.

In the next stage of the opinion cycle, as presidents push their programs, the gloss begins to wear thin. Their proposals inevitably antagonize certain interest groups, and their popularity, predictably, begins to decline. Their public rating may erode further in a third stage if unemployment increases, the president becomes engaged in partisan politics during the midterm elections, or a military operation goes sour. In 1980, for example, many people viewed President Carter's aborted attempt to rescue the American hostages in Iran as an example of his inability to take decisive action at the opportune moment. In November 1980 he lost his bid for reelection.

Since Truman, every president except Eisenhower, Kennedy, and Reagan has left office less popular than when he entered. Throughout the term, however, the presidents' popularity rose and fell in response to numerous unforeseen influences. Truman is said to have been the most and least popular U.S. president, fluctuating between an extraordinarily high rating of 87 percent shortly after he became president and a low of slightly more than 20 percent at one point in his second term. Reagan, recognized as the most effective public relations president since FDR, received only a 37 percent approval rating at the midpoint of his first term, lower than any of the four preceding presidents at that stage of their administrations. But he left office with a 63 percent approval rating—the highest since FDR's 66 percent.

Lyndon Johnson reversed the traditional pattern, receiving low marks for his foreign policy decisions—those pertaining to the Vietnam War—and high marks for his Great Society domestic policies at the start of his presidency. By the end of his administration, his popularity had dropped measurably because of mounting Vietnam War casualties and suspicions that he had lied to the people about the conduct of the war, creating what became known as his "credibility gap."

Traditionally, public evaluation of presidential leadership hinges more on performance than on personal qualities. In this regard, domestic policy issues invariably provoke sharply divided public responses because of the involvement of deeply felt political and personal interests. Big business, for example, reacted unfavorably when President Kennedy forced a roll back in steel price rises in 1962, as did many southerners when the White House enforced the 1954 Supreme Court school desegregation decision.

International events, meanwhile, can cut both ways. As political scientists Richard A. Watson and Norman C. Thomas have noted, dramatic events involving national and presidential prestige—such as Reagan's 1983 Grenada invasion and his air strikes against Libya in 1986—produce a "rally-round-the-flag" phenomenon, with Americans generally supporting their president. However, long-term wars that inflict a heavy toll in casualties, such as those in Korea and Vietnam, can cost the president public support. [18]

How the Public Judges Presidents

Scholars are generally at pains to determine what influences presidential popularity and why. Steven A. Shull, a political scientist, observed, "It seems to be affected by events, the economy, media, the type policy involved, and the style of the president." [19]

The public, not unnaturally, assesses presidents largely from a personal perspective. Favorable opinion may be based on ideological compatibility or simply on whether, as Ronald Reagan suggested, the country seems to be better off than it was under the previous administration.

Among the qualities Americans look for in their presidents is leadership. Americans want chief executives who are steadfast in their convictions—not mired in self-doubts, like Warren Harding, who asked, "Am I a big enough man?" The public clearly prefers activist presidents who perform seemingly superhuman acts of courage and who, for the good of the country, extend their powers to the outermost limits when confronted with war or economic depressions, as did FDR. Americans respect as well the strength of character Truman displayed during the Korean War, particularly in his recalling of Gen. Douglas MacArthur, and during the tensions of the cold war.

Presidential personality, style, and image—that is, how presidents comport themselves and exemplify national values—also are important to the country. Wit counts, too. John Kennedy received high marks both at home and abroad when, during his first official trip to Paris, he introduced himself as the husband of Jacqueline Kennedy, rather than as the president of the United States.

Unfair as it is, presidents susceptible to physical mishaps or clumsiness become victims of public embarrassment. Ford is the most glaring example. Despite his background as a college athlete, he earned a reputation as a bumbler when photographed falling while skiing, hitting his head exiting *Air Force One,* and tumbling down the ramp on arriving in Salzburg, Austria, in June 1975. In his

presidential memoirs, Ford wrote that "every time I stumbled or bumped my head or fell in the snow, reporters zeroed in on that to the exclusion of almost everything else." [20] Carter suffered a similar indignity when he was forced to drop out of a long-distance run because of exhaustion.

To succeed, presidents must exhibit rhetorical prowess—the ability to lift the spirits of people with words and ideas and crystallize a vision for the nation. FDR boosted the country's flagging morale during the Great Depression when he asserted in his 1933 inaugural address, "The only thing we have to fear is fear itself." Kennedy's call to service in his inaugural address in 1961 has become part of the national lore: "Ask not what your country can do for you—ask what you can do for your country."

Americans are most likely to view presidents favorably when they are seen performing ceremonial duties or are projected as personal embodiments of the nation's constitutional and moral values. Such activities include signing legislation, greeting heads of state, welcoming home members of the military wounded in hostile action, or delivering a televised speech dealing with an issue vital to the national well-being. Presidents also invoke a favorable public impression when they are portrayed as family men or pictured in situations common to most Americans, as was Ford in the photograph of him toasting his own English muffins for breakfast.

Eventually, all presidents discover that public opinion can be overpowering. Woodrow Wilson's dream of a League of Nations was destroyed on the shoals of dissenting public opinion. In 1945-1946, after the end of World War II, public pressure to "bring the boys back home" and to demobilize the armed forces was irresistible despite diplomatic imperatives for maintaining a strong military force in Europe. Johnson decided against seeking reelection when it became painfully clear that most Americans were opposed to the Vietnam War. Once the tide of public opinion swept against him at the height of the Watergate scandal, Richard Nixon became the first U.S. president to resign from office. Sometimes, White House public relations plans go awry, as did Ford's anti-inflation campaign featuring buttons labeled "WIN"—whip inflation now. And public impatience to win the release of the American hostages in Iran perceptibly diminished Carter's popular standing and contributed significantly to his defeat in 1980.

Avenues of Communication

Historically, the most significant link between presidents and the American public has been the press. But presidents also have other means of seeking and measuring support for themselves and their policies. Political parties (although more significant in the past than today), the president's own pollsters and public liaison staff, interest groups, and personal appearances both in the United States and abroad are among the other ways the president communicates with the public.

Political Parties

Political organizations first took shape in the 1790s, but not until the election of Andrew Jackson in 1828 did public participation in the parties become widespread. National politics polarized around Jackson and his opposition, and Jackson turned to the public for support. As Bruce Buchanan wrote, "Jackson used his charismatic personality to arouse the consciousness of [the middle] class and focus its attention on the presidency as the instrument for protecting and furthering its interests. In the process, he showed that a president backed strongly by the mass public had the leverage to impose his leadership and make the constitutional system work.... The Jackson presidency was the first great historical demonstration of the contribution made by public support to presidential effectiveness." [21]

By the early twentieth century, throngs of immigrants had moved into the cities, and political machines were held together largely by patronage. Local party organizations, to gain converts and ensure votes, acted as welfare agents, providing jobs, food, loans, and clothes and steering these new Americans through the coils of bureaucratic red tape. Although these functions of the parties changed in the 1930s when the government, under Roosevelt's New Deal, took over many of these tasks, parties remained the principal instrument for selecting and electing presidents until the late 1960s. Because of deep dissension at its 1968 convention, the Democratic party undertook a series of reforms that changed the presidential nominating system and, in a larger context, altered the face of American politics. The party "opened up" the nominating process by augmenting the number of rank-and-file party members as delegates to the national conventions and by accelerating the growth of binding state primaries. The number of primaries grew to 23 in 1972, 30 in 1976, and 38 in 1980, severely limiting the ability of party leaders to handpick delegates. Although Republican party leaders were under less pressure from within to change the rules than were their Democratic counterparts, they too were prompted by state laws to institute reforms that opened the party's nominating process more to rank-and-file voters.

As the parties declined, the role of the media in American politics vastly expanded. Today, it is mainly the media that assess the candidates and, to a degree, select the issues—functions that formerly belonged almost exclusively to the parties. Moreover, the public's impressions of candidates and issues are mostly transmitted through the prism of the news media. Because candidates are less reliant on and less beholden to their party, they run campaigns that are virtually independent of the party but that are quite dependent on the media to project their persona. The media have become the main forum in which the political process is played out.

Critics insist that party reforms have led to unfavorable consequences. Some Democrats assert that under the old system neither George McGovern, Jimmy Carter, nor Michael Dukakis could have been nominated and that the party would not have suffered the damage it did by their political defeats. They additionally stress that the accountability of the new political amateurs and the media representatives is not commensurate with the power of their enlarged roles.

Critics further maintain that national party conventions have evolved into synthetic, made-for-television productions, their outcomes foreordained in the extended primaries. Political scientists William Crotty and Gary Jacobson observed, "The role of the political party in campaigns has given way to the technology of television-centered campaigns built on polls and run by media and public relations experts." [22] For the most part, the conventions

have become ceremonial investitures, an amalgam of politics and show business.

Defenders argue that the reforms tended to democratize the process by opening it to citizen activists and independents, creating new political coalitions. And as Byron E. Shafer has pointed out, the reforms could be seen not only in the identity of the candidates themselves, but "in a shift from party careerists to political insurgents, from insiders to outsiders. [23]

As a consequence of the restructured political process, which diminished the power of machine bosses, the news media became the principal intermediary in the public's relationship with candidates and government officials.

News Media

In 1980 James David Barber described national political journalists as the "new kingmakers" or the "new power brokers." He contends that "journalism took over where the parties left off." Another writer, Stephen Hess, has suggested that the nation is moving "from party democracy to media democracy."

With ample justification, the United States has been called "the first media state." Network television and the national press are no longer simply observers or instant chroniclers of events. Because they interpret as well as report on public affairs, government policy, and popular attitudes, the media have become an integral part of the political process.

The media emerged from the Vietnam War and Watergate more confident—arrogant, in the view of their critics—and freer than ever of some of their self-imposed restraints. Since the war, news organizations have become bigger, more diverse, more influential, and more controversial. In fact, they have become such a participatory ingredient in political life that policy makers and the public alike have a sense that many events do not really take place unless they are witnessed and reported by television and the newspapers or news magazines.

Most presidents enter the White House promising an "open administration" and frequent news conferences. Then, after a relatively brief honeymoon, the president becomes convinced that the media, because of their criticism, are intent on undermining the administration. The media are equally persuaded that the White House in its self-interest is withholding or distorting potentially embarrassing information and seeking to cover up mistakes, errors in judgment, and poorly conceived and executed policies.

Carter's presidency serves as an example. Shortly before his inauguration, Carter said, "If I can stay close to the people of this country . . . I think I have a chance to be a great president." He pledged to hold press conferences every other week. On alternate weeks, as part of the White House's media liaison program, out-of-town editors and broadcasters were invited to Washington to hear administration executives and to meet with the president. Nonetheless, by the end of his administration Carter was holding press conferences less than once a month. Later, he asserted that one of his deepest disappointments as president was "the irresponsibility of the press." [24]

Acknowledging the predictability of relations between the White House and the media, Tom C. Korologos, a congressional lobbyist in the Nixon White House and a transition planner for Reagan, said, "His [Reagan's] relations with the press will be like all presidents. You can put it on a graph. They all start out great, and then one day the White House press secretary comes in and throws his briefcase at the wall. The press thrives on controversy and, in effect, constitutes the opposition government." [25]

Inevitably, what starts out on a harmonious note deteriorates into an adversary relationship. Presidential press conferences occur less frequently. The White House permits only selective interviews with proadministration journalists and cultivates the news media outside of Washington. Finally, the White House circumvents the Washington media by relying more heavily on carefully scheduled presidential speeches and personal appearances, appeals to interest groups, extensive travel, information by news release, and public statements by faithful surrogates.

Television, above all, has changed the relationship between the press and the presidency.

Modern presidents and their advisers are keenly aware that television has increasingly become the medium through which the great majority of voters get their news and form their impressions of public figures. It has allowed presidents to virtually monopolize the political limelight and convey to the American people the impression that they can effectively cope with the problems and crises facing the country.

It has become part of political lore that television enhanced the candidacy of John F. Kennedy in his quest for the White House against Richard Nixon, contributed to Lyndon Johnson's downfall, provided Jimmy Carter with national exposure, and made Ronald Reagan one of the most popular presidents of the twentieth century.

In the pretelevision era, it would have been almost impossible for an outsider from the Deep South with no national identity, such as Jimmy Carter, to suddenly gain the recognition needed to win the presidency. But, as William Lee Miller noted, Carter perceived "the increased importance of the instant, visual, mass communications of signs, signals, and images." [26]

On the negative side, television has significantly altered the political environment in which presidents toil and it can conceivably affect their potential for leadership. Their mental and and physical mishaps are recorded for posterity. Critical coverage can provoke questions about their competence and ability to lead the nation in times of crises, as well as raise doubts about their sincerity and motives. Finally, the constant pressure of being under intense scrutiny and forced to forfeit their privacy serves to sap their energy and consume their time.

Recognizing the positive and negative aspects of the televised presidency, Kenneth W. Thompson, director of the University of Virginia's White Burkett Miller Center of Public Affairs, has stressed that although the power of the media is manifested in every sector of public life "voices continue to be raised asking what its impact will be for good or ill. . . . Only strong institutions and strong leaders can survive the brunt of the media's thrust. A Franklin D. Roosevelt harnessed the media to his ends, a Lyndon B. Johnson or Richard M. Nixon was destroyed. Those who would live in the television age must master it, not be ruled by it." [27]

Measures of Public Support

Presidents are constantly trying to find out what the people are thinking. "What I want," Lincoln once exclaimed, "is to get done what the people desire to have done, and the question for me is how to find that out exactly."

Public opinion can be fickle and is often a source of consternation to public officials. Before the advent of scientific public opinion research in the 1930s, presidents had to rely on crowd reactions, popular sentiment as reflected in White House mail, comments from visitors, editorial positions of the nation's newspapers, observations of friends, and trends in election results. Today, public opinion surveys—conceded to be as much art as science—are part of the political orthodoxy. Refinements in methodology, canvassing techniques, and survey analysis have made polls an indispensable element of campaigning for office and governing once in office.

As defined by veteran public opinion specialist Louis Harris, "Polling is a systematic way of providing intelligence." Others describe it as the best way to make campaign decisions in the most rational way.

Measuring who is ahead and who is behind—the horserace aspect of a campaign—is the most elementary way political polls are used. More specifically, they are used to appraise voter attitudes, identify cutting national issues, help draft campaign strategy, monitor the candidate's strength among the various constituencies, and help determine how the campaign's financial and political resources are to be committed.

Poll findings further provide clues as to where candidates should go to shore up support, what issues they should address, where and how they should run media commercials, what themes they should emphasize to distinguish themselves from the pack.

Richard Wirthlin, President Reagan's pollster, reported that polls help candidates locate opportunities among the sundry constituencies. In 1980, for example, Reagan acted on his survey findings and broke the traditional Democratic coalition by pursuing the votes of blue-collar workers.

Two days before the election, Wirthlin took a poll to measure the probable political consequences should the American hostages be released by Iran before the balloting began. "We found . . . it would have had very little effect on either candidate," he reported. "Knowing that, we kept our campaign very much on [the same] track."

After Reagan took office, Wirthlin's surveys indicated widespread displeasure with administration environmental policies, underscored by controversy involving improper practices within the Environmental Protection Agency (EPA). As a result, to restore credibility and stature to the agency, Reagan appointed the highly regarded William D. Ruckelshaus as EPA director.

Notwithstanding the increased prominence of political polls, no one, including practitioners themselves, contends they are infallible. Indeed, as they proliferate and become more sophisticated, there seems to be more room for miscues and misunderstandings. The margin for error in conducting public opinion surveys is broad and deep: the way the questions are worded, the context in which they are asked, the timing of the poll, whether the sample is large enough to provide a valid reading, whether the findings are correctly analyzed and presented.

Realists recognize that polls are only a snapshot in time and that usually the most beneficial information gained is in spotting movements in public opinion. Even then, polls may be overtaken by events. The *New York Times*/CBS News Poll in February 1984 showed that Democratic presidential candidate Walter Mondale "now holds the most commanding lead ever recorded this early in a presidential campaign by a nonincumbent." That same day, Gary Hart scored an upset victory over Mondale in the New Hampshire primary, overnight turning the contest, at least temporarily, into a two-man race.

While polling is accepted as an essential element of politics, there is suspicion that some politicians depend too much on them and not enough on other sources of information or their own knowledge, experience, and instincts. They may change not only their policy positions, style, and strategy but, in some instances, their political philosophy.

Most successful politicians want to know what public opinion is on any given issue, but will go with their judgment and instinct notwithstanding; they know it is but one of a multitude of factors that envelop most political issues.

George McGovern, the losing Democratic presidential nominee in 1972, who made an unsuccessful bid for the 1984 nomination, offered this view of campaign pollsters: "If you are not careful, they can run the campaign. They have too much influence on some candidates. It's too easy for a candidate to back away from difficult questions based on the findings of his pollster. In that way, they are a threat to a candidate's convictions."

Presidents, for the most part, are attentive to the polls, not simply to secure public affection and boost their popularity, as significant as that may be, but rather to discover opportunities for gain in specific policy areas and detect possible slippage in government performance, thereby allowing them to take remedial action.

Interest Groups

In a speech to the graduating class of Rollins College in 1936, President Franklin Roosevelt declared, "There are ... groups to which almost every man and woman is tied, connected in some way. They are connected with some form of association—the church, the social circle, the club, the lodge, the labor organization, the neighboring farmers, the political party. Even business and commerce are almost wholly made up of groups. It is the problem of government to harmonize the interests of these groups which are often divergent and opposing. The science of politics, indeed, may be said to be in large part the science of the adjustment of conflicting group interests."

Thus Roosevelt acknowledged the interaction between the presidency and the myriad interest groups throughout the United States. He recognized that appeals to the public and Congress are most effective when there is evidence of substantial support from interest groups, many of which have large memberships and are nationally organized and well financed.

Since the Roosevelt era, the number of interest groups has multiplied tremendously. With each emerging concern—arms control, abortion, equal rights, a balanced federal budget, sex and violence on television, noise pollution, the dumping of toxic wastes, consumer protection—new constituencies form organizations to promote, defend, or defeat proposals that would affect their interests.

By the late 1980s, approximately 10,000 professional representatives—or lobbyists—were working in Washington, 7,600 of whom were registered with the clerk of the House, compared with 365 who were registered in 1960. (The statute, which is widely criticized as more loophole than law, allows some special-interest representatives to avoid registration and thus does not indicate the true number of Washington lobbyists.) Among those registered were officers of 1,600 trade and professional associations and labor unions; agents of some 4,000 individual corporations; lawyers and consultants who registered as lobbyists or foreign agents with the Justice Department; and spokespersons for virtually every state and large U.S. city, as well as for many universities and most religious groups. The most recent development is the proliferation of public relations firms in the nation's capital, most of which include lobbyists and special-issue lawyers.

Beginning in the Nixon administration, the White House institutionalized its relationships with interest groups through the establishment of the Office of Public Liaison. The office was formed as a response to the withering of the party system and the collateral emergence of single-issue pressure groups. Presidents recognize that they can no longer rely on traditional political alignments in the promotion of their legislative agenda and executive programs and must seek, issue by issue, the endorsement of floating coalitions.

A critical part of the office's function is regularly to invite various interest group leaders from across the United States to the White House where they are royally treated and briefed on administration policies by top government officials, including White House aides, cabinet members, and the president. Although the White House describes the work of the Office of Public Liaison as an "educational program," it is in effect a lobbying effort based on the expectation that the guests will return home and spread the administration's message, thereby increasing pressure on Congress on behalf of the president's programs. On their part, the interest group participants generally feel they have been given the chance to have their voice heard at the highest level of government.

Presidential Appearances

In the ceremonial role of chief of state, presidents are portrayed as the embodiment of the national interest. Simply the appearance of the president—with the display of the presidential seal and the playing of "Hail to the Chief"—strikes an emotional chord and taps patriotic sentiments among Americans. Whether they voted Republican or Democrat, Americans generally perceive the president as the living symbol of the nation. The chief of state is, further, the country's most familiar and most notable celebrity.

When presidents deliver a major speech, as they do frequently, to national business, labor, veterans, minority, religious, and professional organizations, they are expressing interest in the concerns of these groups, while also addressing the rest of the country. Breakthroughs in transportation and communications technology have offered presidents increased opportunities for going public and for capturing the attention of the electorate. Nixon's trip to China, Carter's town hall meetings and his trip to Panama, Reagan's presence at highly publicized summit meetings with Soviet leader Mikhail Gorbachev and his participation in the glittering centennial celebration of the Statue of Liberty, and George Bush's visit to China shortly after his inauguration all present strong and memorable visual images. The ceremonial presidency plays to a mass audience and is ensured television coverage and front-page headlines. The symbolism and rhetorical flourishes invariably enhance the president's popularity.

The marvel of presidential travel is in the planning and coordination and the assurances taken so that everything goes according to schedule. While the paramount concern is the president's safety and comfort, the objective is to achieve maximum political effect. Stage-managed appearances by the president emphasize the atmosphere and allow the White House to control events, which are avidly televised and reported.

Not infrequently, even the crowd that gathers to greet presidents as they disembark from *Air Force One* is programmed. When Reagan returned from a European trip in June 1982, for example, 50,000 special tickets were distributed to administration officials, federal workers, and employees of the Republican National Committee to guarantee a large welcoming crowd when *Air Force One* landed at Andrews Air Force Base outside of Washington. Although the White House denied any pressure was being applied, "point people" were designated at the various agencies to oversee the turnout. Buses were provided and color-coded tickets printed—yellow for important political figures, green for senior government executives, and white for civil servants and the general public.

Jet travel permits presidents unlimited opportunities to journey to distant capitals and to star in diplomatic dramas, as the world follows each move on the television screen and through the printed press. For the Republic's first 117 years, however, U.S. presidents were expected to remain on American soil to ensure national leadership. Theodore Roosevelt was the first president to venture abroad, sailing to Panama aboard an American ship and, except for a few hours, remaining within U.S. waters. Woodrow Wilson became the first president to cross the seas when he attended the Paris Peace Conference following World War I. He was was severely criticized for his extended absence from the seat of government and the withdrawal of physical protection provided at home. Sen. Lawrence Y. Sherman of Illinois introduced a resolution to declare the presidency vacant whenever the occupant left American soil, but the proposal lacked congressional support.

Wilson's lengthy trip overseas is blamed for his inability to stay in touch with national sentiment concerning the proposed League of Nations and with public attitudes on domestic issues. Not for nearly a quarter of a century did a U.S. president again venture abroad: in 1943 Franklin Roosevelt journeyed to Casablanca aboard a Pan American plane to meet with British Prime Minister Winston Churchill for a wartime conference.

Truman was the first president to popularize domestic air travel but mostly for brief vacation trips to his home in Independence, Missouri. Eisenhower's 1959 "good will" tour around the world generally is recognized as the first presidential trip where favorable publicity appeared to be the primary objective.

Foreign Publics

Under the Constitution, the president has the duties of commander in chief of the armed forces, the power to make treaties and appoint ambassadors with the advice and consent of the Senate, and the authority to deal with other nations. In addition to these formal powers, other factors contribute to the president's preeminence in foreign affairs, including the symbolic nature of the office as a unifying national force, jurisdiction over a huge and highly specialized federal bureaucracy, and high visibility and access to the news media as a means of influencing the public to support White House initiatives.

Presidential supremacy in foreign policy was reinforced with the outbreak of World War II and throughout the ensuing postwar period when the United States abandoned its traditional isolationism and assumed the role of a world power. During the so-called cold war, the United States began massive foreign aid and economic development programs, developed an elaborate network of overseas military bases, and became a leading party to a series of international commitments and collective security pacts.

As it became increasingly evident after World War II that the conduct of U.S. foreign policy affected domestic policy, the nation's economy, the level of U.S. military strength, international trade, and human rights around the world, the president's role as chief diplomat and commander in chief was enhanced. The policies, decisions, and personality of the president, more than of any other single figure, clearly determine the image and credibility of the United States within the international community of nations.

As advances in mass communications and public relations techniques took hold in American society, foreign policy turned more on an enlightened public opinion. "The major decisions in our foreign policy since [World War II] have been made on the basis of an informed public opinion and overwhelming public support," Truman acknowledged.

This trend in a sense had been in motion for several decades. The evolution from secret to open diplomacy following World War I underlined the significance of public opinion in the international arena. In the first of his famous Fourteen Points proposed at the Paris Peace Conference, President Wilson called for "open covenants of peace, openly arrived at, after which there shall be no private international understandings of any kind, but diplomacy shall proceed always frankly and in the public view." Clarifying what he meant by *open diplomacy*, Wilson said, "I meant, not that there should be no private discussions of delicate matters, but that no secret agreements should be entered upon, and that all international relations, when fixed, should be open, aboveboard, and explicit."

Another development that has changed the way sovereign nations deal with one another is "media diplomacy"—the manipulation of the news media and the application of sophisticated public relations to sway international opinion and constituents at home. Formerly, diplomacy was dependent on quiet consultation and private negotiations, but since the 1970s government leaders commonly speak to one another through the media rather than through traditional channels. Television, with its immediate impact, compels heads of government to make quick decisions, often without sufficient mediation and consultation.

Also, with the rise to power of Soviet leader Mikhail S. Gorbachev in 1985 and his policy of *glasnost*, or "openness," the Soviet Union adopted Western-style news and public relations techniques, which sharpened competition between the two global powers for world opinion.

Among the key U.S. institutions involved in this competition is the United States Information Agency (USIA), which falls under the umbrella of the State Department but has its own mandate as the principal voice of the United States abroad. Created in 1953, its essential mission is to portray American values and culture to other countries and explain U.S. government policies and actions. In addition to carrying out a wide variety of cultural and educational programs, USIA advises the president and U.S. representatives abroad on foreign opinion regarding American policies and practices and on other public affairs issues. The agency has branches in 128 countries and lists an estimated 9,000 employees in Washington and overseas.

Operating virtually autonomously within USIA, the Voice of America (VOA) broadcasts news around the world in forty-two languages, with a worldwide audience of at least 120 million. Each week it beams more than 980 hours of news reports and analyses, feature programs, seminar discussions, music, and editorials. In 1985 Radio Marti was launched as a special part of VOA for broadcasting programs scripted solely for audiences in Cuba.

These and the other developments reaching back to Woodrow Wilson and the early movement toward open diplomacy vastly increased the number of players in the formulation, adaptation, and execution of foreign policy. To gain support for their foreign policy programs, modern presidents must now deal not only with Congress but with special interest groups, lobbyists and other representatives of foreign governments, international business and trade corporations, private economic and foreign affairs groups, foreign opposition leaders, U.S. and foreign news media, academic specialists, and social-cultural organizations. Presidents must appreciate that television and other news media are a vital tool in governing and be skilled in their use to win the endorsements of foreign publics.

Notes

1. George C. Edwards III, *The Public Presidency* (New York: St. Martin's Press, 1983).
2. Richard E. Neustadt, *Presidential Power* (New York: Wiley, 1976).
3. Doris A. Graber, ed., *The President and the Public* (Philadelphia: Institute for the Study of Human Issues, 1982).
4. Quoted in Thomas E. Cronin, *The State of the Presidency*, 2d ed. (Boston: Little, Brown, 1980).
5. Clinton Rossiter, *The American Presidency*, rev. ed. (New York: New American Library, 1962).
6. Philip C. Dolce and George H. Skau, ed., *Power and the Presidency* (New York: Scribner's, 1976).
7. Thomas F. Cronin, *The State of the Presidency* (Boston: Little, Brown, 1975).
8. Grant McConnell, *The Modern Presidency*, 2d ed. (New York. St. Martin's Press, 1976).
9. *Washington Post,* November 8, 1984.
10. *Washington Journalism Review* (Fall 1980).
11. Joe McGinniss, *The Selling of the President 1968* (New York: Trident Press, 1969).
12. Emmet John Hughes, *The Living Presidency* (Baltimore: Penguin, 1972), 89.
13. Ibid., 99.
14. John Ehrlichman, *Witness to Power: The Nixon Years* (New York: Simon and Schuster, 1982).
15. Samuel Kernell, *Going Public: New Strategies of Presidential Leadership* (Washington, D.C.: CQ Press, 1986).
16. Douglass Cater, *The Fourth Branch of Government* (New York: Vintage Books, 1965).
17. Quoted in Arthur M. Schlesinger, Jr., *The Coming of the New Deal,* 2d ed. (New York: Houghton Mifflin, 1958).
18. Richard A. Watson and Norman C. Thomas, *The Politics of the Presidency,* 2d ed. (Washington, D.C.: CQ Press, 1987).
19. Steven A. Shull, *Presidential Policy Making* (Brunswick, Ohio: King's Court, 1979).
20. Gerald R. Ford, *A Time to Heal* (New York: Harper and Row, 1979).
21. Bruce Buchanan, *The Citizen's Presidency* (Washington, D.C.: CQ Press, 1987).
22. William J. Crotty and Gary C. Jacobson, *American Parties in Decline* (Boston: Little, Brown, 1980).
23. Byron E. Shafer, *Quiet Revolution* (New York: Russell Sage Foundation, 1983).
24. Jimmy Carter, *Keeping Faith: Memoirs of a President* (New York: Bantam, 1982).
25. Tom C. Korologos, interview with the author.
26. William Lee Miller, *Yankee from Georgia* (New York: Times Books, 1978).
27. Kenneth W. Thompson, ed., *The Media: The Credibility of Institutions, Policies and Leadership,* vol. 5 (Lanham, Md.: University Press of America, 1985).

Political Parties as President-Public Link

Political parties serve by default as links between the president and the people. The Framers of the Constitution did not design a clear president-public connection. They established instead an office of chief executive that was remote from popular influence. Political parties did not exist at the time of the constitutional founding and the Framers envisioned the presidency in nonpartisan terms, so it is not surprising that they did not provide a formal role for political factions.

Parties quickly emerged, however. They became central features of presidential politics and, indeed, the whole of American politics. Their critical functions of linkage or intermediation were exercised primarily in the electoral arena.

Parties linked citizens with rulers. A shared party affiliation could connect the most humble, ordinary citizen with political luminaries such as governors, members of Congress, and even the president of the United States. Parties became the principal channels for participation in the political process. As such they encouraged and facilitated increasingly democratic government in the United States.

Parties also served as vehicles for linking these various public officeholders within the separated-powers system that dispersed them into different branches and levels of government and further positioned them as rivals. The party idea and organization could provide common ground for cooperation among the president, Congress, and, to a lesser extent, the federal judiciary, and even between national and state governments.

Finally, parties connected officeholders with private elites—notable nongovernmental political actors who sought to influence public policy. Largely through campaign contributions, such forces relied on parties to make known their views in the counsels of government.

In the process of presidential selection, political parties serve as gatekeepers, authorizing candidacies through nominations. Without the party nomination, a presidential candidate lacks legitimacy. Conversely, party control over nominations constrains the public's role in the process.

A contemporary assessment of the party-presidency relationship confronts an interesting paradox: the parties persist despite their indisputable loss of influence over campaigns and elections.

By Harold F. Bass, Jr.

Parties do not appear to have the claim on the allegiances of the electorate they once had. Presidents and public can now interact more directly, through institutions such as the communications media, public opinion polls, and pressure groups, with less reliance on political parties. *(See Media, Public Opinion, and Interest Group chapters.)*

The organizational connections between presidency and parties have eroded substantially. This can be attributed to changes in presidential selection procedures and practices, the structure of the presidential office, and the decline of patronage.

Despite their general decline in electoral identification and allegiance, the parties organizationally are renewed and in ascendancy. This can be seen in the establishment and maintenance of permanent headquarters, full-time officers, and the performance of a variety of service functions by both of the national parties and by a growing number of state parties. Presidential aspirants still seek the party nomination to authorize their candidacies, and they run for office under the party label and the symbolism it evokes. Once elected, the president, more than any other individual, embodies the political party in the eyes of the general public, which in large part still identifies with the parties. For all the changes in the president-party relationship, the two remain fundamentally linked.

Historical Perspectives on Parties and the Presidency

The emergence of political parties had a profound and transforming effect on the executive office. The constitutional principle of separation of powers produced a clearly divided governmental structure with three distinct branches: executive, legislative, and judicial. Checks and balances, while blurring these divisions, nevertheless were intended to inhibit cooperation by encouraging rivalries among the branches.

The appearance of national political parties altered this setting. They provided a foundation for coordination, cooperation, and unity. The presidential nominee's position at the head of the party's electoral ticket carried with it, in title at least, the status of party leader. This elevated the chief executive position from that of head of one of

Democratic vice-presidential candidate Lloyd Bentsen, left, and presidential candidate Michael Dukakis acknowledge their nomination at the Democratic National Convention July 22, 1988.

AP

three separate and equal branches to that, in theory, of government leader, through the institution of the political party.

Initially, in the 1790s, American political parties were governmental factions. By 1800, however, they were developing organizational means to appeal to the electorate to support the parties' candidates for public offices. Party organization was taking shape, primarily in the form of loosely linked campaign committees, complemented by the partisan press.

In reaching out to the citizenry, and thus positioning themselves as intermediary institutions linking citizens and government, political parties recognized that the constitutional order rested in part on a foundation of popular sovereignty. By the standards of the day, the states' suffrage requirements were liberal and becoming more so, making it easier for the rank-and-file to vote. Religious tests had been abandoned in the revolutionary era, and property requirements were largely eliminated in the decade of the 1820s. Further, the voters' authority in presidential selection was enhanced by post-1800 changes in the operation of the electoral college.

The establishment of the citizen-government link dramatically increased the president's power position in the political order. By virtue of the selection process, nationwide in scope and increasingly popular in operation, the president could claim a national, popular constituency above and beyond that of any governmental rival. The "people connection" allowed the president to tap into the wellsprings of popular sovereignty that nourished the exercise of political authority in an increasingly democratic society. As "tribune of the people," the president could claim a prerogative not specifically enumerated in the con-

stitutional allocation of governmental power.

These critical transformations began in large measure during the administrations of two early nineteenth-century presidents: Thomas Jefferson and Andrew Jackson.

Jefferson merits credit for originating the presidential role of party leader. He led the Democratic-Republican party before his presidential election in 1800, and he carried this leadership responsibility with him to the White House. As president, Jefferson relied extensively on partisan connections to elicit cooperation from like-minded allies in Congress.

Jackson was a genuine popular hero. Before he entered presidential politics, he had attained widespread acclaim by his military accomplishments in the War of 1812 and the Indian conflicts that followed. In his pursuit of the presidency in 1824 and 1828, he emphasized his appeal to the masses. His party took advantage of this situation by mobilizing supporters under the party banner.

However, these new perspectives on the presidency did not gain widespread acceptance until much later, in the twentieth century, when presidents in general began to reap the political benefits of these developments.

From a different standpoint, the formation of two political parties within a decade of the constitutional founding affected the Framers' design for choosing presidents. In seeking the selection of presidential electors committed to a party ticket, the parties necessitated a constitutional change in the electoral college balloting arrangement. The Constitution originally called for each elector to cast a single ballot. On it were to be placed two names, with only one coming from the elector's state. The name that received the most votes, providing that number composed a majority, would be elected president. The name receiving the next most votes would become vice president. If a tie resulted, or if no name received a majority of votes, the House of Representatives would decide the election.

The first two presidential elections took place absent partisan competition, indeed without any competition. In each instance, George Washington's name appeared on every ballot, while John Adams's name appeared the next most times. Thus, Washington became president, and the vice presidency went to Adams.

In the election of 1796, there was a contest between Adams, supported by the Federalists, and Thomas Jefferson, running under the banner of the Democratic-Republicans. Adams won a narrow victory, so Jefferson succeeded him as vice president.

The presidential contest of 1800 provided a rematch. This time, Jefferson's partisan supporters openly sought the selection of electors committed not only to Jefferson's presidential candidacy, but also to that of running mate Aaron Burr for vice president. In a sense, the Democratic-Republicans were almost too successful. Every elector who voted for Jefferson also voted for Burr, and more voted for Jefferson and Burr than for any other choices. With Jefferson and Burr receiving the same number of votes, the House had to decide which one would be president. Ultimately it chose Jefferson. In the aftermath, Jefferson's partisan supporters in Congress quickly proposed the Twelfth Amendment, ratified in 1804. It called for electors to cast two ballots, clearly differentiating the presidential from the vice presidential vote.

This reform allowed, indeed encouraged, electors to vote for party tickets. As such, it transformed the role of the presidential electors. The Framers had envisioned them as trustees: disinterested, public-spirited elites exercising independent wisdom and judgment. After 1800 the electors acted instead primarily as agents, chosen on party tickets and consistently following the instructions of the victorious party in their state.[1]

The Constitution authorizes each state legislature to determine how that state's electors are designated. At first there was a rough balance between those that opted for legislative selection and those preferring popular election. Increasingly, popular election on party tickets became the norm. By 1836 only South Carolina remained committed to legislative selection, a position it held until after the Civil War. This virtually universal acceptance of popular election of presidential electors enhanced both the connection between the president and the public and the intermediary position of political parties.

The public now had a clear role to play in presidential selection and presidential contenders were dependent on the votes of ordinary citizens. The party, in designating electors committed to the presidential nominee and to be chosen by the voters on that basis, now clearly linked the two.

Virtually from the outset, political parties focused their attentions on election of the president, which contributed strongly to their establishment of national bases. This coordinated and united the diverse factions in the several states.

Thus, the parties transformed American political conflict. At first it was a fight mainly among states. But these rivalries came to be supplanted by party competition, which promoted consensus by reducing the potential for fragmentation from among thirteen states to between two parties.

Origins of Party Labels

Our understanding of political party development in the United States is complicated by considerable confusion surrounding the names of the parties. Contemporary Democrats trace their partisan ancestry back to Thomas Jefferson. In Jefferson's day, however, the party went by two different names, either Republican or Democratic-Republican. By 1830 the dominant wing of a divided Democratic-Republican party, led by President Andrew Jackson, abandoned the "Republican" portion of their label, leaving "Democratic" standing alone ever since.

A quarter-century later, in 1854, antislavery sympathizers forming a new party appropriated the name "Republican." Today's Republicans are their descendants.

The term "Democrat" comes from the Greek word "democratia," a combination of "demos," meaning "common people," and the suffix "-kratia," denoting "strength, power." Thus, "democratia" means "power to the people," or "the people rule."

The term "Republican" derives from the Latin phrase "res publica." It literally means "public thing," or "public affair," and it connotes a government in which citizens participate.

Both party names thus suggest the Democrats' and Republicans' common belief in popular government, conducted by representatives of the people and accountable to them.

The Presidency and Two-Party Competition

A distinctive feature of party competition in the United States is that it is dualistic. In other words, contests ordinarily pit two parties against each other. This is in contrast to the multi-party competition prevalent in many European countries, and the absence of party competition in Communist countries and many of the nation-states of the developing world.

In seeking to explain this phenomenon, scholars have pointed to diverse factors such as tradition, culture, and electoral arrangements. Early on, the political conflicts in America divided the participants into pairs: patriots versus loyalists, Federalists versus Anti-Federalists, Federalists versus Democratic-Republicans. Thus, a tradition of two-party competition developed that hindered the emergence of alternatives.

The American political culture has been cited as a factor in the dominance of the two-party system because it is supportive of accommodation and compromise. This allows diverse interests to ally under a party banner despite significant differences. Absent this spirit of concession, the various groups would form their own, separate political organizations, and a multi-party system would prevail.

Finally, electoral arrangements are critical to an understanding of the two-party system. American elections are for the most part organized on the principle of single-member district, winner take all. Electoral units designate a single individual—the one who receives the most votes—to occupy a public office. The winner-take-all provision frustrates minor parties that, while perhaps capable of assembling sizable numerical minorities, cannot realistically aspire to triumphing in an absolute sense over the two entrenched major parties.

The presidency can be viewed as a special case of, and credited with a critical contribution to, the electoral-arrangements explanation. The constitutional standard of an electoral college majority to elect the president discourages competition from parties that cannot hope to attain the high level of support necessary for victory. As such, it supports the maintenance of the two-party system.

In the early years of the Republic, party competition matched the Federalists led by Alexander Hamilton against the Democratic-Republican followers of Thomas Jefferson. In the wake of the Federalists' demise—caused by Jefferson's conclusive triumphs in 1800 and 1804 and reinforced by the victories of his lieutenant, James Madison, in 1808 and 1812—a brief period of one-party rule ensued. Jeffersonian heir James Monroe presided over this so-called "Era of Good Feelings."

By the mid-1820s, however, intraparty conflict had resulted in the emergence of two rival Democratic-Republican factions. These factions reflected personal ambitions and rivalries in the party leadership, pitting Andrew Jackson and his advocates against an alliance of John Quincy Adams, Henry Clay, and their combined supporters. The Jackson faction represented the emergent claims of the growing southwestern region in party and national politics, as well as those of the lower classes, including immigrants; while Adams in particular spoke for the more traditional regional and socioeconomic elements within the party coalition.

As the Democrats and the Whigs, these erstwhile factions became partisan adversaries in the 1830s. About the time the Whigs died out in the 1850s, a new party, the Republicans, appeared on the scene to challenge the Democrats. Their competition has endured ever since.

Two-party competition has typically taken the form of sustained periods of dominance by one party, measured in terms of control of the presidency. From 1800 to 1860, the Democratic party, in its Jeffersonian and Jacksonian incarnations, ordinarily prevailed in presidential elections. Amid the upheaval of the Civil War, this pattern gave way to one of Republican ascendancy. The rise of the Republican party can be attributed initially to the demise of the Whigs and the self-destruction of the Democrats, both precipitated in large part by the slavery controversy. The ultimately successful prosecution of the Civil War under Republican auspices allowed the party to seize the banner of patriotism, while the Democratic opposition was stained by its Southern roots. Increasingly in the postwar years, the Republican party developed lasting ties with business interests that provided it with solid financial support. The Republican era endured, with few exceptions, until 1932, when it was undermined by the Great Depression. That year marked the beginning of a new Democratic era that clearly lasted two decades.

The presidential elections from 1952 until 1988 departed from the previous patterns in that no party was able to sustain its hold on the White House for more than eight years. Thus, if two-party competition is measured in terms of alternation in the occupancy of the White House, these years constituted an unprecedented era of competitiveness.

In 1988 Republican nominee George Bush's quest to succeed retiring incumbent Ronald Reagan met with electoral approval, guaranteeing the Republicans at least three consecutive four-year terms in control of the White House and suggesting the presence of a new era of Republican dominance in presidential politics.

Parties as Coalitions

Political parties appeal to interest groups, or collections of individuals who share common backgrounds and concerns. Indeed, parties can be seen as broad coalitions of diverse interests: geographic, social, economic, ethnic, and issue. Particularly in presidential elections, parties seek to achieve victory by attracting sufficient electoral support from voters who are members of these groups.

Presidential leadership is part and parcel of the linkages between president and public, and between parties and groups. For example, during the decade of the 1930s, under the New Deal policies of President Franklin D. Roosevelt, the Democratic party assembled under its umbrella a formidable electoral coalition that generally included the South, racial minorities, blue-collar laborers, farmers, and middle-class elements brought low by the ravages of the Great Depression. This party coalition successfully supported Roosevelt's presidential candidacies an unprecedented four separate times. It remained sufficiently intact in 1948 to bring victory to his successor, Harry S Truman. Lingering vestiges of the Roosevelt coalition could be observed in the electoral support for the victorious 1976 Democratic presidential nominee, Jimmy Carter.

Republican responses to this era of Democratic domination entailed successful presidential campaigns by Dwight Eisenhower, Richard Nixon, and Ronald Reagan that appealed to traditionally Democratic voters. The Eisenhower and Reagan appeals in particular were personalistic. Both of these individuals enjoyed popularity that transcended partisanship. In addition, all three benefited from public dissatisfaction with the performance of the Democratic incumbents who preceded them. In each instance, it was fueled by foreign policy problems besetting Democratic administrations: Korea in 1952, Vietnam in 1968, and Iran in 1980.

As presidents, they followed up with efforts to reshape electoral alignments into a new winning coalition of interests under the party banner. Over the years, they achieved significant defections to the GOP in the white South, the middle class, and among blue-collar workers.

Linkage Patterns and Changes

As political parties developed institutionally during the nineteenth century, their intermediary role took on diverse dimensions. In the electoral arena, they structured the vote, providing the voters with alternative choices. Indeed, they effectively controlled the voters' options as well as the routes to public office through their nominations. Without a party nomination, a candidacy lacked credibility and legitimacy.

Their symbols labeled candidates for the benefit of the voters. In an era when literacy rates were much lower than now, and when voters lacked access to much specific personal information about particular candidates, this contribution was critical. The Republican elephant and the Democratic donkey gave voters crucial decision cues regarding the qualities of candidates.

Political parties also provided economic employment and social services for their constituencies. The former occurred through the mechanism of patronage, or appointment to government jobs according to partisan political criteria. Following an election, loyal adherents of the victorious party could claim government positions as spoils.

Significantly, the rise of the "spoils system" occurred in part as a systematic attempt to link the president with the public through the political party. President Andrew Jackson bemoaned the established practice he encountered of elitist careerism in public service. He tried to open public employment to the ranks of ordinary citizens, who provided the foundation of his political support.

As the government grew in size and function, widespread patronage resources gave citizens incentives to establish and maintain party ties. In 1841, for example, the available federal government positions numbered some 23,700. By the 1880s, when the abused and maligned spoils system was reformed, the number of positions had increased about fivefold.[2]

In the nineteenth-century heyday of patronage, practitioners recognized its significance for political parties and enthusiastically defended it in the name of the public good. One of the more flamboyant of the patronage politicians around the turn of the century, George Washington Plunkitt, of New York City's Tammany Hall, perceived the connections as follows:

> First, this great and glorious country of ours was built up by political parties; second, parties can't hold together if their workers don't get the offices when they win; third, if the parties go to pieces, the government they built up must go to pieces, too; fourth, then there'll be h--- to pay.[3]

The social service role assumed by the parties in the latter part of the nineteenth century was exercised primarily by the urban party machines that responded to the needs of the teeming masses of immigrants arriving and residing there. Until the New Deal of the 1930s and the Great Society of the 1960s, neither the federal government nor its state counterparts provided citizens much in the way of help to the needy. The individualistic political culture viewed what has come to be called "welfare" as beyond the pale of the public sector. Such assistance, if any, typically came from private sources such as churches, the Salvation Army, and philanthropists.

Thus, political parties moved into a public void of sorts when they at times directly delivered primary social services: food, clothing, and shelter. More generally, they enabled newcomers to take part in the political process and solicit governmental responses to their needs and interests. It was to the parties that they looked when problems arose that involved the government. Local party leaders pulled strings and provided favors.

As such, political parties served as a channel for social advancement integrating outsiders into the mainstream of society. They attracted constituents who came to rely on the party in meeting daily needs and aspirations for the future and who reciprocated with their loyalties and electoral support.

Within this context, parties came to occupy a central and critical position in the political process. Citizens developed enduring attachments that were manifested primarily by voting for the parties' candidates and otherwise supporting the parties' causes with their energies and resources.

The presidency was significant in these developments. As the most visible party officeholder, the president personified the party in the eyes of the general public. Further, as chief executive, the president authorized the allocation of federal patronage, the bulk of which was distributed through the cabinet-level Post Office Department, a vast operation that extended to virtually every city, town, and village throughout the United States.

Rather quickly, then, in the nineteenth century a system of mutual benefits developed between president and party. A presidential aspirant looked to the party to authorize the candidacy through nomination and depended on its organizational support for victory. Further, an incumbent president looked to the party to promote support for presidential policies.

Besides making available to the party the federal government's patronage resources, the president could be expected to promote the party's fortunes by campaigning for its nominees for other elective offices, shouldering some fund-raising responsibilities, and pushing for enactment of laws to implement the party's public policies. Thus, the presidency provided a critical contribution to the development of the parties as intermediaries.

Party Identification

Voters appear to develop psychological attachments over time to political parties in response to a number of factors.[4] One of those is the success or failure of the president and the presidency in winning adherents to the party cause.

Traditionally, party identifications seem to have taken place relatively early in individuals' lives. Indeed, they have emerged in childhood and in the absence of much specific information about politics. This suggests that political socialization, or the process of learning political and social roles in society, is an important force in the development of party identification.

This early gravitation to one party or another focuses attention on the family as a primary agent in the process. In other words, citizens can acquire party identification by inheritance. This process rarely involves systematic indoctrination on the part of family members. It is normally much more informal and subtle. Children hear parents discussing candidates and issues, and they often come to identify with and share their parents' preferences. Initial, familial influence can be reinforced by a relatively homogeneous environment largely controlled by the family. A focus on inheritance as the foundation for party identification begs the question of why one's ancestors originally developed a party tie. Thus, looking for additional factors associated with party identification, many commentators consider social class, or socioeconomic status, as a major influence.

Social class is a complicated concept. It has both objective and subjective elements. Objectively, class can be defined in terms of wealth, occupation, education, and heritage. Subjectively, class is a function of how one views oneself, and how that individual is viewed, with respect to a relative position within a hierarchical society. According to this perspective, voters are attracted to parties, and parties appeal to voters, on the basis of class interests.

The relationship between class and party in the

Table 1 Social Characteristics and Party Identification: 1984

	Democrats		Independents leaning Democratic	Independents	Independents leaning Republican	Republicans		Party difference	No. of cases
	Strong	Weak				Weak	Strong		
Education									
No high school	27%	18%	9%	14%	8%	12%	10%	23%	494
High school graduate	15	22	12	13	14	14	10	13	775
College	13	20	11	8	14	17	16	0	918
Income									
Lower third	24	21	13	13	10	11	9	25	635
Middle third	17	20	12	10	14	15	12	10	690
Upper third	12	19	9	8	27	18	16	−3	623
Occupation									
Service	25	26	12	12	8	10	7	34	264
Blue collar	19	20	12	12	14	12	10	17	744
White collar	17	21	8	10	16	14	14	10	293
Professional	13	18	10	9	14	19	18	−6	629
Farm	10	17	7	18	12	18	16	−7	98
Religion									
Jews	29	31	14	8	10	4	6	50	52
Catholics	19	23	10	14	12	11	10	21	571
Protestants	16	19	9	9	13	18	14	3	1,355
Race									
Blacks	33	32	14	11	6	1	3	61	242
Whites	15	19	11	11	14	17	14	3	1,900
Region									
South	21	23	9	14	11	11	9	24	740
Non-South	15	19	12	10	13	17	14	3	1,473
Sex									
Female	18	22	10	10	11	15	12	13	1,256
Male	16	17	13	12	14	15	13	5	980
Subjective Class									
Working	19	23	12	12	12	13	8	21	1,082
Middle	15	18	10	9	13	17	17	−1	1,043

Source: Center for Political Studies, University of Michigan; data made available by the Inter-University Consortium for Political and Social Research. Cited in Frank J. Sorauf and Paul Allen Beck, *Party Politics in America,* 6th ed. (Glenview, Ill.: Scott, Foresman, 1988), 175.

Note: Totals cumulate horizontally to 100 percent, minus apoliticals. Party difference is calculated by subtracting the percentage of strong and weak Republicans from the percentage of strong and weak Democrats. Negative numbers indicate a Republican advantage in the group.

United States is complex and inconclusive. In comparison with European societies, class consciousness is relatively weak; class mobility is relatively high. There have always been substantial cross-cutting cleavages along class and party lines. Nevertheless, it is fair to say that today's Democratic party is identified with and appeals to the poor and working-class elements of American society to a greater extent than is the case for the Republican party. The converse is also true, with the Republican party drawing greater support from and reflecting the interests of the upper echelons of society.

Tables 1 through 4 provide data regarding party identification in the American electorate. In nationwide polls, members of the public were asked about their social characteristics, their party identification, and their voting behavior. The poll results indicate, for example, that in 1984 27 percent of those surveyed who lack a high school education identified themselves as strong Democrats, while

only 13 percent of college graduates did so. In contrast, while only 10 percent of the respondents who lacked a high school education considered themselves strong Republicans, 16 percent of the college graduates did so. Thus, one can demonstrate a positive relationship between level of education and party identification, warranting the assertion that the Democrats draw more support than do Republicans from the less-educated elements of American society. *(See Table 1, Social Characteristics and Party Identification: 1984, this page.)*

Demographic factors such as region, religion, race, and sex also influence party identification. Among these, regionalism appears in decline. Years ago, the Democratic party received unquestioning support from most southerners. At least at the presidential level, this is no longer the case. In 1984 only 44 percent of those southerners surveyed identified themselves as Democrats. Even more tellingly, only once between 1964 and 1988 had a Democratic presi-

Table 2 Party Identification of American Adults: 1952-1984

	1952	1956	1960	1964	1968	1972	1976	1980	1984
Democrats									
Strong	22%	21%	20%	27%	20%	15%	15%	18%	17%
Weak	25	23	25	25	25	26	25	23	20
Independents closer to Democrats	10	6	6	9	10	11	12	11	11
Independents	6	9	10	8	10	13	14	13	11
Independents closer to Republicans	7	8	7	6	9	10	10	10	12
Republicans									
Weak	14	14	14	13	14	13	14	14	15
Strong	13	15	15	11	10	10	9	8	12
Others	4	4	3	2	2	2	1	3	2
	101%	100%	100%	101%	101%	100%	100%	100%	100%

Source: Center for Political Studies, University of Michigan; data made available through the Inter-University Consortium for Political and Social Research. Cited in Frank J. Sorauf and Paul Alan Beck, *Party Politics in America*, 6th ed. (Glenview, Ill.: Scott, Foresman, 1988), 167.

Note: Percentages are based on surveys of the national electorate conducted in October of each presidential election year.

dential nominee won the once-solid South, and that was favorite son Jimmy Carter in 1976. Similarly, the Republicans' traditional midwestern base has experienced erosion.

Clear racial and religious distinctions can be seen among partisans. Oftentimes, however, these may stem mostly from underlying class and regional differences. For example, the Democratic party receives disproportionate support from racial minorities, as evidenced by the report that 65 percent of the blacks polled in 1984 considered themselves Democrats, but only 4 percent styled themselves Republicans. Since this racial group tends to be located at the lower end of the social-class ladder, however, it is not always clear whether minority or class status is the determining factor.

Similarly, Catholics and Jews have historically supported the Democrats, while nonsouthern Protestants have leaned in the Republican direction. But at least some of these differences can be attributed more directly to class. This was traditionally the case for Democratic-disposed immigrant Catholics and Southern Baptists. Among the latter, the class factor reinforced an even stronger and more fundamental regional one.

In recent years, students of voting behavior have discerned the presence of a "gender gap," a divergence in the partisan tendencies of men and women. Women currently appear more likely than men to support the Democratic party.

Ideology and issues also help shape party attachments. Voters who consider themselves more liberal tend to gravitate in the Democratic direction, while conservatives lean toward Republicanism. In taking issue positions, political parties seek to elicit support from like-minded groups and individuals. For example, an antiabortion party platform plank invites opponents of abortion to flock to the party banner.

Attractive nominees on the party ticket, especially at the presidential level, can lead voters to identify with a party. For post-World War II Republicans dispirited by a long series of defeats, their hope for the future was expressed in the slogan, "I Like Ike," a reference to the personal popularity of their 1952 presidential nominee, Dwight Eisenhower. More recently, the popularity of two-term winner Ronald Reagan often overcame the pull of party allegiance. The term "Reagan Democrats" described

his appeal to working-class individuals who normally would not vote for a Republican candidate.

The successful candidates' performance in public office, again especially at the presidential level, looms as an important consideration. Public approval of President Franklin Roosevelt's leadership through the travails of the Great Depression and World War II catapulted the Democratic party into an enduring position of dominance. Conversely, President Richard Nixon's involvement in the Watergate scandal had a detrimental influence on the support levels enjoyed by the Republican party.

A series of empirical voting studies in the 1950s demonstrated a high degree and substantial significance of party identification and party loyalty in electoral behavior. More recently, studies consistently show that this psychological identification with party is waning. Where straight-ticket voting once prevailed, voters demonstrate increasing inclinations to split their tickets.[5]

Indeed, these tendencies toward weakening party identification and increased ticket-splitting help explain why recent Republican presidential nominees generally have been successful despite apparently greater popular support for the Democratic party. In particular, white southerners are prone to retain their traditional party identification and vote Democratic in congressional, state, and local elections and yet vote Republican at the presidential level.

Party Decline

Party decline can be attributed to a number of important developments.[6] One is the explosion of mass media of communication that brings an abundance of information about politics and politicians to an increasing literate electorate. Thus fortified, voters become much less dependent on the party symbol as a guide in choosing among candidates.

Another is the decline of patronage, diminishing a once-potent motivation for party loyalty. The spoils system institutionalized in the early nineteenth century came under increasing attack after the Civil War. Sentiment for the merit principle for government service grew steadily. It found expression in the 1883 Civil Service Reform Act that

Table 3 Presidential Voting among Party Identifiers: 1952-1984

	1952	1956	1960	1964	1968	1972	1976	1980	1984
Democrats									
Strong	84%	85%	90%	95%	85%	73%	91%	86%	87%
Weak	62	62	72	82	58	48	74	60	67
Independents closer to Democrats	60	68	88	90	52	60	72	45	79
Independents	—	—	—	—	—	—	—	—	—
Independents closer to Republicans	93	94	87	75	82	86	83	76	92
Republicans									
Weak	94	93	87	56	82	90	77	86	93
Strong	98	100	98	90	96	97	96	92	96

Source: Center for Political Studies, University of Michigan; data made available by the Inter-University Consortium for Political and Social Research. Cited in Frank J. Sorauf and Paul Allen Beck, *Party Politics in America*, 6th ed. (Glenview, Ill.: Scott, Foresman, 1988), 199.

Note: The table shows the percentages of each category of partisans who reported a vote for their party's candidate for president. To find the percentage voting for the opposing party's candidate or some other candidate, subtract the entry from 100 percent. Individuals who did not vote or did not vote for president are excluded.

resulted in some 10 percent of federal government employees being classified under merit coverage.

From this small base, the classification coverage grew steadily to its current level of more than 90 percent. But while the percentage of civil service positions gradually increased, more patronage positions became available as the federal government grew. Still, in a century's time, the percentages of patronage versus classified positions in the federal executive have reversed. State and local governments have tended to follow suit. As a result, as Tammany Hall's Plunkitt feared, no longer could the party establish and maintain ties with citizens by holding out prospects of jobs and the status they entailed.

Yet another factor is the advent of the welfare state. Traditionally, the public sector, or government, affected a laissez-faire, or hands-off, posture in the realm of social services. Since the New Deal of the 1930s, however, government in general and the federal government in particular has assumed widespread responsibilities in this area. In doing so, it has supplanted the urban political machines that had built enduring commitments to party through the delivery of social services formerly unavailable from the public sector.

Another pertinent element is change in the methods by which political parties nominate candidates. For much of the nineteenth century, the party organization exercised tight control over this process. It served as a gatekeeper, commanding the route to public office. Thus aspirants had to receive the endorsement of the party organization to achieve their ambitions.

In the name of democratic reform, however, the Progressive movement around the turn of the twentieth century advocated broader popular participation in the nomination process. The Progressives' preferred method was the direct primary, a party election whereby voters chose the party's nominee to contest the general election.

The Progressives proved successful. The primary has become the standard method of party nominations, with the notable exception of the presidential contest. Even here, the Progressive influence can be seen in the early twentieth-century appearance of presidential primaries in a handful of states and in their dramatic proliferation since 1968.

By enhancing popular participation, presidential primaries strengthen the relationship between the president and the public. On the other hand, primaries open the party's nomination to candidates not necessarily approved by the party organization, and perhaps even antagonistic toward it. They deprive the organization of a traditional responsibility—one that provided a major foundation for the power of the party. Thus, many commentators view the party primary as destructive of the organization and a major factor in the decline of party as an intermediary between president and public.

Party Organization

The formal machinery of the party parallels government organization in the United States. At every level of government in our federal system—national, state, and local—there is a corresponding unit of party organization. Throughout, the lower levels of the organization generally designate membership for the higher levels.

Traditionally, most party power rested with the state and local organizations. They dominated the national parties, which were essentially holding companies. In recent years, this balance has shifted, centralizing power at the national level. This centralization has been made formal, especially by the Democrats, through a codification of national party responsibilities in the party's rules and procedures.

The institutions of party organization are the convention, the committee, the chair, and the headquarters staff. The first three typically exist at all levels, with the fourth appearing only occasionally in localities.

National Level

National party organization activity traditionally centered on the presidency. It had relatively little control over the operations of the state and local entities. More recently, it has become increasingly superfluous to presidential politics and removed from them. However, it has assumed increasing supervision over the lower levels. In the wake of these historic shifts, national party organization today appears stronger and more vital in many respects than ever before, though less relevant to the presidency.

Table 4 Straight-ticket Voting among Party Identifiers: 1952-1984

	1952	1956	1960	1964	1968	1972	1976	1980	1984
Democrats									
Strong	86%	84%	87%	80%	72%	66%	—	62%	69%
Weak	69	72	74	53	43	38	—	39	46
Independents closer to Democrats	56	58	56	37	32	28	—	23	38
Independents	56	43	65	53	24	28	—	21	25
Independents closer to Republicans	65	56	51	33	43	30	—	28	33
Republicans									
Weak	72	69	68	44	49	40	—	35	41
Strong	85	83	79	71	74	60	—	61	59

Source: Center for Political Studies, University of Michigan; data made available by the Inter-University Consortium for Political and Social Research. Cited in Frank J. Sorauf and Paul Allen Beck, *Party Politics in America*, 6th ed. (Glenview, Ill.: Scott, Foresman, 1988), 201.

Note: The table shows the percentages of each category of partisans who reported voting a straight ticket in state and local elections. To find the percentage splitting their tickets, subtract the entry from 100 percent. Individuals who did not vote or did not vote in state and local elections are excluded. The question was not asked in 1976.

Convention

Party organization at the national level dates back to the Jacksonian era, when the nominating convention appeared on the scene. Replacing the discredited congressional caucus as a nominating device, the quadrennial convention brought together state delegations to name the party's presidential ticket.[7]

The convention delegates also agreed upon a statement of party principles and issue stances, or platform, on which the party's nominees could run in the upcoming election. The gathering served as a massive party rally, where rival factions could be conciliated and unified, and enthusiasm generated, in preparation for the general election campaign. The convention provided a national institutional identity, serving as the party's voice and authority.

In the nineteenth century, state representation at the national convention followed the electoral college formula, itself an extension of the Constitutional Convention's Great Compromise on congressional apportionment. In the bicameral Congress, the House of Representatives was apportioned according to population, and the Senate according to state equality, two senators for each state. Under this arrangement, delegate seats at the nominating convention were allocated in proportion to the states' representation in Congress: a mixture of population plus state equality.

In the twentieth century, both major parties adopted formulas that weight representation according to the states' previous electoral support for the party. In other words, a positive record of support for the party's nominees produces bonus representation at the convention.

For example, for the Republicans in the 1980s, each state had a core of delegates assigned as a multiple of the size of its congressional delegation. Each received a specified number of at-large delegates. Each state got additional delegates if it had Republican governors, senators, and a party majority in its congressional delegation. A final bonus provision gave the state more representation if its electoral votes had gone to the GOP nominee in the previous presidential election. Nonstate units (District of Columbia, Puerto Rico, Virgin Islands, and Guam) received varying at-large delegates.

The Democrats in recent years have moved beyond the bonus system to embrace two alternative representational principles. First, they have systematically sought through affirmative action to give representation to a variety of population groups. These include women, racial minorities, and age cohorts. Second, they have seated ex officio "superdelegates," party officeholders chosen apart from the normal delegate-selection processes.

Over the years, the conventions have grown dramatically. Early conventions drew fewer than 300 delegates. In contrast, contemporary Democratic conventions bring together more than 4,000, and today's Republicans assemble more than 2,000. Twenty cities have been the convention sites through 1988, some more than once—such as Chicago, San Francisco and Miami.

In the nineteenth century state party organizations tightly controlled the selection of convention delegates. Around the turn of the century, the Progressive movement pushed for popular selection of delegates through a party primary. While a few state parties adopted this mechanism, most kept the party organization in charge.

However, some epochal reforms within the Democratic party after 1968 lodged far more effective party authority at the national level than had been the case and dramatically increased the number of state parties electing delegates through primaries. These reforms also, along with other coinciding trends, transformed the character of convention decision making. Party voters essentially choose the nominee in primaries and caucuses, leaving the convention little to do except ratify the voters' choice.

As a result every major party convention since 1952 has resulted in a first-ballot victory. In 1988 Republican George Bush and Democrat Michael S. Dukakis wrapped up convention majorities through delegate-selection contests in the states well in advance of the convention. For them and their parties, the convention's nominating role was a mere formality.

Increasingly, the modern convention has become a media event, heightening its traditional party rally function. The target of attention has shifted, however, from the party activists in the hall to the vast television audience viewing the prime-time proceedings. The convention gives the nominee a forum to kick off the general election campaign by demonstrating presidential leadership qualities to

In 1972, when Democratic vice-presidential nominee Thomas Eagleton, left, withdrew from the ticket, the Democratic National Committee formally nominated a replacement, Sargent Shriver.

both party and public. This can be achieved through actions such as the choice of a running mate, acceptance of the nomination with a forceful speech, and general management by the nominee and the campaign staff of the events of the convention week.

The national convention endures as the formal/legal nominator of the presidential ticket and as the apex of authority within the party. It remains a quadrennial event, though the Democrats experimented with midterm conventions in 1974, 1978, and 1982. These meetings were designed to stimulate discussion and development of party positions on issues. The party now has abandoned this experiment, restoring the traditional four-year gap between conventions.

Committee

An institution convening for a few days every four years can hardly exercise power and authority within a political party. Early on, in the 1840s, the Democratic national convention established a national committee to oversee the conduct of the presidential campaign and to guide the party's fortunes between conventions. Subsequently, when the Republican party formed a few years later, it adopted a similar organizational arrangement.[8]

These national committees consisted of representatives of the state and local parties. At the outset, the principle of state equality was established: one member from each state party. In the 1920s both parties expanded committee membership to two representatives from each state—one male and one female. This revision clearly responded to the Nineteenth Amendment that denied states the power to discriminate according to sex in establishing voter qualifications.

In 1952 the Republican party departed from the historical commitment to state equality as a representational principle. That year, its national convention voted to give ex officio national committee membership to party chairs from states that (1) supported the Republican nominee for president, (2) selected a majority of Republican House members and senators, or (3) selected a Republican governor. This reform gave added weight to those states that consistently voted Republican. Subsequently, the GOP returned to the principle of state equality by designating all state party chairs as committee members. Additionally, the District of Columbia, Guam, Puerto Rico, and the Virgin Islands came to be treated like states for representational purposes.

In the early 1970s the Democratic party abandoned state equality by adopting weighted representation and dramatically expanding the committee's membership. Table 5 indicates the current composition of the national committees.

While the convention formally designates the national committee, in practice it ratifies state-level decisions regarding membership. State parties utilize a variety of means for choosing their representatives, usually according to their own rules and/or state laws. In most states, the state convention selects them. Alternatively, the state committee, the national convention delegation, or the party voters through a primary may be authorized to do so. Members serve a four-year term beginning with adjournment of the national convention and ending with adjournment of the following convention.

Party rules require the Democratic National Committee to meet at least once a year, while the Republican National Committee is supposed to meet at least twice a year. Typically, the party chair calls meetings, but each party provides for alternative avenues whereby meetings can be called, such as by the executive committee or a stipulated percentage of the membership.

The committee's major collective function is the election of officers, chief of which is the party chair. Beyond formally designating its leadership, the committee as a collective body has little to do. Most of its assigned functions are undertaken by the chair and headquarters staff, with the committee customarily authorizing and ratifying these decisions.

One noteworthy assignment was to fill vacancies that occur before the election in the nominations for president and vice president. If a convention's nomination is vacated for any reason, legally it falls to the national committee to meet and fill it. Thus, in 1972, when Democratic vice-presidential nominee Thomas Eagleton withdrew, the Democratic National Committee, on the recommendation of presidential nominee George McGovern, formally nominated R. Sargent Shriver for the second spot on the ticket. A somewhat similar situation had developed for the Democrats in 1860, when their vice presidential nominee declined the nomination and the national committee replaced him.

Chair

The position of national party chair has high visibility and significance within the party organization. To the general public, its occupant stands as a symbol and spokesperson for the party. To the president, the chair is a top-level presidential appointee who links White House and party and through whom the president traditionally has exercised considerable party leadership.[9]

Selection. The national committee formally elects its top officer, traditionally at a meeting immediately following the national convention. This established the presumption that the term of office was four years. In practice, few national party chairs have served that long. Within-term vacancies have been exceedingly common, especially in the chair of the party that lost the presidential election.

The Democrats continue to elect their party chair after

the convention. In the 1980s the Republicans decided to elect the chair in January of each odd-numbered year, thus reducing the term of office to two years and somewhat isolating chair selection from the contest for the party's presidential nomination.

By custom and practice of a century's standing, the national committee has deferred to the party's presidential nominee in electing its chair. The usual procedure has been for a delegation from the committee to call on the nominee to solicit a recommendation. The committee would then convene to ratify that choice. This practice initially developed to tie the nominee's campaign with the national party effort. It had the effect of placing the party leadership under the nominee's authority.

After the election, the president-elect can continue to claim that prerogative. Thus, for the party whose nominee occupies the White House, the position of chair remains in effect a presidential appointment. Its incumbent serves at the pleasure of the president, with the national committee compliantly endorsing the president's choice.

Thus, in practice, the only times the national committee has acted on its own in choosing its chair have been in cases of vacancies occurring between nominating conventions when the party does not control the presidency. Even here, the influence of former or potential nominees, along with congressional party leaders, cannot be discounted.

The significance of the Republican party's realignment and limitation of the term of the party chair is not yet clear. However, it is doubtful that it will fundamentally reorient established patterns and practices.

For much of its existence, the chair has been a part-time position, with no definite eligibility requirements. But in most cases the incumbent has been a state party leader, a member or former member of Congress, a political associate of the presidential nominee, or a combination of the three. George Bush, a former House member who headed the GOP in the last two years of the Nixon administration, is the only national chair who went on to become president. (See Table 6, National Party Chairs, p. 24, and box, The Party Chair as Candidate for National Office, p. 25.)

In the 1970s both major parties began requiring that the chair position be full time and salaried. This action appears to have been in response to an increasing tendency to place legislators, parttime by definition, in that office. It relates to the increasing institutionalization of the national organization, whose members consider themselves ill-served by part-time leaders with primary loyalties to other elements within the party. Moreover, with the increasing amount of responsibility and activity located at the national level, the party headquarters requires full-time leadership.

Backgrounds. The early chairs were often men of considerable wealth. While sizable personal fortunes have not been a disqualification in recent years, they are no longer quite so common. Since World War I, the following chairs have come from the ranks of state party leaders, most of whom were state chairs: Republicans Will Hays, Hubert Work, Claudius Huston, John Hamilton, Harrison Spangler, Arthur Summerfield, Wesley Roberts, Ray Bliss, Mary Louise Smith, Richard Richards, and Frank Fahrenkopf; Democrats James Farley, Ed Flynn, Robert Hannegan, Howard McGrath, Frank McKinney, Jean Westwood, and Charles Manatt.

A congressional connection can be found for a number of national chairs. In the twentieth century, national chairs

Table 5 Composition of the National Party Committees: 1989

	Number of members
Democratic National Committee	
National committee officers	9
Chair and highest-ranking officer of opposite sex from each state, District of Columbia, and Puerto Rico	104
Chair and highest-ranking officer of opposite sex, national committeeman and national committeewoman from Guam, Virgin Islands, and American Samoa	12
Cochairs and highest-ranking officers of opposite sex, national committeemen and national committeewomen of Democrats Abroad	8
Members apportioned to states and equivalent units on basis of current national convention apportionment formula	200
Auxiliaries	
Democratic Governors Association (3)	
Congressional Parties (4)	
Democratic Mayors Conference (3)	
Young Democrats (3)	
National Federation of Democratic Women (3)	
Democratic County Officials Conference (3)	
Democratic State Legislative Leaders Association (3)	
National Democratic Municipal Officials Conference (3)	25
Additional Members	45
Total	403
Republican National Committee	
National committeeman, national committeewoman, and a chair from each state and from the District of Columbia, Guam, Puerto Rico, and the Virgin Islands	162
Total	162

Source: The Charter and the Bylaws of the Democratic Party of the United States, and *The Rules of the Republican Party.*

with congressional experience before, during, and/or after their party organization leadership are Republicans Mark Hanna, Henry Payne, Harry New, Simeon Fess, Everett Sanders, Joseph Martin, Carroll Reece, Hugh Scott, Leonard Hall, Thruston Morton, William Miller, Rogers Morton, Robert Dole, George Bush, William Brock, and general chair Paul Laxalt; Democrats James Jones, Thomas Taggart, George White, Cordell Hull, Howard McGrath, Henry Jackson, and Fred Harris.

Apart from Congress, the national-level political office from which the most chairs have been associated has been that of postmaster general. The list of chairs who had served previously, subsequently, or simultaneously as head of the Post Office consists of Democrats James Farley, Frank Walker, Robert Hannegan, and Lawrence O'Brien, and Republicans Marshall Jewell, Henry Payne, George Cortelyou, Harry New, Frank Hitchcock, Will Hays, and Arthur Summerfield.

Table 6 National Party Chairs

Name	State	Years of service	Name	State	Years of service
Democratic party			**Republican party (continued)**		
B. F. Hallett	Massachusetts	1848-1852	J. Donald Cameron	Pennsylvania	1879-1880
Robert McLane	Maryland	1852-1856	Marshall Jewell	Connecticut	1880-1883
David A. Smalley	Virginia	1856-1860	D. M. Sabin	Minnesota	1883-1884
August Belmont	New York	1860-1872	B. F. Jones	Pennsylvania	1884-1888
Augustus Schell	New York	1972-1876	Matthew S. Quay	Pennsylvania	1888-1891
Abram S. Hewitt	New York	1876-1877	James S. Clarkson	Iowa	1891-1892
William H. Barnum	Connecticut	1877-1889	Thomas H. Carter	Montana	1892-1896
Calvin S. Brice	Ohio	1889-1892	Mark A. Hanna	Ohio	1896-1904
William F. Hartity	Pennsylvania	1892-1896	Henry C. Payne	Wisconsin	1904
James K. Jones	Arkansas	1896-1904	George B. Cortelyou	New York	1904-1907
Thomas Taggart	Indiana	1904-1908	Harry S. New	Indiana	1907-1908
Norman E. Mack	New York	1908-1912	Frank H. Hitchcock	Massachusetts	1908-1909
William F. McCombs	New York	1912-1916	John F. Hill	Maine	1909-1912
Vance C. McCormick	Pennsylvania	1916-1919	Victor Rosewater	Nebraska	1912
Homer S. Cummings	Connecticut	1919-1920	Charles D. Hilles	New York	1912-1916
George White	Ohio	1920-1921	William R. Wilcox	New York	1916-1918
Cordell Hull	Tennessee	1921-1924	Will Hays	Indiana	1918-1921
Clem Shaver	West Virginia	1924-1928	John T. Adams	Iowa	1921-1924
John J. Raskob	Maryland	1928-1932	William M. Butler	Massachusetts	1924-1928
James A. Farley	New York	1932-1940	Hubert Work	Colorado	1928-1929
Edward J. Flynn	New York	1940-1943	Claudius H. Huston	Tennessee	1929-1930
Frank C. Walker	Pennsylvania	1943-1944	Simeon D. Fess	Ohio	1930-1932
Robert E. Hannegan	Missouri	1944-1947	Everett Sanders	Indiana	1932-1934
J. Howard McGrath	Rhode Island	1947-1949	Henry P. Fletcher	Pennsylvania	1934-1936
William M. Boyle, Jr.	Missouri	1949-1951	John Hamilton	Kansas	1936-1940
Frank E. McKinney	Indiana	1951-1952	Joseph W. Martin, Jr.	Massachusetts	1940-1942
Stephen A. Mitchell	Illinois	1952-1954	Harrison E. Spangler	Iowa	1942-1944
Paul M. Butler	Indiana	1955-1960	Herbert Brownell, Jr.	New York	1944-1946
Henry M. Jackson	Washington	1960-1961	B. Carroll Reece	Tennessee	1946-1948
John M. Bailey	Connecticut	1961-1968	Hugh D. Scott, Jr.	Pennsylvania	1948-1949
Lawrence F. O'Brien	Massachusetts	1968-1969	Guy George Gabrielson	New Jersey	1949-1952
Fred Harris	Oklahoma	1969-1970	Arthur E. Summerfield	Michigan	1952-1953
Lawrence F. O'Brien	Massachusetts	1970-1972	C. Wesley Roberts	Kansas	1953
Jean Westwood	Utah	1972	Leonard W. Hall	New York	1953-1957
Robert Strauss	Texas	1972-1977	H. Meade Alcorn, Jr.	Connecticut	1957-1959
Kenneth Curtis	Maine	1977-1978	Thruston B. Morton	Kentucky	1959-1961
John White	Texas	1978-1981	William E. Miller	New York	1961-1964
Charles Manatt	California	1981-1985	Dean Burch	Arizona	1964-1965
Paul Kirk	Massachusetts	1985-1989	Ray C. Bliss	Ohio	1965-1969
Ronald H. Brown	Washington, D.C.	1989-	Rogers C. B. Morton	Maryland	1969-1971
			Robert Dole	Kansas	1971-1973
			George Bush	Texas	1973-1974
			Mary Louise Smith	Iowa	1974-1977
Republican party			William Brock	Tennessee	1977-1981
Edwin D. Morgan	New York	1856-1864	Richard Richards	Utah	1981-1983
Henry J. Morgan	New York	1864-1866	Paul Laxalt		
Marcus L. Ward	New Jersey	1866-1868	(general chair)	Nevada	1983-1986
William Claflin	Massachusetts	1868-1872	Frank Fahrenkopf	Nevada	1983-1989
Edwin D. Morgan	New York	1872-1876	Lee Atwater	South Carolina	1989-
Zachariah Chandler	Michigan	1987-1879			

Source: Hugh A. Bone, *Party Committees and National Politics* (Seattle: University of Washington Press, 1958), 241-243; updated by author.

Gubernatorial linkages are slightly less frequent. In the nineteenth century, three incumbent governors simultaneously served as national party chairs: Republicans Edwin Morgan, Marcus Ward, and William Claflin. Five former governors later occupied the party chair: Republicans Marshall Jewell, John Hill, and Paul Laxalt; Democrats Howard McGrath and Kenneth Curtis. Two former party chairs went on to serve as governors: Democrats Robert McLane and George White.

Until the 1970s the party chair was exclusively the province of white males. Democrat Jean Westwood broke this pattern in 1972, followed by Republican Mary Louise Smith in 1974. The Democrats shattered precedent in 1989 and chose a black, Ronald Brown, as chair. The GOP also avoided stereotypes, choosing as chair Lee Atwater, 37, a former rock 'n' roll guitarist.

The Party Chair as Candidate for National Office

Traditionally, the national party chair performed in the arena of organizational politics and eschewed personal participation in electoral politics at the presidential level. Democratic national chair James A. Farley's candidacy for the 1940 presidential nomination constituted a major and singular departure from established practice. Since 1960, however, the incumbent national party chair frequently has figured in speculation surrounding the composition of the party's presidential ticket. This connection has taken three forms: (1) the chair's availability for the vice-presidential nomination; (2) consideration of the party chair position as a consolation prize for a loser in the vice-presidential sweepstakes; (3) the presence of former party chairs in the field of contenders for the party's presidential nomination.

These modern patterns first emerged in 1960, when Sen. Thruston B. Morton of Kentucky, the Republican national chairman, was a finalist on nominee Richard Nixon's list of vice-presidential prospects. Passed over in favor of Henry Cabot Lodge, Morton retained the chairmanship.

On the Democratic side in 1960, nominee John F. Kennedy placed Sen. Henry M. Jackson of Washington on his short list of potential running mates. After he opted for Lyndon B. Johnson, Kennedy tapped Jackson for the DNC chairmanship for the duration of the campaign. When his nomination met with vocal opposition at the convention, Johnson received word from the Kennedy camp that should he decline the offer, he could have the party chairmanship.

In 1964 Republican nominee Barry M. Goldwater named as his running mate the incumbent national party chair, Rep. William E. Miller of New York. As of 1989 Miller remained the only incumbent chair ever named to a major party ticket.

The year 1968 marked the return of Richard Nixon to the Republicans' presidential ticket. Nixon seriously considered Rep. Rogers C. B. Morton of Maryland, younger brother of Thruston, as his vice-presidential partner, before settling on Spiro T. Agnew. When a vacancy occurred in the chairmanship following the general election, Nixon recommended Morton for the post.

In the Democratic contest that year, Sen. Fred Harris of Oklahoma lost out to Edmund S. Muskie as Hubert H. Humphrey's choice of running mate. Harris then unsuccessfully sought the party chairmanship that on Humphrey's suggestion went to Lawrence F. O'Brien. Harris's persistence paid off when he was named chair in January 1969 amid speculation that he was positioning himself for a future presidential bid.

In 1972 O'Brien figured prominently in convention-week speculation for the vice-presidential spot that went to Sen. Thomas Eagleton of Missouri. When Eagleton resigned the nomination shortly afterward, O'Brien again was mentioned as a possible choice, though the slot eventually went to R. Sargent Shriver.

When Richard Nixon resigned in 1974, Gerald R. Ford became president, creating a vacancy in the vice presidency. Ford considered appointing George Bush, then the incumbent Republican national chair, but instead he chose Nelson Rockefeller. Ford dumped Rockefeller from the ticket at the 1976 convention, replacing him with a former national chair, Sen. Robert Dole of Kansas. One of the individuals Ford passed over, John B. Connally, was offered the party chairmanship as a consolation prize, but Connally reportedly rejected the offer. The Democratic presidential field that year included former party chair Harris.

The 1980 Republican nomination contest featured the candidacies of two former party chairs, Bush and Dole. After both lost out to Ronald Reagan and Bush became Reagan's running mate, the ticket's victory made Bush the first former party chair to be elected vice president.

In 1988, with Reagan's second term due to expire, Bush and Dole resumed their presidential rivalry. Early in the campaign season rumors had former senator Paul Laxalt of Nevada, who held the position of general chair of the Republican party from 1982 through 1986, as a possible contender; but Laxalt never entered the fray. Bush prevailed, and his November victory made him also the first former party chair to be elected president.

From the late 1950s through the mid-1970s, several House and Senate members were national party chairs. The visibility of the office made it attractive to electoral figures who sought the role of party spokesman. But the decision by both parties in the 1970s to make the chair a full-time position was likely to diminish this connection in the future.

Other Officers. Besides designating a chair, the national committee selects a number of other officers. The Democrats elect three vice chairs (two of whom are of the opposite sex of the chair), a treasurer, a finance chair, a secretary, and other appropriate officers as they deem necessary. The full committee is also empowered to choose an executive committee, determining its size, composition, and term of office.

The Republicans choose a cochair of the opposite sex, along with eight vice chairs—a male and a female from each of four different regional state associations: West, Midwest, Northeast, and South. They also select a secretary, treasurer, and such other officers as they desire. Other collective leadership structures include the chair's executive council and the executive committee, with party rules stipulating procedures for selection and responsibilities.

Activities. There is a distinction between the status and activities of the national chair whose party nominee occupies the White House and the one whose party is out. The in-party's chairs serve under the party leadership of the president. Out-party chairs have no obvious party superior, yet they occupy ambiguous positions with respect to the congressional party leadership.

The role of the in-party chair has undergone major changes over the past fifty years. Once, the national chair was a central actor in presidential politics. By and large, this is no longer the case. Both in-party and out-party chairs today are far more involved in directing party-building endeavors—national, state, and local—than was previously typical. This has come about because of changes in both the presidency and the political parties.

In the past the national chair customarily directed the party campaign, of which the presidential race was the central feature. The expectation of tying together the overall party effort and the specifically presidential campaign underlay the development of the custom whereby the national committee began soliciting the presidential nominee's recommendation for its chair. Operating out of party headquarters, the president's choice would direct the campaign.

More recently, the presidential nominees have instead developed and relied on personal campaign organizations. The reasons include strategic considerations related to declining party identification in the electorate, federal election laws effectively mandating the establishment of separate organizations, and, most important, changes in the nature of nomination campaigns.

Years ago, nomination campaigns were low-key efforts designed to elicit the support of a relative handful of party chieftains, who in turn controlled state delegations at the convention. With the advent of primary contests to select delegates, prospective nominees must develop full-scale campaign organizations well in advance of the convention.

The road to the convention nomination now proceeds through delegate-selection primaries in well over thirty states, where campaign organizations are tried and tested. The eventual winner normally will be inclined to continue to operate through that organizational vehicle in the general election campaign that follows.

This development relegates the national organization to the periphery of the campaign effort. It similarly places the chair outside the inner circle of campaign decision makers. Thus, a major role traditionally performed by the party chair has been rendered negligible.

At the outset, national chairs had important patronage responsibilities. The chair claimed the spoils of electoral victory for the party loyalists. The traditional association between the chair and the postmaster generalship pertained directly to this task, because the Post Office provided an abundance of government jobs to be distributed among the party faithful. By the time of the Nixon administration, the Post Office's patronage position had long since been decimated by civil service expansion. In 1971 the department was restructured as the Postal Service, a government corporation, removing it from both the cabinet and party politics.

Throughout the government, the establishment and expansion of the merit system has drastically reduced the available patronage. Moreover, the types of positions now available tend to be less appropriate for party organization claimants. Thus, the role of the party chair as patronage dispenser has become passé.

Party chairs in days gone by also served their presidents as key political advisers. They kept chief executives in touch with the perspectives of their counterparts in statehouses and city halls.

Modern presidents have perceived much less need for such advice. They now have a sizable personal staff of aides they can rely on as advisers and intermediaries with other political leaders. Polling organizations provide presidents with an abundance of data about the public pulse. Here again, the traditional role of the chair has been supplanted.

Developments within the party organization also have worked to distance the chair from the presidential inner circle. Party chairs have always operated under a norm of neutrality toward competing candidacies for the presidential nomination. Usually, this norm was conveniently ignored by in-party chairs serving as presidential appointees and pursuing the interests of their sponsors. As the parties have come to be more bureaucratic and institutional, the expectations regarding neutrality are growing stronger. Federal election laws reinforce the pressure for the chair to remain neutral.[10] Thus, modern party chairs are less likely to occupy the traditional role of key presidential adviser.

The chair's role of fund raiser endures today, but in vastly altered form and more removed from presidential politics. Nineteenth-century chairs tended to be wealthy individuals who made major personal contributions to the presidential campaign, bankrolled a limited party operation that supplemented the campaign, and prevailed upon their similarly disposed friends and associates to do likewise.

The growing costs of presidential campaigns have placed financing them beyond the means of a relative handful of individuals, even those of immense personal wealth. Further, federal election laws limit the financial contributions of individuals. They also provide for public funding of presidential campaigns.

National party headquarters operations have also grown beyond the capacity of the chair personally to subsidize them. Thus, while contemporary chairs continue to perform a significant fund-raising function, they do so in an altered fashion that is oriented toward party building and somewhat distanced from the presidential arena.

Both national committees have for many years established finance committees and designated individuals to chair them. The Republicans began doing so in the 1930s, and the Democrats followed suit some two decades later. These individuals, while under the authority of the chair, nevertheless operate separately and thus relieve the chair of many traditional fund-raising responsibilities.

As these traditional roles have diminished in importance, other time-honored functions have endured and even increased. Three identified by political scientists Cornelius Cotter and Bernard Hennessy are those of *image-maker*, *hell-raiser*, and *administrator*.[11]

Public relations has always been a major responsibility of the party chair. In the nineteenth century, many national chairs came from newspaper backgrounds. While this has been much less the case since World War I, a sensitivity to and a flair for public relations continue to be expected of the chair.

The chair seeks to promote a positive public image for the party, to position its actions and objectives in the best possible light. This can be done by personally assuming the role of party spokesperson. Such a chair will regularly make the rounds of the network television interview shows such as "Meet the Press" and "Face the Nation" and will be readily available for interviews and comments to reporters. In addition, the chair acts as a good-will ambassador for party unity and expansion. Chairs uncomfortable with personal appearances will nonetheless sponsor similar efforts by other voices for the party.

The chair as hell-raiser is the partisan's partisan. Such a figure will seek to satisfy the expectations of the party faithful by flailing away at the opposition party and righteously defending the party against detractors' assaults. Presidents often rely on their party chairs to emphasize this party leadership role. Doing so enables presidents to appear above partisan battles. However, it also reduces the party's significance as a link between president and public.

As administrators, party chairs supervise the activities of the national headquarters—a role that has grown with the headquarters' expansion. The current requirement that the chair's position be full time and salaried also serves to emphasize the administrative aspects of the job.

Headquarters

In the nineteenth century, party operations were conducted largely within the context of the convention and the presidential campaign.[12] The chief responsibilities of the committee and its chair were to prepare and conduct the quadrennial nominating convention and direct the ensuing presidential campaign. Once the nominations were completed, headquarters would be established, usually in New York City, and the campaign led by the party chair. After the election, the organization would be largely disbanded. The committee would meet perhaps once a year; at other times the national party would exist in the person of the chair. The pace would pick up again when plans had to be made for the forthcoming convention.

In the 1920s both national parties established year-round headquarters operations with paid staff. The Republicans took the lead here. In the ensuing years, they would continue to emphasize organizational development more than their Democratic counterparts. Initially, both parties rented office space in Washington, D.C. During the Nixon administration, the Republicans moved into their own building adjacent to the House Office Buildings on Capitol Hill. In the 1980s the Democrats did the same, opening their permanent offices just a few blocks away.

Both parties have expanded their staffs and scope of operations, which swell temporarily before presidential elections. In the intervening years, the staff size remains relatively high. Political scientists Cornelius Cotter and John Bibby have assembled figures indicating that since 1950 the Republicans have never had fewer than eighty paid employees, and the Democrats, never fewer than forty. Further, off-year staffing for both parties has averaged in excess of seventy.[13]

With this increased staff capacity, the national party has been shifting its emphases away from its traditional responsibilities toward party-building activities. But tasks related to the planning and conduct of the convention persist. The committee issues the convention call, which stipulates procedures for delegate apportionment and selection, along with temporary convention rules. It designates the membership and leadership of preconvention committees and designates key convention presiders and speakers. It establishes the site, date, and order of business, though with in-party committees the White House normally has a significant say in these determinations.

The national headquarters retains some presidential campaign responsibilities. The Democratic party charter formally authorizes it to conduct that campaign.[14] The nominee's own campaign organization, however, typically assumes the brunt of the campaign effort, relegating the party organization to the periphery. Nevertheless, operations of a contemporary presidential campaign are sufficiently broad that there is plenty of activity to occupy the time and energy of an expanded national committee staff throughout the fall campaign.

It is outside the arena of presidential politics, however, that party headquarters are making increasingly significant contributions, primarily in campaign assistance and other services to the state and local parties. The national parties are now actively engaged in candidate recruitment. They offer training sessions and make available a wide variety of information and expertise for the benefit of the parties' nominees. These include research, polling, data processing, direct mail, consultants, and money in vast quantities.[15]

Here again, the Republicans were the pioneers, initially under the leadership of Ray Bliss, party chair from 1965 to 1969. The same approach was emphasized by William Brock, chair from 1977 to 1981. The Democrats have followed suit since the late 1970s.

State and Local Levels

There are of course substantial variations among the fifty state and countless county and subcounty units of the political parties. Their structural components typically replicate the national pattern: convention, committee, chair, and, in recent years, headquarters staff.[16] At the lower levels, the pattern persists, though with the omission of headquarters staffs.

State Conventions

State conventions ordinarily meet once every two years, preceding the scheduled elections. They bring together representatives of the lower-level party units and vary in size. Most draw under a thousand delegates, but several exceed this total. In 1978 more than 7,300 delegates assembled for the Virginia Republican convention.

The advent and acceptance of the direct primary in this century has almost completely taken from these bodies what was originally one of their primary responsibilities—nominating candidates for statewide offices. Contemporary conventions may elect party officers and adopt a party platform. During presidential election years, the state conventions traditionally played an important role in the selection of the state parties' delegates to the nominating convention. Party reforms have substantially reduced this role.

State Committees

State party committees also vary in size, from under fifty to more than five hundred. California, the biggest, assembles more than 800 members. As is the case at the national level, the state committees are charged with leadership selection and guiding the party's fortunes between conventions. By and large, these tasks are delegated to chairs and headquarters staffs. Many state party committees also designate executive committees to act for them.

State Chairs

State party chairs can be categorized into in-party and out-party groups, depending on whether the party's nominee holds the governorship. In-party chairs can be further subdivided into those who act as political agents of their governors and those who act independently. In many state parties, the convention or the committee defers in selecting

How States Allocated Democratic Delegates in 1988

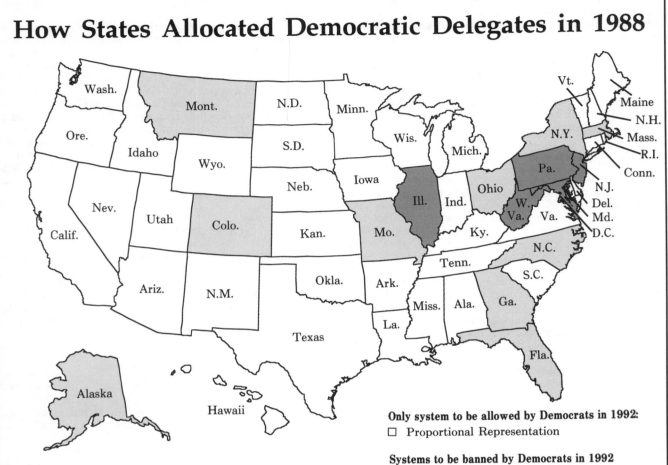

Only system to be allowed by Democrats in 1992:
☐ Proportional Representation

Systems to be banned by Democrats in 1992
■ Direct Election
☐ Bonus

The Democratic national convention at Altanta in 1988 approved rules changes to ensure that the party's presidential delegates in 1992 would be elected to more closely reflect one-person, one-vote.

One change would reduce the number of uncommitted "superdelegates," who had moved overwhelmingly in mid-1988 to the eventual nominee, Massachusetts Gov. Michael S. Dukakis. Another would require delegates to be divided among candidates to reflect their share of a state's primary or caucus vote. Banned would be delegate-allocation systems used in 1988 that gave an extra reward to the winner.

Those systems benefited Dukakis in a number of states. He won four of the five states that held direct election primaries (where voters balloted directly for district delegates and winner-take-all was possible). And he won six of ten states with bonus systems (where the winner in each district won one delegate before the rest were divided proportionally).

In 1988 Democrats in most of the megastates used one of these two systems of awarding delegates, but in 1992 they must join the rest of the country in allocating their delegates proportionally to reflect the primary or caucus vote.

The table below compares the percentage of the primary vote that Dukakis and Jesse L. Jackson received in 1988 with the share of delegates they won under the various systems of delegate allocation. Each candidate's delegate total is based on the number he won as a result of primary voting and does not include delegates gained after other candidates or from the uncommitted ranks.

Maryland had a hybrid system, electing district delegates by direct election and statewide delegates by proportional representation. (Puerto Rico's direct election primary results are included in the tabulations.)

Primary Results in 1988 (percent)

	Dukakis		Jackson	
Primaries	Primary vote	Delegates	Primary vote	Delegates
Direct election	46	56	29	12
Bonus	43	54	28	30
Proportional representation	40	43	30	34

a chair to the wishes of the governor or the gubernatorial nominee. Party building is a primary concern of state party chairs, who also are involved in fund-raising and campaign-related activities.

State Headquarters

Contemporary state party chairs usually operate out of year-round party headquarters occupied by small but full-time, paid staff. This development is relatively recent, dating back to the early 1960s. Political scientist Robert Huckshorn attributes this phenomenon to four factors. One is the increase in party competition at the state level, especially in the South. Another is the growth of technology that has inspired state parties to take advantage of new methods and approaches in electoral politics.

A third factor is pressure from the national parties and government. Reforms in the selection of delegates to the national convention have imposed procedural guidelines on the state parties that require considerable attention to detail. Federal campaign finance legislation also has imposed stringent reporting guidelines.

Finally, Huckshorn contends that increased communication among the state chairs in recent years, taking the form of meetings under formal organizational auspices, has encouraged chairs lacking headquarters facilities to emulate those who do. The result is an increased bureaucratization of the state parties.

Local Party Organization

At the local level, the components of convention, committee, and chair exist amid vast variations. The legendary urban party machines are essentially extinct. Nevertheless, some retain a residual and relative strength. In Chicago, for example, remnants of the once-powerful Daley organization linger. Elsewhere, some local parties are but organizational shells, with positions unoccupied and handfuls of officials quietly tending to procedural regularities. Here as at the other levels, election campaigns provide the primary arena for party activity. A recent comparative study found few signs of organizational decline among local parties.[17]

State and Local Parties and Presidential Politics

More so than today, the past relationship between state and local party organization and the presidency centered on presidential selection. After the national convention became the nominating vehicle in the 1830s, and until recently, state and local party leaders tightly controlled the selection of convention delegates and effectively instructed their delegations in voting on nominees. Thus, astute presidential candidates sought the support of these grass-roots political leaders.

The preconvention presidential campaign typically consisted of relatively low-key efforts by candidates and managers to line up commitments from the party bosses. In turn, the bosses had options such as jumping aboard a bandwagon, backing favorite sons, or remaining uncommitted in hopes of ultimately tipping the balance at a divided convention.

Conventions in those days featured "smoke-filled rooms" where the party leaders gathered to wheel and deal for the presidential nomination. Thus, the victor would be beholden to the bosses who had authorized the outcome. Around the turn of the century, Ohio's Mark Hanna epitomized power brokers of this type.

In the years immediately preceding World War II, Frank Hague of New Jersey and Boss Crump of Memphis, Tennessee, represented the breed. As late as the 1960s, Mayor Richard Daley of Chicago still embodied the traditional pattern.

In campaigns of this era the presidential nominee relied heavily on personnel resources that the state party leaders could mobilize. Old-time campaigns were much more labor-intensive than they are today. Until about 1960 the state party leaders were able to provide the necessary campaign workers.

Following the campaign, the victorious party's bosses would claim the federal patronage as a reward for their workers. Thus, through the spoils system, the presidential-selection process clearly linked the state and local parties with the presidency.

Fundamental changes have altered this traditional linkage process. Party reforms beginning in the Progressive Era around the turn of the century, and picking up steam after 1968, have drastically diminished the role of state party leaders in designating and controlling delegations to the national convention. Delegates formerly hand-picked by party leaders now are mostly chosen through primaries and participatory caucuses.

In presidential primaries, party voters sometimes vote directly for convention delegates. In many states, they do so in conjunction with a vote for the presidential candidate of their choice. Convention delegates slots usually go to supporters of the various presidential candidates in proportion to their electoral support.

In the caucuses, local party activists gather at specified locations in voting precincts to register their support for particular presidential candidates. Each precinct will send representatives to a county-level assembly in proportion to the initial division of support for the various contenders. At the county level, candidate supporters will be selected, again proportionally, to attend congressional district and finally state conventions. There the national convention delegates will be chosen from among the survivors of the earlier trials. The state parties also provide for at-large representatives to be chosen at the state level.

Thus, presidential candidates are considerably less likely to rely on the state leaders' support. Instead, they will emphasize appeals to pressure group leaders and party activists in the electorate who, through presidential primaries and participatory caucuses, have the controlling say in delegate selection. The delegations so chosen will be more under the direction of candidate and pressure group organizations, lessening the state party leaders' influence on the convention's choice.

Modern presidential campaigns are capital and technology intensive. Where once party workers rang doorbells to solicit support, today through television candidates themselves appear in living rooms throughout the nation.

The expansion of civil service and consequent reduction of patronage resources also has helped to disengage state and party leaders from the presidency. This is not to say that the state and local parties have declined organizationally. Indeed, there is considerable evidence to the contrary.[18] But their organizational activity no longer relates so clearly to the presidency as it once did.

Strom Thurmond, left, ran for president under the Dixiecrat party label in 1948. Twenty years later, George Wallace ran under the American Independent party banner.

National-State Party Relations

National parties of the past were weak and lacking in resources compared with the state and local political organizations, primarily because the federal system decentralized power in general and party power in particular.[19] In recent years, a dramatic "nationalization" has taken place as the national parties expanded authority and influence over their state counterparts. The two parties have taken different paths to similar ends. The Democrats have reformed party rules that primarily address delegate-selection procedures for the national convention. The Republican approach has been less legalistic, concentrating instead on making the state parties more reliant on the national party for needed services.[20]

The Democrats' altered course began in the late 1940s in the context of uncertainty about the loyalty of certain southern state parties toward the national ticket and platform. Twice in a twenty-year period, sizable elements of the southern Democratic party bolted to follow a regional favorite son.

In 1948 several southern delegations walked out of the national convention following the passage of a controversial platform plank supporting black civil rights. After the convention, several southern state parties held a rump assembly and nominated South Carolina governor Strom Thurmond to head a "Dixiecrat" ticket in the presidential election. Thurmond won four states and thirty-nine electoral votes.

In 1968 Alabama governor George Wallace mounted a presidential bid under the American Independent party label. He carried five states and won forty-six electoral votes.

During the two decades of conflict over the loyalty issue, the national party demanded that the state units guarantee support for the convention's decisions. To put teeth in this demand it threatened not to seat noncomplying state delegations at subsequent conventions.

Initially, this controversy was closely associated with the issue of civil rights for blacks. The 1964 Democratic national convention resolved to prohibit racial discrimination in delegate selection to the 1968 convention. This constituted a historic assertion of national authority over what had previously been the state parties' exclusive prerogative. It also authorized the national chair to appoint a committee to assist the state parties in complying with this new guideline.

This committee and the 1968 convention, along with a new group established by the latter, the Commission on Party Structure and Delegate Selection, broadened the issue beyond that of black civil rights to embrace more generally popular participation in delegate selection and other party activities. These various proposals were accepted by the Democratic National Committee and the party's 1972 convention. They culminated at the 1974 midterm convention in the adoption of a charter that clearly subordinates the state parties to their national counterpart. As amended, this charter and accompanying bylaws remain in force as the party's "constitution."

The nationalization of the Republican party has placed much less emphasis on formal rules. Where the national Democrats have mandated reform in delegate selection, the Republicans have merely recommended it. In practice, however, many of the Democratic party guidelines have been incorporated by state legislatures into laws, so that they are similarly binding on the state Republican parties.

The national Republican party has amassed a formidable financial foundation that allows it to bestow "favors," such as monetary assistance and campaign and party-building expertise, that bind state and local parties to the national organization. Therefore, while the Republicans have not formally altered their party structure, they too have positioned the national organization in the dominant position.

Notes

1. Nine isolated instances of "faithless electors," or those who did not follow partisan instructions, have been identified since 1796. The most recent occurred in 1988. Congressional Quarterly, *Presidential Elections Since 1789*, 4th ed. (Washington: Congressional Quarterly Inc., 1987), 147.
2. Herbert Kaufman, "The Growth of the Federal Personnel System," in Wallace Sayre, ed. *The Federal Government Service*, 2d ed. (Englewood Cliffs, N.J.: The American Assembly, Prentice-Hall, 1965), 41-43, provides a table, "Extension of Competitive Civil Service, 1884-1963," which sets the total number of federal government employees in 1884 at 131,208. His source was the Commission on Organization of the Executive Branch of Government, *Report on Organization of the Executive Branch of Government* (February, 1955), 97-98.
3. William A. Riordan, *Plunkitt of Tammany Hall* (New York: Dutton Paperback, 1963), 13.
4. This discussion follows the outline of the presentation by Frank J. Sorauf and Paul Allen Beck, *Party Politics in America*, 6th ed. (Glenview, Ill.: Scott, Foresman, 1988), 167-187.
5. The most important single statement of the concept and significance of party identification is found in Angus Campbell et al., *The American Voter* (New York: Wiley, 1960), ch. 5-7. For a general consideration of more recent findings attaching less significance to party identification, see Norman H. Nie, Sidney Verba, and John R. Petrocik, *The Changing American Voter* (Cambridge, Mass.: Harvard University Press, 1976). On the phenomenon of ticket-splitting, see Walter DeVries and Lance Tarrance, Jr., *The Ticket-Splitter: A New Force in American Politics* (Grand Rapids, Mich.: Eerdmans, 1972).
6. The party-decline thesis finds expression in Walter Dean Burnham, *Critical Elections and the Mainsprings of American Politics* (New York: Norton, 1970); Gerald M. Pomper,

"The Decline of the Party in American Elections," *Political Science Quarterly* 92 (Spring 1977): 21-41; William J. Crotty and Gary C. Jacobson, *American Parties in Decline* (Boston: Little, Brown, 1980); and Martin P. Wattenberg, *The Decline of American Political Parties* (Cambridge, Mass.: Harvard University Press, 1984).

7. The traditional role and status of the national party convention is developed at length in Paul T. David, Ralph M. Goldman, and Richard C. Bain, *The Politics of National Party Conventions* (Washington: Brookings Institution, 1960).

8. Two classic works on the national party committees are Hugh A. Bone, *Party Committees and National Politics* (Seattle: University of Washington Press, 1958); and Cornelius P. Cotter and Bernard C. Hennessy, *Politics Without Power: The National Party Committees* (New York: Atherton, 1964). Also see *The Charter and the Bylaws of the Democratic Party of the United States* (Washington, D.C.: Democratic National Committee, 1987); and *The Rules of the Republican Party* (Washington, D.C.: Republican National Committee, 1984).

9. Generally, see Cotter and Hennessy, *Politics Without Power*, chs. 4-5, for a consideration of the traditional role and status of the national party chair.

10. Cornelius P. Cotter and John F. Bibby, "Institutional Development of Parties and the Thesis of Party Decline," *Political Science Quarterly* 95 (Spring 1980): 6-7.

11. Cotter and Hennessy, *Politics Without Power*, 67-71, 78-80.

12. See Bone, *Party Committees and National Politics*, ch. 2; Cotter and Hennessy, *Politics Without Power*, ch. 6-9; Cotter and Bibby, "Institutional Development of Parties," 2-9.

13. Cotter 14. *The Charter and Bylaws of the Democratic Party*, 3.

14. *The Charter and Bylaws of the Democratic Party*, 3.

15. Sorauf and Beck, *Party Politics in America*, 144.

16. Sources for this discussion include Malcolm E. Jewell and David Olson, *American State Parties and Elections*, rev. ed. (Homewood, Ill.: Dorsey, 1982), ch. 3; Robert J. Huckshorn, *Party Leadership in the States* (Amherst: University of Massachusetts Press, 1976); and Cornelius P. Cotter et al., *Party Organizations in American Politics* (New York: Praeger, 1984).

17. Cotter et al., *Party Organizations in American Politics*, ch. 2.

18. Ibid., passim.

19. See E. E. Schattschneider, *Party Government* (New York: Rinehart, 1942), 129-133; Morton Grodzins, "American Political Parties and the American System," *Western Political Quarterly* (December 1960): 974-998.

20. Cotter and Bibby, "Institutional Development of Parties," 13-20; Charles Longley, "Party Reform and Party Nationalization: The Case of the Democrats," in *The Party Symbol: Readings on Political Parties*, ed. William Crotty (San Francisco: Freeman, 1980), 359-378; John F. Bibby, "Party Renewal in the National Republican Party," in *Party Renewal in America*, ed. Gerald Pomper (New York: Praeger, 1981), 102-115.

Selected Bibliography

Bibby, John F. "Political Parties and Federalism: The Republican National Committee." *Publius* (Winter 1979): 229-36.

——. "Party Renewal in the National Republican Party." In *Party Renewal in America*, 102-115. Edited by Gerald M. Pomper. New York: Praeger, 1981.

Bone, Hugh A. *Party Committees and National Politics*. Seattle: University of Washington Press, 1958.

Burnham, Walter Dean. *Critical Elections and the Mainsprings of American Politics*. New York: Norton, 1970.

Campbell, Angus, Philip E. Converse, Warren E. Miller, and Donald E. Stokes. *The American Voter*. New York: Wiley, 1960.

Cotter, Cornelius P., and John F. Bibby. "Institutional Development of Parties and the Thesis of Party Decline." *Political Science Quarterly* 95 (Spring 1980): 1-27.

——, James L. Gibson, John F. Bibby, and Robert J. Huckshorn. *Party Organizations in American Politics*. New York: Praeger, 1984.

——, and Bernard D. Hennessy. *Politics Without Power: The National Party Committees*. New York: Atherton, 1964.

Crotty, William J., and Gary C. Jacobson. *American Parties in Decline*. Boston: Little, Brown, 1980.

David, Paul T., Ralph M. Goldman, and Richard C. Bain. *The Politics of National Party Conventions*. Washington: Brookings Institution, 1960.

Flanigan, William H., and Nancy H. Zingale. *Political Behavior of the American Electorate*, 6th ed. Dubuque, Iowa: William C. Brown, 1987.

Huckshorn, Robert J. *Party Leadership in the States*. Amherst: University of Massachusetts Press, 1976.

Jewell, Malcolm E., and David M. Olson. *American State Parties and Elections*, rev. ed. Homewood, Ill.: Dorsey, 1982.

Longley, Charles. "Party Reform and Party Nationalization: The Case of the Democrats." In *The Party Symbol: Readings on Political Parties*, 359-378. Edited by William J. Crotty. San Francisco: Freeman, 1980.

Polsby, Nelson W. *Consequences of Party Reform*. New York: Oxford University Press, 1983.

Pomper, Gerald M. "The Decline of the Party in American Elections." *Political Science Quarterly* 92 (Spring 1977): 21-41.

Price, David E. *Bringing Back the Parties*. Washington, D.C.: CQ Press, 1984.

Wattenberg, Martin P. *The Decline of American Political Parties*, 1952-1980. Cambridge, Mass.: Harvard University Press, 1984.

Wekkin, Gary D. "National-State Party Relations: The Democrats' New Federal Structure." *Political Science Quarterly* 99 (Spring 1984): 45-72.

Presidents and the News Media

In the various roles of chief of state, head of government, commander in chief, and party leader, modern American presidents must be effective communicators. To promote their programs and policies, they must be able to forge a bond with the electorate and earn its trust and confidence. This presidents do largely by "going public" and by managing the news media. As a former White House aide noted, "presidential power is communications power." [1]

Communication has become an integral part of politics and the governing process to the extent that its use has become institutionalized. Because of the revolution in mass communications, presidents have been persuaded to change their political styles and governing procedures. Television, especially, has enhanced their ability to project their message and mobilize public sentiment. Correspondingly, television subjects them to microscopic scrutiny and tends to magnify their defects, hence diminishing some of the mystique of the office. In the main, however, it provides them with a marked advantage over their critics and rivals.

Today, an incumbent president enjoys constant media exposure. The president's voice is the most distinct in public affairs, the president's face the most familiar. The chief executive is the prime news personality in the country; each official act and most of the president's personal activities are reported and photographed by the news media and disseminated around the world. No other celebrated figure can match the president as a national attraction, thus ensuring that the electorate will listen and frequently heed what the White House has to say about public policy.

In a sense, the presidency has evolved into a form of theater in which the chief executive is the most visible and compelling actor on the American stage. Accordingly, one student of the presidency has observed, "The whole of the White House is an institution for communicating on behalf of the President." [2]

Specifically, political scientist Doris Graber has noted, the news media perform four basic functions for presidents. They keep them informed about breaking events, including developments in other parts of the government; they keep presidents attuned to the major concerns of the American people; they enable presidents and their staffs to "convey their messages to the general public as well as to political elites within and outside of government"; and they allow chief executives to "remain in full public view on the political stage," thereby ensuring that their human qualities and professional skills are thoroughly displayed. [3]

Thus, the media age has contributed toward the making of a more visible and personalized presidency.

Historical Background

The tradition of a free press in the United States is almost as old as the nation itself. It has become part of the national heritage, protected by the Constitution and woven in the country's social fabric.

From the early colonial years, the press—primitive by today's standards and politically partisan—was recognized as a force in the affairs of the citizens and their governmental representatives. James Madison perceived a free press as an essential pillar of democracy. "Whatever facilitates a general intercourse of sentiments," he wrote, "as good roads, domestic commerce, a free press, and particularly a circulation of newspapers through the entire body of the people ... is favorable to liberty." [4]

Madison, along with Alexander Hamilton and John Jay, wrote *The Federalist Papers* to enlist support for the new Constitution. Thomas Paine vigorously promoted separation from the crown in his provocative pamphlets, such as *Common Sense*. He also penned the *Crisis* papers, one of which contained the memorable line, "These are the times that try men's souls."

Universal acceptance of the notion that a free society cannot endure without a free exchange of ideas and information was not achieved easily. The struggle dates back at least to 1690 when the first colonial newsletter, *Publick Occurrences Both Foreign and Domestick*, was published in Boston by Benjamin Harris, who had fled to the New World after being pilloried in London for printing anticrown pamphlets. His small, three-page publication lasted only one issue because he had neglected to obtain the "countenance of authority" required by the royal governor of Massachusetts. Harris further offended the governor, as well as Puritan officials in Boston, by offering an account of the corruption of Indians by colonists and suggesting that the king of France had an affair with his son's wife.

During this period, the British crown viewed the press

By Dom Bonafede

and the spread of knowledge as a threat to its rule and discouraged the dissemination of public prints. This autocratic attitude was reflected in remarks by his majesty's governor in Virginia: "I thank God we have no free schools nor printing, and I hope we shall not have these hundred years. For learning has brought disobedience and heresy and sects into the world, and printing has divulged them and libels against the government. God keep us from both." [5]

In 1704 the *Boston News-Letter,* put out by John Campbell, the local postmaster, appeared under the notice that it was being "published by authority." The imprimatur, of course, meant that the paper was allowed to exist only with the benevolence of the royal governor. Accordingly, the paper was exceedingly dull and cautious in its reports, which consisted mainly of old news, death notices, summaries of church sermons, and notices of ship arrivals and departures.

To Campbell, the paper had been merely a sideline. In 1719 he lost his job as postmaster and his successor promptly began a new paper, the *Boston Gazette.* Incensed by the competition, Campbell wrote of the rival paper, "I pity [its] readers. Its sheets smell stronger of beer than of midnight oil." [6]

The incident thus served as a preface to the circulation wars that would mark the newspaper business in the late nineteenth and and early twentieth centuries. It was not until 1721, with the publication of the *New England Courant* by James Franklin, that criticism of the reigning authority began to seep into the American press. Franklin dared to publish without the approval of the colonial authorities and because of his temerity was thrown into prison and later prohibited from publishing a newspaper without prior sanction. He evaded the restriction by appointing his younger brother Benjamin as publisher. Young Ben had been an apprentice printer at twelve, and, though he was still little more than a boy, his intellect, unceasing curiosity, and grasp of public affairs, as well as his deft way

with words, served to make the paper a success. He and his brother had a falling out, however, and Ben moved to Philadelphia, where at twenty-three he began the *Pennsylvania Gazette.*

Benjamin Franklin's colorful personality and prominent role in the birth of the new nation have tended to overshadow his accomplishments as a creative journalist. He published one of the first American magazines, launched the first newspaper chain, and founded the first American foreign-language papers. Franklin additionally was one of the first advertising copywriters. One of his newspaper ads, which in those days looked similar in print to the news items, plugged a product called "Super Fine Crown Soap": "It cleanses fine Linens, Muslins, Laces, Chinces, Cambricks, with Ease and Expedition, which often suffer more from the long and hard rubbing of the Washer, through the ill qualities of the soap than the wearing." Interestingly, the soap was made by his brothers John and Peter.

Above all a patriot, Benjamin Franklin urged his fellow colonialists to join in a confederation and in 1754 drew and published what is considered the first American editorial cartoon: a reptile divided in separate parts, each representing one of the colonial states, over the caption, "Join, or Die."

By the early 1700s printing was an established, honorable craft; Ben Franklin demonstrated that journalism could be a respectable calling.

Evolution of Press Freedom

In a landmark case that exemplified the tension between the Colonies and crown, John Peter Zenger, publisher of the *New York Weekly Journal,* noted for its outspoken criticism of the British-born royal governor of New York, was charged with seditious libel in 1734. His attorney, Andrew Hamilton, argued that contrary to Brit-

In 1754 Benjamin Franklin drew what is considered the first American editorial cartoon. In his *Pennsylvania Gazette,* Franklin published the drawing of a reptile divided into separate parts, each representing one of the colonial states.

ish law—which held "the greater the truth the greater the libel"—truth could be used as a defense against libel and that a jury, not a royal magistrate, should decide questions of libel. The jury agreed, thereby striking a symbolic blow for press freedom.

Even so, a philosophical doctrine espousing freedom to exchange ideas and express views different from those of governing authorities developed more slowly among the public than the press. By the mid-eighteenth century more than a dozen independent weekly newspapers, necessarily small because of poor transportation and the need to set type laboriously by hand, had been established, mostly in port towns. Published mainly by printers and postmasters, they were directed at the educated, well-off urban classes and the political and commercial elites, who could afford the relatively high subscription rates. The "news" generally consisted of shipping and mercantile announcements, the promotion of special interests supported by the publisher, and information culled from old British newspapers brought in by ship.

But as the conflict between the Tories and patriots became more intense, the papers grew in numbers and circulation, and the press began assuming more of a significant role in the changing social and political realm. The papers were basically political, some siding with the Colonies and others with the crown, and all openly endorsing a particular faction, cause, party, or personality.

Their contents were distinctly editorial in tone, with a good deal of opinion. Personal attacks and biased information were common fare. No effort was made to disclose the closed-door deliberations of government bodies, yet editors of the early press risked imprisonment with their heavily caustic and bitterly critical editorials. By the time of the Revolutionary War, publishers were recognized as influential public figures, and newspapers went to an estimated 40,000 colonial homes.[7]

As rebellious fervor against British rule gathered momentum, many of the colonial papers, though divided on numerous issues, openly opposed stringent impositions by the crown, notably the 1765 Stamp Act, which was intended to replenish the royal coffers depleted by the war against France. The act levied a penny tax per issue upon each newspaper. The colonial publishers angrily denounced the tax as an infringement on their freedom and as an example of taxation without representation. The opposition voices were so forceful that within a year Parliament repealed the act.

With the beginning of the revolutionary war in 1775, the colonial press, comprising about thirty-seven papers, remained polarized between the crown and the revolutionists, with most favoring the latter. Several new papers sprang up while others went out of business; by the war's end in 1783 about thirty-five papers were being published regularly.[8] That same year the *Pennsylvania Evening Post and Daily Advertiser* was converted from a weekly to become the first American daily newspaper.

Party Newspapers

Following the Revolutionary War, newspapers in the new nation transferred their partisan leanings to the debate and controversy over the powers of the central government, manifested in the struggle between the Federalists under the banner of Alexander Hamilton, Washington's chief lieutenant, and the antifederalist Democratic-Republicans led by Thomas Jefferson. In essence, the Federalists favored a strong national government and the Democratic-Republicans, a league of more or less independent states.

The Founders by now were aware of the usefulness of the press and found expression of their views in the "party press"—newspapers and journals that sided with them and served their political purposes in mobilizing public opinion.

In his campaign to promote the Federalists' cause, Hamilton established the *Gazette of the United States*. Not to be outdone, Jefferson recruited Philip Freneau, "The Poet of the Revolution," ostensibly to act as a paid "translator" but in reality to publish a party newspaper, the *National Gazette*. Name-calling and vitriolic language were not uncommon in the pages of these and other papers of the time.

It is highly unlikely, however, that the Founders ever envisioned that the press would attain the lofty prominence it has or that it would become the "Fourth Branch of Government." The struggle for press freedom in the early years of the Republic, as reflected in the press duels between Hamilton and Jefferson, was part of a more ambitious struggle to form a constitutional government and a manifestation of the self-interests of the men who participated in the fight.

Furthermore, even those patriots who advocated press freedom also insisted on press responsibility. They were convinced that the press should be free to publish without prior restraint but should not be immune from sanctions for publishing false and malicious calumnies against the government.

In his defense of Zenger, attorney Andrew Hamilton told the jury that "Nothing ought to excuse a man who raises a false charge or accusation, even against a private person, and that no matter of allowance ought to be made to him who does so against a public magistrate."[9]

Benjamin Franklin himself declared in reference to journalists guilty of libeling government officials, "We should, in moderation, content ourselves with tarring and feathering and tossing them in a blanket."[10]

Testing the Limits

In 1798 the press became embroiled in the dispute between the Federalists and Jeffersonian Democratic-Republicans when, at a time when war with France appeared imminent, Congress passed the Sedition Act. Endorsed by the Federalist administration of John Adams, the legislation, notwithstanding the First Amendment, provided penalties of up to two years in prison and a fine of $2,000 for writing, printing, or uttering "false, scandalous and malicious" statements against the government or Congress. To the Democratic-Republicans, the act was an attempt by the Federalists to create a one-party press and one-party government. Over the next two years ten editors of Republican newspapers were convicted of violating the law. It expired in March 1801 when Jefferson assumed the presidency and pardoned all those prosecuted under its provisions.

As American government scholar James Q. Wilson observed,

> The debate over the Sedition Act was the first effort by the new republic to define the acceptable limits of public criticism of government. The Federalist position was that the First Amendment, while it prohibited censorship (such as the government preventing a newspaper from publishing a story), did not prohibit punishing a newspaper for having printed a false and malicious story. Just as individual citizens had the right to sue a newspa-

per for publishing a libelous story about them, so also the government had the right to sue a newspaper for libeling it.[11]

Jeffersonians did not contend that the press should be immune from any government controls. Rather they argued that the First Amendment did not authorize the federal government to punish the press for seditious libel. Jefferson claimed that punishment for "the overwhelming torrent of slander" in the press was "the exclusionary right" of the states. Thus, as Wilson observed, "The first major debate over the meaning of the constitutional freedoms conferred on those who wrote and spoke was in large measure a debate over states' rights."[12]

The Supreme Court never reviewed the convictions under the Sedition Act; the issue of criminal libel remained mired in confusion, and the scope of the First Amendment was left undetermined.

While Jefferson perceived the press as performing an educational function necessary for self-government and regarded free expression as one of man's inalienable natural rights, he also appreciated its pragmatic capabilities. In an effort to counter the *Gazette of the United States*, established by Alexander Hamilton to promote the Federalists' cause, Jefferson recruited Philip Freneau, "The Poet of the Revolution," to create *The National Gazette*, which became the voice of the Anti-Federalists and Washington's strongest critic.

After becoming president, Jefferson persuaded a young printer, Samuel Harrison Smith, to start up the *National Intelligencer*, as his administration's party organ, subsidizing him with government printing contracts.

Newspapers continued to grow as the country entered the new century. By 1800 there were more than 230 newspapers in the United States, and most large cities had at least one daily newspaper.

Throughout the nineteenth and twentieth centuries, the press expanded beyond the most fertile imagination into the mass media, largely because of advanced technology, the imperatives of public policy and private enterprise, and the recognition that communications had become a vital social, political, and cultural force as the world assumed the proportions of a "global village."

Rise of New Forms of Media

Historically, American journalism has passed through a succession of epochal cycles. The first of these saw fundamental changes in the print media, which for centuries had served throughout the world as the public's main sources of news and information. In the twentieth century, the advent of electronic journalism brought Americans even closer to their government and its leaders.

Mass-Circulation Newspapers

Advocacy journals of the colonial era served as a vehicle for narrowly defined political interests. "News" was primarily something on which to tie editorial opinions.

Then, with the birth of Jacksonian democracy in 1833, the party press began to wane and the penny press, aimed at the mass of the American populace, emerged. Its appearance resulted from a fortunate combination of factors: the development of high-speed presses that enabled publishers to print thousands of copies of a newspaper cheaply and quickly, an increase in the level of literacy, and the rise of self-supporting urban workers. Also, the invention of the telegraph in 1844 meant that news could be disseminated almost immediately; in 1790 it took more than ten days for news of an event in Boston to be published in Philadelphia.

These changes gave rise to mass circulations and increased advertising, hence publishers did not have to rely so much on political subsidies for operating revenues. Also, in the period from Jackson to Lincoln, presidents were generally unskilled in mastering the press as a political vehicle.

The end of the party press was sealed in 1860, when the Government Printing Office was established, thereby terminating their profitable printing contracts. The growth of professional Washington news bureaus and the realization by editors that their influence did not depend on party affiliation gave the coup de grace to the party press in the United States.

Forerunner of the penny press was Benjamin H. Day's *New York Sun*, which cost one cent compared with six cents for most other dailies. Penny papers that followed included James Gordon Bennett's *New York Herald* and Horace Greeley's *New York Tribune*. The country's first popular, commercialized newspapers, they played up human interest, crime, and social injustice and enticed an untapped audience from among the middle levels of society. By cutting across social class and political party lines, they attracted advertisers who relied on a broadly based clientele. They further expanded the scope of the news, with firsthand reports of national and foreign events, thus shaping a journalistic concept that would become an enduring element of the American press.

Aside from their common characteristics, each paper and publisher was distinctly individualistic.

The *Sun* specialized in short, breezy items about local

Library of Congress

Horace Greeley used his newspaper for crusades and causes. His *New York Tribune* was the first major paper to endorse the abolition of slavery and the first to introduce a separate editorial page.

people and domestic occurrences. One of the paper's most popular features, called "Police Office," carried reports of local people arrested for drunkenness and boisterous behavior.

Bennett, who viewed himself as a reformer, pursued an aggressive editorial policy and broadened the *Herald* to include financial news and sports reporting.

Greeley preferred to use his newspaper for crusades and causes. He called the *Tribune* "the great moral organ" and, using it as such, he exposed slum conditions in New York, advocated women's rights, and opposed capital punishment, alcohol, and tobacco. Greeley's *Tribune* was the first major paper to endorse the abolition of slavery and the first to introduce a separate editorial page. As romanticized in legend, Greeley advocated the western expansion of the country.

Within a decade after the emergence of the penny press, the combined circulation of all U.S. dailies climbed from 78,000 to an estimated 300,000. It was during this period that news reporting acquired special characteristics as a vocation. Interviewing became an integral tool of news gathering. Bennett's *New York Herald* created a sensation when it published an interview with the madam of a "fancy house" where a murder had occurred. As a result of the *Herald*'s stories, a young suspect was released by the police.

During this period, worldwide news agencies were formed—the Associated Press in 1848 and Reuters, the British wire service, the following year.

As the number of newspapers increased, editors relied more on the wire services for news beyond their local community and range of coverage. But since the wire services served numerous client newspapers of various editorial viewpoints, they confined themselves to reporting news in a straight, impartial manner, without commentary or opinion. This emphasis on objectivity soon became a sacred tenet of American journalism.

Civil War Coverage. Perhaps more than any other single event, the Civil War prompted sweeping changes in journalistic practices. The overwhelming demand for news sent newspaper sales soaring, and editors began trying to gain exclusive news and satisfy a popular appetite for the latest happenings.

Reporting of wars and foreign affairs up to the mid-nineteenth century was largely haphazard. Editors simply plagiarized war news from foreign newspapers. English papers employed junior military officers at the front to send letters, which more often than not were slanted and full of self-aggrandizement.

Accorded the honor of being recognized as one of the first notable war correspondents was William Howard Russell, of the *Times* of London. His account of the charge of the Light Cavalry Brigade during the Crimean War in 1854 remains memorable in the annals of journalism— "... In diminished ranks, with a halo of steel above their heads, and with a cheer which was many a noble fellow's death cry, they flew into the smoke of the batteries...." [13]

As noted by Phillip Knightley, author of *The First Casualty*, "Russell's coverage of the Crimean War marked the beginning of an organized effort to report a war to the civilian population at home using the services of a civilian reporter." [14]

The American Civil War shortly afterward afforded the opportunity to report a massive conflict on a grand scale, helped by the fact that during the early 1860s there

Mathew Brady was the foremost pioneer of modern photography. His photographs offered a vivid visual account of the Civil War and served as an example for succeeding generations of photojournalists.

Library of Congress

were an estimated 50,000 miles of telegraph lines throughout the eastern part of the country.

Some 500 correspondents covered the war for the North alone; the *New York Herald* reportedly put more than sixty correspondents in the field and spent nearly $1 million on the coverage. The *New York Tribune* and *New York Times* each dispatched at least twenty reporters to the fighting zone. Many British and European newspapers devoted almost as much space to the war as the American press.

Modern photography also came into being during the war. Mathew Brady followed the Northern armies and took thousands of photographs, although unfortunately the newspapers were unable to print them because they lacked the equipment and technique. Yet, Brady's photographs offered a vivid visual account of the war and served as an example for succeeding generations of photojournalists.

But because of a confluence of factors—erratic mail service and interrupted telegraph transmissions, heavy-handed censorship, the inexperience of many reporters, and the unethical conduct of others—the reporting of the war was often biased, inaccurate, sensationalist, and propagandistic. Nevertheless, it established war correspondence as a distinct brand of reporting and vastly expanded journalism's horizons.

Pulitzer and Hearst. With the burgeoning of the industrial revolution and the growth of the United States as a fledgling world power, the mass-circulation journals of Joseph Pulitzer and William Randolph Hearst, pandering to blatant sensationalism and chauvinistic sentiments, flourished during the late nineteenth century and early decades of the twentieth century. Massive tides of immigrants were entering the United States and editors designed their newspapers to meet changing social conditions and boost readership. They provided glaring headlines, splashy "reform" crusades, circulation stunts, large doses of cheap melodrama, and lurid tales of sin and sex.

As powerful "press lords," Hearst and Pulitzer extended their influence deep into politics and government by appealing to a mass audience.

Pulitzer promoted his *New York World* as the "people's champion" and its editorial pages, reflecting the paper's independence and crusading spirit, endorsed income and inheritance taxes and regulary sided with labor unions in strike situations. It was a leading voice against industrial monopolies and political bossism. An exposé by the *World* in 1905 of corruption and embezzlement by "money interests" in the life insurance industry led to regulatory legislation in New York State. In foreign affairs, the paper opposed the annexation of the Philippines and U.S. imperialism in the Caribbean. Pulitzer himself was elected to Congress in 1884 but resigned after a few months because service in Washington kept him away from overseeing his beloved *World*.[15]

Espousing programs and policies even more radical than those of Pulitzer, his chief competitor, Hearst and his *New York Journal* attacked the "criminal trusts" and came out in favor of the nationalization of coal mines, railroads, and telegraph lines. He supported a graduated income tax, election of U.S. senators by popular vote rather than by state legislatures, and improvement of the public school system. He endorsed William Jennings Bryan for president in 1896 and 1900. When President McKinley was assassinated by an anarchist in 1901 with a copy of the *Journal* in his pocket, the public was reminded of the paper's vitriolic assaults against McKinley, and Hearst judiciously changed the name of the paper to the *American*.

A man of monumental ego, Hearst frequently sought elective office and in 1904 made a vigorous drive for the Democratic presidential nomination on an antitrust platform. He narrowly lost the nomination when some of his delegates were denied credentials. He served two terms in Congress but was defeated in elections for New York governor and mayor of New York City.

The popular fervor whipped up by Hearst against Spanish colonial rule in Cuba prompted journalism scholar Frank Luther Mott to write that it was highly probable, "If Hearst had not challenged Pulitzer to a circulation contest at the time of the Cuban insurrection, there would have been no Spanish-American War." [16]

Before World War I, Hearst's papers sought to keep America out of the conflict. They harassed President Wilson's policies with slogans such as "America First" and "No Entangling Alliances." According to one biographer, John K. Winkler, the publicity campaigns Hearst fashioned around the slogans "possibly postponed for many months our entry into the war." Winkler further observed that after the war Hearst "used every atom of his influence to rally sentiment against the League of Nations and Woodrow Wilson saw his hope for outlawing war go down into dust." [17]

In 1932, near the end of his flamboyant career, Hearst was instrumental in the selection of Franklin Roosevelt as the Democratic presidential nominee. Hearst originally supported John Nance Garner of Texas for the nomination. When it became apparent that the Chicago convention was deadlocked, Hearst, who was at his palatial home at San Simeon, California, was persuaded by FDR's campaign manager, James A. Farley, to call Garner and have him release his California and Texas delegates to Roosevelt. On the fourth ballot, California cast its forty-four votes for FDR. "Hearst had named a President," one writer observed, and Garner agreed to be FDR's running mate.[18]

Pulitzer, who abandoned the excesses of sensationalism in the last years of his life, apologetically acknowledged that if a newspaper were to have "any influence, to accomplish anything worthwhile, it was necessary to have a great circulation." To Pulitzer, his *World* was a force for good. He maintained, "The *World* should be more powerful than the President. He is fettered by partisanship and has only a four years' term." [19]

Occupying a special niche in the archives of American journalism is the account of Hearst's sending illustrator Frederic Remington to Cuba to cover the Spanish-American War. Remington cabled: "Everything is quiet. There is no trouble here. There will be no war. Wish to return." Hearst, according to legend, wired back, "Please remain. You furnish the pictures and I'll furnish the war."

Whether fact or fable, the story reflects the flavor of "yellow journalism." More important, it presaged the expanding influence of the press in public policy affairs, as well as its own sense of self-importance.

To a large degree, Hearst and Pulitzer were mythmakers with a thirst for power and wealth. They were giants in their field, for they more than anyone else understood and foresaw the awesome potential of mass circulation newspapers. For good or ill, they set the pattern for modern American newspapers with dramatic exposés of public abuses and the graphic use of headlines, illustrations, color printing, and, later, photographs. Their papers were self-portrayed as champions of the people. The formula suited a time of national consciousness, and circulations skyrocketed. After turning the *St. Louis Post-Dispatch* into a highly respected newspaper, Pulitzer brought the *New York World* in 1883 for $346,000; by 1886 its circulation topped 250,000, making it the most widely read newspaper in the city, and before long it was reputed to be worth $10 million.

Hearst, after successfully running the *San Francisco Examiner*, bought the *New York Journal* and immediately engaged in a newspaper war with Pulitzer, hiring away some of the *World*'s best writers and illustrators. Within two years, the *Journal* surpassed the *World*'s circulation.

Ironically, this period of racy journalism also marked the beginning of the ascendancy of the *New York Times* as one of the premier newspapers in the country. Begun in 1851 on an investment of $51,000, the paper gained a reputation for thoughtful, objective journalism under its legendary early editor, Henry Raymond. On the brink of bankruptcy in 1896, the *Times* was bought by Adolph Ochs, who would launch a dynasty that would make the paper a social and political force and a model of journalistic excellence.

Heyday of the Tabloids. As early as 1897 the muckraking journalist Lincoln Steffens concluded after surveying the American press that "Journalism today is a business." [20]

With advances in newspaper photography and the bold use of editorial cartoons and illustrations, tabloids became the rage in New York during the jazz era of the 1920s. World War I secured the U.S. dominance in international affairs, the country was entering a decade of prosperity, and its attention was captured by the movies, "flapper" girls, airplanes, gangsters, sports heroes, and Prohibition. In the forefront of the tabloids during the "Roaring Twenties" were the *Daily News*, *Daily Graphic*, and Hearst's *Daily Mirror*. They offered the readers a pastiche of gossip, inside tidbits about the rich and famous, sex and crime stories, advice to the lovelorn, horoscopes, and sports. The writing was short, simple, and explicit, and the compact size made tabloids easy for people to handle while on the subway or bus.

They read about the party hosted by a Broadway producer at which a nude dancing girl cavorted in a bathtub full of champagne; of the Hall-Mills murder trial in New Jersey, in which a minister's widow was accused of slaying her husband and his choirsinger paramour; of the superhuman athletic feats of Babe Ruth, Jack Dempsey,

Bill Tilden, and Gertrude Ederle; of how a corset salesman by the name of Judd Gray conspired with Ruth Snyder in disposing of the unwanted Mr. Snyder.

Writing about "the war of the tabloids" in *The Press in America*, Edwin Emery reported that when Charles Eliot, former Harvard University president, and Rudolph Valentino, "the Sheik" of Hollywood fame, died in August 1926, the *Daily News* gave Valentino six pages of space and Eliot a single paragraph. Blared one tabloid headline: "Valentino Dies With Smile as Lips Touch Priest's Crucifix."[21]

The Gray-Snyder murder trial particularly exemplified the unrestrained "jazz journalism." Following their conviction, one of the tabloids published an artist's conception of what the pair would look like strapped in the electric chair. The *Graphic* promoted an exclusive about the condemned Ruth Snyder that remains a classic example of journalistic bad taste: "Don't fail to read tomorrow's *Graphic*. An installment that thrills and stuns! A story that fairly pierces the heart and reveals Ruth Snyder's last thoughts on earth; that pulses the blood as it discloses her final letters. Think of it! A woman's final thoughts just before she is clutched in the deadly snare that sears and burns and FRIES and KILLS! Her very last words! Exclusively in tomorrow's *Graphic!*"

Photographs were forbidden of the actual execution, but the *Daily News*, in what many critics condemn as one of the most infamous episodes in American journalism, had a photographer strap a tiny camera to his ankle and take a picture an instant after the current was turned on. The enlarged photo took up the entire front page of the January 14, 1928, *Daily News*. As Emery noted, the paper "sold 250,000 extra copies, and then had to run off 750,000 additional pages later."

The preoccupation of the tabloid press with sex, crime, and entertainment in the Roaring Twenties extended to politics. The papers played up the Teapot Dome oil lease scandal that plagued the administration of Warren G. Harding, the first newspaper publisher to become president. Calvin Coolidge was painted in the press as "Silent Cal" because of his New England taciturnity, and Herbert Hoover was voted into office amid the constant reminder that the Republican party had promised two chickens in every pot and two cars in every garage.

The 1920s were made to order for journalistic sensationalism, which reflected the spirit of the times. The country's cry was "back to normalcy"; people wanted to forget the war years and concentrate on "living." Political conservatism and laissez-faire policies prevailed throughout the nation.

Competitive Media. During this same period, new claims were staked on the U.S. news audience with the rising popularity of radio and the creation of *Time* magazine in 1923 by Henry Luce and Briton Hadden, two young Yale graduates who felt there was a need to condense and provide focus to the news.

Politicians were quick to seize on radio as a useful tool to further their objectives. In 1920 station KDKA of Pittsburgh broadcast the returns of the Harding-Cox presidential election. By 1922 there were some 600 stations on the air and three million sets were available to listeners by the time of the 1924 presidential election. Presidential contests would forever be changed. Presidents henceforth would need to be skilled practitioners of the new medium to gain office and effectively govern.

By the end of the decade, tabloid journalism went into decline. Largely because of the intense competition, the rising costs of distributing a large number of daily editions, and the new technology, the tabloid papers were not highly profitable. The Wall Street crash of 1929 and the onset of the Great Depression that left millions unemployed changed the national atmosphere. This was evident in the rise of interpretive reporting during the 1930s and 1940s, partly in response to FDR's revolutionary New Deal legislation. Americans needed to understand the meaning and significance of events and developments. Roosevelt was keenly aware of this and relied on the press to deliver his message and gain public support.

It was a period of transition in both politics and journalism. In 1933 the American Newspaper Guild was established, changing forever the labor-management relationship between owner-publishers and working journalists.

During World War II, Edward R. Murrow showed how radio news could be shifted from the studio to the scene of the event and became a role model for succeeding generations of electronic newscasters.

Following the war, the arrival of television, coupled with the counterculture revolution of the 1960s, ushered in a new mode of journalism in which inhibitions on the press were markedly relaxed. Emphasis was on the intimacies of private lives, on personal style, and on imagery and symbolism. Anecdotal, "fly-on-the-wall" reporting, popularized by author-journalist Theodore H. White in his "Making of the President" series, revolutionized political reporting. Objectivity, once a sacred sacrament of American journalism, gave way to a more personalized, opinionated advocacy reporting.

Murrow, one of broadcasting's legendary figures, revolutionized radio journalism with his personalized live reports from bomb-ravaged London during World War II. Afterward, his radio documentary series, "Hear It Now," subsequently transformed with the growth of television to "See It Now," and his highly popular "Person to Person" interview program probed national issues and served to underscore the potential influence of the electronic medium on public policy. In a March 9, 1954, broadcast of "See It Now," Murrow openly condemned the witch-hunting tactics of Sen. Joseph R. McCarthy, R-Wis. (1947-1957), thus initiating his downfall. The broadcast, one of the most controversial in broadcast history, changed the course of American journalism, as well as the national political scene.

Up to that point, the press had generally published with traditional journalistic objectivity McCarthy's unsubstantiated charges that certain Americans in and out of government were engaged in subversive activities. Objectivity, or the simple recitation of facts, had long been rooted in American journalism. Beginning in the last half of the nineteenth century, the major newspapers endorsed the concept to gain a broad spectrum of readers and not offend any faction with partisan opinion or bias. The wire services particularly were strong advocates of objectivity since they sought to solicit clients of all stripes. Adherence to the standard was based as much or more on economics than on professional idealism.

The "New Journalism," employing a highly impressionistic style of writing and other literary devices such as reconstructed dialogue and the writer's own perceptions, became the vogue. At the same time, tabloid journalism was revived and renamed "supermarket journalism." Tabloids, such as the *National Enquirer* and *National Star*, highlighting "intimate secrets" of celebrities, were popularly sold at supermarket checkout counters.

Meanwhile, the role of the news media and the organizational structure of the journalistic community underwent vast changes. The press's persuasive impact in the Vietnam War and the Watergate scandal made the public aware of its influence on popular opinion and public policy. The advent of television and changes in social patterns and work habits led to the demise of numerous newspapers, especially afternoon dailies. Within a decade, the number of daily circulation papers dropped from 1,764 in 1978 to 1,654 in 1989, and 97 percent of U.S. cities were being served by only one daily newspaper.

Total daily newspaper circulation slipped from 63.3 million in 1984 to 62.5 million in 1986. Advertisers, however, continued to spend more with newspapers than with television—$27.0 billion on newspapers in 1986 compared with $22.4 billion on TV.

The News Conglomerates. Most surviving newspapers enjoyed unprecedented profits, leading to a wave of newspaper purchases by major news organizations and corporate investors, thus reducing the number of independent, individual owners and family-owned news properties. By 1988 an estimated 70 percent of U.S. dailies were owned by large chains and big-name news organizations, such as Rupert Murdoch's News Corporation Ltd., Gannett, Knight-Ridder, Hearst, Cox, Scripps-Howard, *New York Times*, *Los Angeles Times*, and *Washington Post*.

Inevitably, the emergence of media conglomerates raised disturbing questions as to whether the diversity of American journalism, acknowledged as the basis of its strength, was being diluted by a concentration of ownership. The American press has experienced radical changes from the colonial era to the nuclear age, but the recognition that a free flow of information is vital to the sustenance of a democratic society remains constant.

No relationship in presidential life is more ambiguous, more unpredictable and volatile, or more serious in consequences. The American concept of freedom of the press owes more to Thomas Jefferson than any other public figure, yet while defending the principle he was at the same time a severe critic of the press, maintaining that "advertisements . . . contain the only truths to be relied on in a newspaper." A century and a half later, Dwight D. Eisenhower, scarcely disguising his disdain for the press by cautioning his cabinet members not to believe everything they read in the newspapers, nevertheless defended their First Amendment rights. He publicly proclaimed, "I . . . will die for the freedom of the press." [22]

The built-in tension between presidents and media representatives is muted by mutual recognition that neither can perform their assigned functions without the assistance of the other. Presidents must communicate with the public to garner popular support for their programs and policies; the press must receive the cooperation of the White House to accurately report and assess events and developments at the highest level of government.

Wire Services

In the tradition of the wire service reporter, there is a "deadline every minute." The wire services—known also as news agencies or press associations—are wholesale purveyors of news, photographs, and features. The world—including city halls, state legislatures, Washington, Wall Street,

Hollywood, and distant foreign capitals—is their beat. Their clients are mainly newspapers, news magazines, and broadcast stations, of which not even the richest and biggest have the resources to completely cover the globe.

Because their media clients operate under various time zones, and because of the intense competition between them, the wire services are under constant pressure to be first with the news. Some editor, somewhere, is rushing to meet a deadline and needs the most recent news development to provide a well-balanced, up-to-the-minute account of what is happening in the world.

The two major news agencies in the United States are the Associated Press (AP), the nation's largest news-gathering organization, and United Press International (UPI); together they provide much of the news offered by the print and electronic media. Even the giant news organizations, with their own corps of domestic and foreign correspondents, rely on the wire services to achieve thorough coverage.

Founded in 1848 when several New York newspapers decided to pool their manpower to reduce the costs of covering ships coming in from Europe, the AP expanded into a nonprofit cooperative of subscribing publications and broadcast stations. Under AP bylaws, members are obligated to share their news with the AP for possible distribution to other members. Each member pays AP for the service, based on its size and circulation and amount of editorial material provided; thus, a large newspaper such as the *New York Times* will pay more for the service than a small-town paper.

In 1907 newspaper chain owner E. W. Scripps began operating the United Press, and two years later Hearst founded the International News Service (INS). In 1958 United Press absorbed the International News Service and changed its name to United Press International.

UPI, unlike AP, is a privately owned company that sells its news services on a contract basis according to a formula similar to its chief competitor's. While AP has been the foremost wire service for many years, UPI gained a reputation for journalistic aggressiveness. It was the first to recognize the potential market among broadcast stations.

Both AP and UPI utilize a large network of domestic and foreign bureaus, many of which operate around the clock. AP, which has been increasing its lead over the financially ailing UPI since the mid-1970s, employs an estimated 1,600 reporters, editors, and photographers stationed at some 100 regional domestic bureaus and 60 foreign bureaus. It serves about 1,500 U.S. newspapers and more than 6,000 radio and television stations. Overall, it files a reported three million words a day, reaching one billion people worldwide through 15,000 news outlets. Its Washington bureau alone is said to transmit an average of 200,000 words and 300 photographs each day. [23]

Besides their general news wire, the press associations have special wires for sports, financial, and regional news, as well as a radio-TV wire written in broadcast style for easy delivery on the air.

Wire service reporters follow certain rules in writing straight news stories. They are principally concerned with communicating facts and are instructed to be as accurate and concise as possible and to separate news from opinion. Since their readers and listeners have varying interests and span the ideological spectrum, they place a high value on objectivity and impartiality. Analysis and interpretation are avoided—unless clearly labeled as such.

Because the AP and UPI reporters are writing for a broad audience, they usually delete local references or generalize about them. They must get to the heart of the story almost immediately to grasp the attention of fast-acting editors and to tell the story in a minimum number of words in inverted pyramid style (with the most important information at the top) so that it can be cut from the bottom if necessary. In keeping with newspaper trends, however, the wire services in recent years have placed greater emphasis on enterprise reporting and made more of an effort to offer in-depth reports.

In line with long-established practice, AP and UPI transmit separate stories on the same topic for morning and afternoon papers on A.M. and P.M. cycles to ensure that they are not duplicated and are updated with fresh leads and new information.

Several major newspapers and chains have formed syndicates of their own to sell their stories and services to other press organizations, among them the *New York Times*, *Los Angeles Times-Washington Post*, *Copley*, and *Knight-Ridder*. They do not try to compete with the wires on "spot" stories, but rather offer background, analytical, and feature material. Some chains, such as Gannett, operate internal news services that send editorial material to all member papers.

Two foreign news services, Reuters, the British press agency, and Agence France-Presse, the French wire service, are comparable to AP and UPI and even have some U.S. clients. Numerous other countries have national news services, such as the Soviet Union's Tass and the People's Republic of China's Hsinhua news agency. National wire services are often government controlled and sometimes used for propagandistic purposes.

For years U.S. news agencies transmitted their stories over leased telegraph circuits to domestic subscribers who received them on teleprinter machines. Satellite technology, however, has vastly speeded up the transmission process; where teleprinter machines typed out 66 words a minute, computer-based equipment can print more than 1,200 words a minute.

UPI has had at least three changes in ownership since merging with INS in 1958, during which it experienced a turnover in editorial leadership and a constriction in operations. It further suffered a loss of some of its clients, leading to speculation that it might fold or revamp its editorial services.

Magazines

Magazines have served as a supplemental form of information to newspapers since colonial times. In 1741 Andrew Bradford published *American Magazine*, the first publication of this type to appear in the Colonies, beating Benjamin Franklin's *General Magazine and Historical Chronicle* by a few days. Both publications, however, soon folded because of financial difficulties.

For the next century and a half, numerous successors, mainly monthlies, emerged, but most failed to survive because of a lack of advertising and a limited editorial vision devoted principally to literature and contemporary social manners. Some few, nevertheless, made their mark by expanding their appeal and coverage to include questions of public policy, among them *Graham's Magazine*, under the direction of Edgar Allan Poe, the *Saturday Evening Post*, and *Godey's Lady's Book*, a pioneer for women's rights, which by 1850 had a circulation of more than 150,000.[24]

During the mid-1800s the *Nation*, *Atlantic*, and *Harper's Weekly*, which in 1863 published reproductions of Mathew Brady's Civil War photographs, came into prominence. In 1870 *Harper's*, with the help of Thomas Nast's searing editorial cartoons, contributed toward the downfall of the "Tammany Hall" political machine controlled by William "Boss" Tweed.

In 1879 Congress lowered postal rates for periodicals, thus stimulating broader distribution of newspapers and magazines. Shortly afterward, publishers ushered in the era of mass-circulation magazines by restructuring editorial content to bring the publications into harmony with the popular tastes and interests of the rising American middle class. Designed to appeal to a broad audience, magazines were easier to read, more entertaining, and, significantly, cheaper to buy than the restricted circulation magazines. S. S. McClure founded *McClure's* in 1893 and charged fifteen cents a copy, about half the regular magazine rate at that time. The same year Frank Munsey dropped the price of his magazine, *Munsey's*, to ten cents. Munsey, in the tradition of the yellow journalists of that day, was primarily interested in making a profit. Then, in 1897, Cyrus H. K. Curtis bought the *Saturday Evening Post* for $1,000 and began to sell it at five cents a copy.

Soon after the turn of the century, the *Ladies' Home Journal* became the first magazine to reach a circulation of one million. By 1912 circulation of the *Saturday Evening Post* soared to nearly two million.[25]

During this period, "muckraking" journalism—a term coined by President Theodore Roosevelt—reached its zenith. Published in national magazines of opinion, muckraking journalists specialized in essay-type, in-depth revelations of political corruption, social injustice, industrial abuses, and other ills accompanying the meteoric economic and population growth of the country. In contrast to the sensation-seeking "crusading" press of the time, they were motivated by a keen sense of morality and a rising social consciousness. Among the muckraking exposés, published in *McClure's*, were Ida M. Tarbell's "History of the Standard Oil Company" and Lincoln Steffens's "The Shame of the Cities."

During the first half of the twentieth century, magazine sales boomed, notwithstanding the introduction of movies, radio and television programs, and paperback books. Following World War I news magazines, pictorial magazines, and digests, such as the *Reader's Digest*, sprang up. *Newsweek* and *U.S. News*, copying a format inaugurated by *Time*, appeared in 1933. Publishers were now shifting the emphasis on sales from subscriptions to newsstands.

In 1936, following the successful debut of *Time* thirteen years earlier, Henry Luce launched *Life*, a dazzling, innovative pictorial magazine that was to revolutionize the visual media. Luce perceived *Life* as offering a "window on the world." The magazine led to a new journalistic genre—photojournalism—and enhanced the professional stature of news photographers. Inspired by *Life*, *Look* magazine appeared in 1937.

But by the early 1970s both *Life* and *Look* would cease weekly publication, killed by a medley of factors, including high production costs, the competition from television, and the trend toward specialized magazines appealing to specific audiences. The latter included magazines such as women's—*Cosmopolitan*, *Ms.*, *Glamour*, and *Good Housekeeping*; men's—*Playboy*; celebrity and personality—*People* and *Us*; science—*Scientific American* and *New En-*

gland Journal of Medicine; history and culture—*National Geographic* and *Smithsonian*; family living—*Better Homes and Gardens.*

By the late 1980s there were more than 100 magazines dealing with farming alone and at least 2,500 devoted to business, including *Business Week, Fortune, Nation's Business,* and *Forbes.* At the same time, an increasing public awareness of politics and public affairs sustained the popularity of magazines such as the *New Republic,* the *Nation,* and *National Review,* as well as those dealing in factual accounts and objective analyses, such as *Congressional Quarterly* and *National Journal.* There were also about 150 city magazines.

Although many mass-circulation magazines, such as *Collier's,* folded, the magazine industry has generally enjoyed economic prosperity. In 1986 more than 320 million copies of magazines were printed per issue in the United States and three magazines—*Reader's Digest, TV Guide,* and *National Geographic*—each topped ten million in circulation.

Radio

In 1920 Pittsburgh station KDKA went on the air to report the election returns of the presidential race in which Warren G. Harding defeated James M. Cox. It marked the first time that radio news of a significant event was broadcast. From then on the airwaves would serve as the foremost instant chronicler of events and rituals and forever change the way people perceive the world beyond their immediate reach. Over succeeding decades radio would stir the imagination and provide news and entertainment for a vast majority of Americans.

At first radio was largely conceived as a fad; indeed, many thought of it as an extension of the telephone. Only a half-million radio sets were sold in 1924. The next year some two million sets were purchased. Throughout these early years, sales of radio equipment formed the most lucrative aspect of broadcasting; the principal promoters were less visionaries than commercial investors.

But with the formation in 1926 of the National Broadcasting Company (NBC), a wholly owned subsidiary of the Radio Corporation of America (RCA), and the network that in 1927 became known as the Columbia Broadcasting System (CBS), a vast communications structure linking stations for simultaneous broadcasts began to take shape. By 1934—the same year the Mutual Broadcasting System was established—radio had evolved into an advertising medium. A half-century later there were roughly a half-billion working radio sets in the United States and about ten thousand radio stations in operation.

The American Broadcasting Company (ABC) was established when NBC, which dominated national radio, was forced by the Federal Communications Commission (FCC) to give up one of its two networks, the Red or the Blue. NBC sold the Blue Network in 1943 to Edward J. Noble, who renamed it the American Broadcasting Company in 1945.

Radio had several pioneering fathers: Guglielmo Marconi, who developed a wireless transmitter in 1901; Lee de Forest, the inventor of a vacuum tube that amplified voice and music transmissions; David Sarnoff, one of the first to recognize radio's potential and a dominant figure in the growth of RCA; and William Paley, scion of a cigar company fortune, under whose direction CBS became a powerful communications empire.

As a new communications vehicle, radio required a new style of writing. Radio scriptwriters wrote for the ear, newspaper reporters for the eye. Radio writing was conversational in tone, with short, direct sentences in the active tense, minus complex explanations and literary flourishes.

Entering directly into the living room, radio cultivated an intimate bond between speaker and listener; the two shared a common interest. People had to schedule their time to conform with radio's schedule; hence, at a given hour, millions of listeners gave their attention to the same program, making radio a universal communications medium.

Another major difference is that broadcasting uses the public airwaves and, as a result, is subject to government licensing and regulation through the Federal Communications Commission—in contrast to newspapers and magazines, which are virtually unregulated because of First Amendment freedoms. An FCC radio license is renewable every seven years (and every five years for television). Created by Congress in 1934 as an outgrowth of the 1927 Federal Radio Commission, the FCC stipulated that broadcasting stations must "serve the public interest, convenience and necessity."

In one of its most significant policy actions, the FCC instituted the "fairness doctrine," requiring broadcasters to present a variety of viewpoints on controversial issues of public importance. Opponents favoring a deregulation of the broadcast industry maintained that the doctrine served to stifle the very democratic debate it was designed to promote and that the intense competition among the large number of stations precluded the necessity to mandate fairness. After years of controversy, the FCC on August 4, 1987, voted unanimously to abolish the fairness doctrine on the grounds that it restricted the free speech rights of broadcast journalists. Earlier, a congressional majority, led by Sen. Ernest F. Hollings, D-S.C., sought to enact the doctrine into law, but President Reagan on June 20, 1987, vetoed the measure. "In any other medium besides broadcasting, such federal policing of the editorial judgment of journalists would be unthinkable," Reagan said in rejecting the legislation.

Supporters of the proposal maintained that radio and television rely on a limited public resource—the electromagnetic spectrum—and that the doctrine was necessary to ensure that minority viewpoints were aired. Reagan and other opponents argued that because of advancements in communications technology the public had a large number of alternative information sources available—including more than 10,000 radio stations, about 1,600 television stations, and an estimated 7,700 cable television systems.[26]

Left standing was the equal-time rule, which required broadcasters who sell air time to one political candidate to sell equal time to the candidate's opponent. The Federal Communications Commission, incidentally, does not regulate the networks because they do not use the airwaves but instead use privately leased lines to relay programs to individual stations.

The "golden age of radio" is measured from the mid-1920s to the end of the 1940s. During that quarter of a century mystery and action-adventure shows such as "Gangbusters" and "Ellery Queen" were among the most popular programs. Radio also had soap operas, such as "Our Gal Sunday," and, for young listeners, "Jack Armstrong, the All-American Boy." The first successful radio situation comedy, "Amos 'n' Andy," went on the air in 1930.

President Calvin Coolidge's inauguration in 1925 was heard coast to coast on a twenty-one-station hookup. In 1933 President Roosevelt spoke directly to the American electorate and solicited its support in the first of his radio fireside chats.

And in one of the most memorable incidents in the annals of radio, on October 30, 1938, Orson Welles triggered a panic with a production of H. G. Wells's play *War of the Worlds*. Although a fictional account, it made many listeners believe that alien creatures from Mars were invading the United States, causing wholesale confusion and traffic jams in New Jersey by people fleeing their homes. Above all, the show demonstrated the power of radio.

Included in the pantheon of early radio celebrities, whose names were familiar to most U.S. households, were news broadcasters Lowell Thomas, H. V. Kaltenborn, Floyd Gibbons, Gabriel Heatter, Elmer Davis, Walter Winchell, and Edwin C. Hill, as well as Graham McNamee and Ted Husing, who were best known as sportscasters. Perhaps the greatest was Edward R. Murrow, whose vivid, eyewitness accounts of the Battle of Britain during World War II brought the war home to millions of Americans and continue to stand as classic examples of radio reporting. Murrow's economy of language and ability to evoke drama in unfolding events remain unmatched.[27]

Murrow was personally responsible for arranging the first radio world news roundup on March 13, 1938, while war hovered over Europe, with live pickups from London, Paris, Berlin, Rome, and Vienna for relay to New York. In his memoirs, William L. Shirer, who was hired by Murrow to help cover the war for CBS, wrote that the breakthrough "helped radio news broadcasting abruptly come of age. . . . From that hasty development sprang the principal format of broadcast news—first over the radio, then over television—as we have known it ever since." [28]

The explosive emergence of television dimmed the golden age of radio. Many media observers predicted that radio would soon become an anachronism. But while radio lost massive advertising revenues to television, it continued to thrive, mainly on news reports, talk shows, and music played by disc jockeys, many of whom became the medium's new celebrities. The development of miniature transistors and the proliferation of automobile radios further contributed to its enduring popularity.

Television

Television, the most glamorous and extravagant medium, ironically lacks a rich early history to match its pervasive presence in contemporary American society. Following experimentation in the 1920s and 1930s, commercial television burst on the scene in the late 1940s without difficult birth pangs. Radio provided an already established network and station structure, as well as news and entertainment formulas that television would adopt. The star system had earlier been introduced by movies and radio. Advertisers, conditioned by radio, were lined up. Even the appropriate government regulatory agency, the FCC, was ensconced and prepared to deal with the new medium.

Television's principal contribution was its technical competence. By 1938 David Sarnoff was able to announce that home television was "now technically feasible." The following year, NBC, owned by RCA, offered a public demonstration of television at the New York World's Fair.

But the technological advancements that made home TV possible were developed long before its public unveiling. Two scientists credited with the development of television were Vladimir Zworykin, who perfected a primitive television tube, the idonoscope, in 1932, and Philo Farnsworth, who invented the electric camera in 1930.

The FCC received its first application for a commercial TV license from a Milwaukee newspaper in 1939. The permit was granted in 1941, along with licenses for nine other stations. At the time, radio was riding a crest of popularity and the public consensus was that TV could never replace radio. Many thought of it as a toy. Filmmakers did not take it seriously. During the new invention's infancy, performers had to wear heavy, green makeup to appear "normal" to the TV camera and take salt tablets because of the heat from the blazing lights.

World War II interrupted TV's development, but by January 1948 the nation had 102,000 television sets and by April the number more than doubled. Ten years later, four out of five American homes had TV sets. By the 1980s there was no part of the United States that could not receive some TV signal. An estimated 98 percent of all American homes had at least one TV set and nearly half had two or more sets. There were more TV sets in the country than telephones or bathtubs.

FCC regulations limit the number of broadcast enterprises that one owner may hold to twelve AM radio stations, twelve FM stations, and twelve television stations. The TV stations, however, cannot cover more than 25 percent of the country's TV households.[29]

The FCC further prohibits the cross-ownership of a TV station and a daily newspaper in the same market. The intent of the rules was to encourage decentralized or local ownership and preclude a concentration of media ownership. Critics, however, contended that the regulations were counterproductive and not necessary to preserve diversity of media ownership and that they further raised questions concerning protection of free speech under the First Amendment. It was additionally argued that the cross-membership prohibition contributed to the decline of competing dailies in large markets.

Networks and Ratings. In the forefront of the television era were the three national networks—ABC, CBS, and NBC—which focused primarily on entertainment to draw large audiences and attract advertisers. Essentially, the networks are program distribution companies that buy shows from television production companies, such as Music Corporation of America, Disney, Universal, and 20th Century Fox. They then distribute the programs to the independently owned local stations across the country with which they are affiliated. Advertisers pay the networks to include commercial announcements with the programs. In turn, the networks pay the stations a portion of their advertising fees for running the programs and commercials. The local stations can further sell time between programs to local advertisers. With apparent justification, local TV stations are sometimes referred to as "money-making machines."

Central to the marriage of television with advertising is the ratings systems, because the larger the audience the higher the advertising income. Shows with high ratings charge more for commercials than shows with low ratings. In 1986 total advertising revenue for television amounted to $22.4 billion (compared with $27.0 billion for newspapers, $7.0 billion for radio, and $5.4 billion for magazines).[30]

The cost of a TV commercial varies widely from station to station. The average thirty-second network commercial in prime time costs about $150,000, but the price can go to twice that figure for a top-rated show. For a thirty-second spot during a Superbowl championship football game, the cost can even be more than a half-million dollars.

Audience feedback, which determines ratings, is monitored by two major marketing research firms, A. C. Nielsen and Arbitron. Basically, each surveys a representative sample of households nationwide. Viewers, broken down demographically, keep diaries to indicate their viewing habits. To enhance the precision of the findings, researchers in 1987 began experimenting with "peoplemeters," hand-held electronic devices that viewers punch to record the channel being watched.

Like radio, TV had its "golden age." The decade of the 1950s was a period of rapid expansion and daring innovation, during which some of the medium's most celebrated stars reigned on the TV screen in vaudeville-like variety shows. They included Ed Sullivan's "Toast of the Town," "Arthur Godfrey's Talent Scouts," and "Texaco Star Theater," featuring Milton Berle, who became known as "Mr. Television." Popular dramas were performed live on programs such as "Studio One," "Robert Montgomery Presents," and "Kraft Television Theater," inasmuch as videotape would not be invented until near the end of the decade. A new genre, the "adult western," attracted a loyal following, and among the favorites were "Gunsmoke," "Wagon Train," and "Maverick."

In 1951 Murrow premiered "See It Now," a program that explored controversial issues of the day. Murrow also narrated a memorable CBS documentary, "Harvest of Shame," which focused on the tragic condition of American migrant farm workers. The first successful big-money TV quiz show, "The $64,000 Question," went on the air in 1955. Four years later, scandal swept the television industry when it was disclosed that the quiz show was rigged; as a result, the networks became more aware of their ethical responsibilities.

Public Affairs vs. Entertainment. Almost from its beginning, television has exerted a powerful influence in public affairs, especially at the presidential level. Madison Avenue advertising techniques were adopted to fashion Eisenhower's TV commercials in the 1952 campaign. That same year Richard Nixon, Eisenhower's running mate, paid NBC $75,000 for network time to defend himself—in what became famous as his "Checkers" speech—against charges that he had misused campaign contributions. (Checkers was his pet dog, given to him as a gift and which he said he would keep notwithstanding his critics.) The televised speech is generally credited with saving Nixon's political career.

In 1956 the networks extensively covered the Eisenhower-Stevenson campaign. And in 1960 Kennedy and Nixon engaged in the first TV presidential debate.

Congress, on the other hand, was slow in grasping the importance of television as a political instrument, with the result that it was less able to compete as a coequal with the executive branch.

The Senate allowed broadcast coverage of committee hearings in the early 1950s and among the early examples were the 1950-1951 Kefauver hearings on organized crime and the 1954 Army-McCarthy hearings. In 1966 Sen. J.

William Fulbright, D-Ark. (1945-1974), chairman of the Foreign Relations Committee, held televised hearings to inquire into White House policy on the Vietnam War. The House first permitted television coverage of a committee hearing in 1974. For fifty-four days the nation watched as the House Judiciary Committee heard testimony on impeachment charges against President Nixon.

Although the House trailed the Senate in opening committee hearings to live broadcast coverage, it was the first to authorize coverage of its actual sessions. After many years of internal debate, the House in 1979 set up a closed-circuit television system that permits cable subscribers in many communities to see gavel-to-gavel coverage on the C-SPAN cable network. The Senate followed suit several years later.[31]

Television by the late 1950s and early 1960s was acknowledged as a highly popular and effective caterer of news. Many network newscasters became household names, notably Walter Cronkite, Eric Sevareid, Chet Huntley, David Brinkley, John Chancellor, Howard K. Smith, and Harry Reasoner.

In a sense, television was both a style-setter and a reflection of the incumbent American life style. Beginning in the early 1970s adult comedies such as "All in the Family" and "M*A*S*H*" ventured into areas previously off-limits, such as abortion, homosexuality, premarital sex, drug addiction, and racial prejudice. Next, the networks offered "Dallas" and other prime-time soap operas that typically dealt with rich and powerful families and were spiced with sex scenes. Situation comedies, drawing on popular predecessors such as "I Love Lucy" and "The Honeymooners," were revived in the 1980s, among them "The Bill Cosby Show" and "Family Ties." Action-adventure programs also made a comeback in contemporary settings, including "Hill Street Blues" and later "Miami Vice," which were aimed at a young, aware audience.

As an ubiquitous visual medium, television stirs the imagination of viewers and adds to their knowledge by providing a window on places and events. The unparalleled sensation of watching man walk on the moon, the poignant drama surrounding President Kennedy's assassination, and the heartsick anguish felt in viewing the *Challenger* space shuttle explosion remain indelible in the minds of Americans. Television brought the Vietnam War into living rooms and raised viewers' consciousness over the issue. The televised Watergate hearings in 1973 and the Iran-contra hearings in 1987 served as a public education into shadowy operations of government. And Mikhail Gorbachev's 1987-1988 meetings with President Reagan in Washington and Moscow, as viewed through the prism of television, offered a rare glimpse of a new type of Soviet leader.

For all that, the limitations of television are as exceptional as its benefits. It is a transitory medium, concerned almost exclusively with the moment as it rushes from one story to another; hence, there is little continuity or coherent perspective in the march of events. Television speaks in captions and turns issues into slogans and converts complexities into bite-sized superficialities. With television, everything is magnified, every news item is front-page news because there are no back pages on the screen or different sizes of headlines to suggest the significance of a story. In contrast to the print medium, which attempts to impose a kind of order out of chaos, television creates an emotional impact. Spurred by the craving for high ratings, television allows sensations to dominate, rather than reflection and reason. By the late 1980s the average American household had its TV set on for about seven hours a day. It remained uncertain, however, how long viewers were actually watching and whether they fully absorbed what they were seeing and hearing.

Nevertheless, television broadens viewers' horizons and changes their way of seeing things and their concept of reality. Its impact on American culture, politics, and government is universally recognized, if unclear as to degree and quality.

Cable and Public TV. Advances in electronic technology, notably the satellite transmission of video signals, provide alternate systems of news, educational, and entertainment programs for home viewers who pay for the service. Cable TV, or CATV (community antenna television), began as a means to bring commercial TV signals into isolated communities. It soon became apparent, however, that the coaxial cable had the capability of using numerous channels for a variety of specialized programs, including sports, news, movies, shopping tips, educational instruction, and government information.

In 1956 only about 400,000 U.S. homes had cable TV; in 1967 the number grew to three million, and by 1988 more than half of the nation's TV households were linked to cable systems. Cable TV broke the near-monopoly enjoyed by the broadcasting networks, which by 1989 had lost nearly 20 percent of their prime-television audience because of the competition. Among the popular cable systems were CNN (Cable News Network), offering round-the-clock news, and C-SPAN (Cable Satellite Public Affairs Network), specializing in public service programs, including gavel-to-gavel coverage of Congress. Each of the cable networks devoted more air time to the 1988 national presidential conventions than any of the three major commercial networks, thus in a sense preempting the latter's traditional role.

Another development in the broadening use of television was Congress's creation in 1967 of the Corporation for Public Broadcasting. As set up, public, or noncommercial, television and radio are nonprofit and depend on a mixture of public and private financing. A separate Public Broadcasting Service, a cooperative association of local stations, produces TV programs, often in collaboration with foreign broadcast systems, and acts as sort of a network for distributing TV programs. Among public television's biggest hits were "Sesame Street," "Civilisation," and "The Forsythe Saga." Popular programs from British television included "Upstairs, Downstairs" and "The Adams Chronicles."

In radio, the stations are linked by the National Public Radio system, which produces and distributes programs.

Public broadcasting system members in 1987 included 394 noncommercial television stations and 296 noncommercial FM radio stations.[32] Overall the hallmark of public broadcasting is its emphasis on cultural affairs, classical drama, experimental programs, academic discussions, political analysis, documentaries, and minority-oriented shows.

White House Press Corps — Early Years

Presidents since George Washington have had relations with the press of one kind or another, ranging at various times from mutual cordiality to tense adversary relationship. From the colonial era until now there has been no break in the relationship, which has evolved into one unlike that of any other head of state in the world. Nowhere else is the press literally quartered in the same house as the nation's chief executive, thus symbolizing the importance of communications and public opinion to democratic government.

As former presidential aide Douglass Cater observed, "No monarch in history has had a retinue like that which gathers about the American President and calls itself the White House press corps. The reporters hang about his antechamber with the indolence of courtiers at some feudal court keeping those who pass in and out—Governors, Cabinet members, Senators, Ambassadors—under constant surveillance and interrogation. They dog the President's every step and turn his most casual public conversation into a mass meeting. They follow him wherever he goes." [33]

In keeping with his aloof nature, Washington had little direct contact with the partisan press of the day and occasionally voiced criticism of it. "Newspaper paragraphs unsupported by other testimony, are often contradictory and bewildering," he once maintained.[34]

On another occasion, he declared, "We have some infamous Papers, calculated for disturbing if not absolutely intended to disturb, the peace of the community." [35]

Notwithstanding his wary view of the press, Washington knew the importance of an informed public opinion; he sensed its role in deciding the fate of the proposed new Constitution and he advocated favorable postal rates for newspapers. He was a regular reader and often used the press for personal advertisements, including one that read: "A COOK—Is wanted for the family of the President of the United States. No one need apply who is not perfect in the business, and can bring indubitable testimonials of sobriety, honesty, and attention to the duties of the station." [36]

Inevitably, the adulation bestowed upon Washington as the new nation's revolutionary war hero and first president soon was tempered by sharp criticism and bitter innuendoes by partisan journals. He was accused of unlawfully appropriating land belonging to his friend, Lord Fairfax. In papers such as the *Aurora*, published by Benjamin Bache, the New York *Argus*, Boston *Chronicle*, Richmond *Examiner*, *Kentucky Herald*, and *Carolina Gazette*, Washington was censured for "stately journeying through the American continent in search of personal incense," putting on royal airs, hosting "court-like levees" in "queenly drawing-rooms," and preferring the seclusion of a monk. Tom Paine, who had fallen on hard times, accused him in print of being "treacherous in private friendship . . . and a hypocrite in public life."

Noting Washington's irritation with such press accounts during a cabinet meeting, Thomas Jefferson wrote:

> The President was much inflamed, got into one of those passions when he cannot command himself, ran on much on the personal abuse which had been bestowed on him, defied any man on earth to produce one single act of his since he had been in govmt which was not done on the purest motives . . . that by gold he had rather be in his grave than in his present situation. That he had rather be on his farm than to be made emperor of the world and yet they were charging him with wanting to be king.[37]

Hence, a pattern was set in which succeeding presidents recognized the necessity of dealing with the press, even at their own peril, to ensure an informed national constituency and mobilize popular support.

From Printers to Professionals

The development of the news media, from print to radio and thence to television, has become one of the determinant factors in how presidents and their initiatives are presented and promoted. And just as the political process has changed, so have the journalists who cover Washington and the White House.

During the early years of the Republic, newspapers were mainly subsidized, highly partisan political organs published by printers who were more accomplished in mechanical than intellectual matters.

In his travels throughout America in 1831, Alexis de Tocqueville was admittedly impressed that almost every hamlet had a newspaper. But he noted that their publishers were "generally in very humble position with a scanty education and vulgar turn of mind." He further remarked on the papers' "open and coarse appeals to the passions of the readers." [38]

The early publishers, for the most part, were accorded little social and professional status. Most began as printer apprentices. They were unskilled as writers. Reporting, as subsequently defined to mean the collecting and disseminating of news and information, was unknown. Newspaper producers largely relied on letters, travelers, ship crews, other papers, and official sources for their material.

Oddly, newspapers then showed meager interest in chronicling events involving the new government. When the nation's capital was transferred from Philadelphia to Washington in 1800 there were no correspondents on hand. Gradually, the genesis of a Washington press corps began to take shape in the form of editors who visited the backwater town while Congress was in session. Their reports were sent back to their papers as letters, which more often than not reflected their personal bias and were printed under pseudonyms.

Efforts had previously been taken to establish newspapers in Washington but none succeeded, although nearby Georgetown and Alexandria each boasted a journal. Within weeks after the seat of government moved to Washington, several newspapers appeared, the most important being the *National Intelligencer*, which became the official organ of the Democratic-Republicans led by Jefferson.

The paper's young editor, Samuel Harrison Smith, who had moved from Philadelphia where he published the *Universal Gazette*, sought permission to report the proceedings of Congress. The request was initially denied but later approved, and reporters were allowed to attend the legislative sessions. Indeed, for some time, Smith's stenographic reports were the only printed records of congressional proceedings and were the ancestor of today's official *Congressional Record*.

During the War of 1812 the offices of the *National Intelligencer*, now under new ownership, were sacked and burned by the British. After a few days' inconvenience, the paper resumed publication.

Credited with being one of the first Washington correspondents according to modern terms was Nathaniel Carter, a senior editor of the New York *Statesman and Evening Advertiser*. He went to Washington in 1822 to provide what he described as "the latest intelligence of every description which can be obtained at the seat of government." [39]

The same year, Elias Kingman arrived in Washington from Rhode Island and for the next forty years operated a news bureau from which he served newspapers all over the country. Shortly thereafter, Col. Samuel L. Kapp, of the *Boston Galaxy*, appeared in the capital and began to furnish news to his paper and others.

Many of their journalistic contemporaries wrote under pseudonyms, including Matthew J. Davis, who appeared in print as "The Spy in Washington," and Nathan Sargent, whose pen name was "Oliver Oldchild." [40]

Still, for the first several decades of the nineteenth century, newspapers were written for the classes rather than the masses; they published less domestic than foreign news and were not sold on the streets. Many journals appeared to promote a particular political interest or public figure and just as suddenly disappeared. Among them was the *Atlantic World*, which was established in 1807 to support the political ambitions of Aaron Burr but survived only a few months.

Also, many New York papers of that day relied mainly on written accounts by members of Congress for coverage of legislative activities in Washington. The notion of regularly paying reporters to serve as a paper's staff observer and chronicler did not emerge until the mid-1820s. About that time, a Congressional Press Gallery was established, presaging a profound change in press-government relations. The lawmakers' action recognized the blossoming influence of the press in public affairs.

Even so, the growth of professional journalism and the creation of a Washington press corps as recognized today were slow and erratic. Newspapers favored by Washington administrations received government printing contracts and other patronage. Reporting was considered a seasonal occupation and its practitioners were often hired by the month at wages ranging from twelve to twenty dollars, including food and lodging. Sometimes, they were paid space rates—that is, according to how many column inches of their copy was published. Frequently, they left the provincial capital city on the Potomac mudflats as soon as Congress adjourned.

Shortly after his assumption of the presidency, Andrew Jackson and a group of his friends launched the Washington *Globe* as the voice of the new administration under the editorial direction of Amos Kendall, publisher of the Kentucky *Argus*. Kendall soon became a principal adviser to Old Hickory. One incensed House member of that period said of Kendall, "He was the president's thinking machine, his writing machine—aye, and his lying machine." [41]

Popularized News

A member of the pioneer Washington press corps at the time was James Gordon Bennett, who later became a legendary figure in American journalism as founder and editor of the New York *Herald*. Bennett's specialty, which became a characteristic element of the penny press, was writing lively accounts of Washington society and intimate details about the lives of well-known people. He is credited with popularizing the news and liberating the press from party control.

In 1841 Bennett, after becoming head of the *Herald*, set up the first Washington newspaper bureau with regular courier service to New York. Before long, Benjamin Day's New York *Sun* and Horace Greeley's *Tribune* followed his lead.

The period just before and during the Civil War gave impetus to the formation of an institutionalized Washington press corps and changed the course of American journalism. The bitterly contested 1824 presidential campaign between John Quincy Adams and Andrew Jackson focused news attention on Washington. Personal journalism supplanted the partisan press. The first telegraphic news dispatch, sent from Washington to the Baltimore *Patriot* on May 25, 1844, revolutionized press operations.

Above all, the press was designed to appeal to a mass audience, rather than a select segment of society, and this audience wanted to read more about important political figures. For the first time a reporter was assigned full time to cover a president-elect, a step that led to the creation of the modern White House correspondent. The reporter was Henry Villard, of the Associated Press, who in 1865 accompanied Lincoln from Springfield, Illinois, to Washington.

The Civil War created an insatiable demand for news and prompted sweeping changes in journalistic practices. In his 1975 book *The First Casualty* Phillip Knightley described the massive effort to cover the fighting:

> Some 500 [correspondents] went off to report the war for the North alone. The New York Herald put sixty-three men into the field and spent nearly one million dollars in covering the war. The *New York Tribune* and the *New York Times* each had at least twenty correspondents, and smaller papers, in such places as Cincinnati and Boston, all had their own men at the front. European war correspondents, such as William Howard Russell of *The Times* of London and Georges Clemenceau of *Le Temps*, were there, and many European newspapers devoted almost as much space to the war as did the American press.[42]

Several correspondents earned their reputations covering the war, among them H. Whitelaw Reid, of the *Cincinnati Gazette*, who later became publisher of the *New York Tribune*; John Russell Young, who marched with the Army of the Potomac; Sylvanus Cadwallader, of the *New York Herald*, who was present when Lee surrendered to Grant at Appomattox; George Smalley, of the *New York Tribune*, who wrote a stirring account of the Battle of Antietam; and Henry Villard, who voiced his opinion to Lincoln about what he felt was wrong with the Union Army.

The poet Walt Whitman, while serving as a nurse with the Union Army, also filed dispatches for the *New York Times*. In the main, however, the competent correspondents were vastly outnumbered by those in their ranks who were ill-trained, unethical, or dishonest. Most made no pretense at maintaining objectivity and were given to hyperbole and chauvinistic exaggeration: skirmishes were reported as glorious victories and retreats as strategic withdrawals before an enemy force vastly superior in numbers.

According to one study, "Sensationalism and exaggeration, outright lies, puffery, slander, faked eye-witness accounts, and conjectures built on pure imagination cheapened much that passed in the North for news."[43]

Gen. William Tecumseh Sherman particularly viewed the press as a pariah and on occasion threatened to treat correspondents as spies. In their defense, the correspondents contended they were hampered by poor communications, strict censorship, and uncooperative military officers.

Nevertheless, the war underscored to newspaper publishers that enterprise reporting and getting the news ahead of the competition was a way to build up circulation. Correspondingly, the war elevated journalism to a position of importance. By war's end reporters were solidly ensconced as part of the institutional scene in Washington. In "Recollections of a Washington Newspaper Cor-

The first reporter ever assigned to cover a president-elect full time, Henry Villard followed Abraham Lincoln in 1865, thus becoming a forerunner of the modern White House correspondent.

Illinois State Historical Library

respondent," Francis A. Richardson noted how cabinet officials, members of Congress, and government executives now sought out reporters of the major newspapers at their favorite retreats along Washington's Newspaper Row.[44]

Emblematic of journalism's elevated stature, President Andrew Johnson agreed to an interview with J. B. McCullagh, of the *St. Louis Globe-Democrat*, and permitted the reporter to quote him directly—the first time a president agreed to be formally interviewed for a newspaper story.

How Presidents Dealt with the Press

Presidents, who are constantly reminded of their power and prestigious rank, become exasperated because they cannot control the news media, even though they can to a large degree set the news agenda. This inability exposes their vulnerability and tends to mock the grandeur of their office.

All presidents, at some time or another, become frustrated at what they perceive as unfair treatment by the press, even while acknowledging its vital function in a free society. This sensitivity, often resulting in a strained relationship between the two institutions, is part of the baggage of the presidency and dates back to its beginnings.

How presidents respond when they feel mistreated by the press varies according to their personal temperaments, their relationship with members of the news media, their interpretation of the role of the press, and the particular state in their presidency. The period when they serve also has a bearing: early-nineteenth-century presidents, for example, could simply avoid personal contact with the press, an obvious impossibility in the television age. Among the various reactions of recent presidents beleaguered by the press, Nixon compiled an "enemies list," Kennedy canceled the White House subscription to the *New York Herald Tribune*, and Reagan rarely held formal press conferences toward the end of his presidency.

Propaganda Tool

Early presidents—including George Washington, John Adams, Thomas Jefferson, and later Andrew Jackson—felt unfairly abused and slandered by opposition journals. They sought to circumvent the daily litany of lies and vitriol by favoring their own partisan newspapers, which were equally biased, as the dominant source of presidential news.

The press, it should be stressed, was largely a propaganda tool at that time. The notion of the press as an independent news medium had not yet been developed. Essentially, newspapers were vehicles designed to advance the interests of the various political factions. Nonetheless, contemporaries recalled that the colonial newspapers had been a potent weapon in the fight for freedom from British rule and were keenly aware of their force and influence on public opinion.

Up to the Jacksonian era, U.S. presidents had little or no association with the press as direct sources of news. All, however, were conscious of the importance of informed public opinion and eagerly endorsed party newspapers supporting their administrations. John Adams briefly toyed with the idea of establishing a government gazette, as was the common practice among European governments.

While some of the early presidents, such as Adams and Madison, frequently contributed articles and essays to favorite newspapers, Jefferson vigorously refused to offer his writing to the public prints. He cautioned recipients of his letters not to make their contents public and occasionally boasted that he did not read the papers—yet he always seemed to know what was being printed in them.

Washington was an avid newspaper reader and the partisan excesses of the press offended his sense of decorum and nationalistic zeal, provoking him to complain that the "calumnies" against his administration were "outrages on common decency." [45] His antagonism toward the press, however, was mainly confined to personal correspondence and private conversation. Throughout his public life, he was the particular target of bitter criticism in the *Aurora*, published by Benjamin Franklin Bache, known as "Lightning Rod Junior" in reference to his illustrious grandfather. In one notable incident, Bache printed in detail the provisions of a treaty that John Jay negotiated with the British in 1795.

Bache denounced the secret pact in a separate pamphlet and accused President Washington of having "violated the Constitution and made a treaty with a nation abhorred by our people. . . ." [46]

In the original draft of his Farewell Address, Washington attacked the press, but he deleted the criticism at the urging of Alexander Hamilton. He did, however, remark on the significance of an informed public, stating, "In proportion as the structure of a government gives force to public opinion, it is essential that public opinion should be enlightened."

Washington personally arranged that his Farewell Address be exclusively published on September 19, 1796, in the *Pennsylvania Packet and Daily Advertiser*, cited by historians as the nation's first daily newspaper.

John Adams felt so maligned by the colonial press that he signed into law the notorious Alien and Sedition acts, which served as a gag law on the press and led to the imprisonment of several editors. Highly unpopular and clearly unconstitutional, the legislation, which was subsequently overturned, helped hasten the demise of the Federalist party.

Jefferson exalted freedom of the press as "one of the great bulwarks of liberty," but he was not above using the press for political purposes. It was while serving as Wash-

ington's secretary of state that Jefferson was instrumental in enlisting the poet-journalist Philip Freneau to act as a paid "clerk for foreign languages" in his office. This was a charade for Freneau's real mission, which was to establish the *National Gazette* as an editorial voice in opposition to the Federalist party of Washington and Hamilton.

After becoming president, Jefferson induced Samuel Harrison Smith to set up the *National Intelligencer* as an organ of his administration. It remained the preeminent newspaper in the country for more than a decade, serving the Jefferson Republican cause well and faithfully.

Another future president, James Madison, was a coauthor of the *Federalist* papers. The persuasive essays he, Hamilton, and Jay wrote contributed greatly to the adoption of the new government. Renowned as the "father" of the Constitution, Madison deserves equal credit for his advocacy of the Bill of Rights. He was a defender of a free press and one of the first public men to perceive the value of bipartisan reporting and commentary. [47]

Andrew Jackson used the press aggressively for partisan purposes. As a vital element of his restructuring of the party system and the presidency, he surrounded himself with a coterie of friends and advisers, which became known as the "Kitchen Cabinet." Included were Amos Kendall and another established editor, Francis P. Blair. Midway in Jackson's first term, his friends began the Washington *Globe*, with Kendall and Blair the guiding spirits. The paper promptly received lucrative government printing contracts, federal officeholders with salaries of $1,000 or more a year were expected to subscribe, and before long it changed from a semiweekly to a daily.

It was widely recognized that the voice of the *Globe* was that of Jackson, the head that of Blair, and the ideas those of Kendall. One of Blair's ploys was to reprint favorable articles that Jackson allies were suspected of planting in rural journals. And at one point fifty-seven journalists were reported to have been on the government payroll during Jackson's administration.

Even before the end of Jackson's term, the *Globe* began promoting his heir apparent, Vice President Martin Van Buren. Alongside the dynamic, forceful, and strong-willed Jackson—"Old Hickory"—Van Buren came across as a dandified political opportunist whose career was promoted by the Albany *Argus*, in which he had a personal financial interest.

Although Van Buren had the support of several leading newspapers, few presidents have been so bitterly assailed by the press, at least in part because of his aristocratic pretensions. Like today's new media, the press examined Van Buren's past with a fine-tooth comb—once it became apparent that he would succeed Jackson. The story was revived that he was the natural son of Aaron Burr. The New York *American* warned of "the great and menacing evil, the blighting disgrace of placing Martin Van Buren, illiterate, sycophant, and politically corrupt, at the head of this great republic." Davy Crockett, the frontiersman and Alamo defender who became a member of Congress, wrote,

> Van Buren is as opposite to General Jackson as dung is to a diamond. . . . When he enters the Senate chamber in the morning, he struts and swaggers like a crow in a gutter. He is laced up in corsets, such as women in a town wear, and, if possible, tighter than the best of them. It would be difficult to say from his personal appearance, whether he was man or woman, but for his large red and gray whiskers. [48]

During his presidency, Van Buren broke tradition by receiving and talking with a few reporters, including James Gordon Bennett. But the meetings were perceived more as audiences than as news interviews, as currently defined.

The 1840 presidential campaign offered a glimpse of the future with its emphasis on imagery and slogans. Whig candidates William Henry Harrison, hero of an 1811 battle against Tecumseh, and John Tyler ran under the war cry of "Tippecanoe and Tyler, too." Their campaign emblem was the log cabin, a readily recognized symbol of the young nation's vision, virility, and pioneering spirit. In reality, however, Harrison was neither born in a log cabin, nor was his home built of logs, except for one section.

James K. Polk, the first dark-horse candidate to become president, preferred to remain out of the public eye and was little known to the national electorate except through the news journals. Although he mistrusted the press, he was cognizant of its influence, and like his predecessors he used a favorite newspaper, in this case the Washington *Union*, as a platform for his administration.

Commenting in his diary on an editor who had broken a confidentiality, Polk wrote, "He meant no harm, I am satisfied. It is a constitutional infirmity with him, I believe, that he cannot keep a secret: all he knows, though given him in confidence, he is almost certain to put into his newspaper...." That, in essence, reflected his convictions about journalists.

Franklin Pierce, in acknowledgment of the increasing role of the press in public affairs, supplied newspapers with advance copies of his December 1854 message to Congress—a customary practice today.

The last president to rely on a special newspaper as an official administration voice was James Buchanan. The party press had been withering since the Polk regime and its demise was inevitable. Among the contributing factors was the invention of the telegraph, which led to formation of the wire services and the growth of Washington news bureaus staffed by enterprising journalists. "Objective reporting" began to take root as a professional standard. Another factor was the increased use of the press for advertising, which provided newspapers with financial revenue independent of the patronage of presidential administrations. Finally, in 1860 the Government Printing Office was established, eliminating the profitable printing contracts on which many papers subsisted.

Civil War and Reconstruction

Abraham Lincoln rarely sought publicity for the sake of self-aggrandizement but he was acutely aware of the importance of public opinion and the forces that shaped it. He was a faithful newspaper reader and an occasional contributor to local journals early in his career. Throughout his public life, he developed a cordial relationship with the press and often corresponded with journalists and sometimes sought their counsel, although he did not speak directly to them for publication. Prominent among the journalists with whom he frequently dealt were Horace Greeley, of the New York *Tribune*, who often tried the president's patience; Col. John W. Forney, publisher of the Washington *Chronicle* and Philadelphia *Press*, a friend and confidant; and Henry J. Raymond, editor of the New York *Times*.

Lincoln further believed, however, that he had to go beyond the press to measure public aspirations and find out what the people were feeling and saying. Hence, twice a week he held open White House receptions where ordinary citizens could meet him, express their sentiments, and air their grievances. "I call these receptions my public-opinion baths," he said, "... and, though they may not be pleasant in all particulars, the effect as a whole is renovating and invigorating to my perceptions of responsibility and duty. It would never do for a President to have guards with drawn sabres at his door, as if he fancied he were, or were trying to be, or were assuming to be, an emperor." [49]

Lincoln's paramount concern was the salvation of the Union. During the Civil War he permitted censorship and suppression of the press on a scale not seen since the founding of the Republic. Editors of antiwar papers—"Copperheads," as opponents of the war were called—were sometimes thrown in jail without formal charges against them. Telegraph companies were monitored, and Union generals were allowed to control the activities, movements, and access of correspondents on their own initiative. In the white-hot passions of the time, mobs occasionally destroyed the offices of antiwar newspapers and tarred and feathered their editors.

While recognizing the need to curb press activities that might aid and comfort the enemy, including news dispatches revealing troop movements and other details that endangered the lives of Union soldiers, Lincoln frequently displayed moderation in his attitude toward the press. On one occasion, General Sherman, whose antipathy toward the press was well known, arrested a *Tribune* correspondent and would have had him shot as a spy if the president had not intervened. In another instance, Gen. Ambrose E. Burnside ordered the suspension of the Chicago *Times* because of its Copperhead sentiments and its undisguised enmity toward Lincoln, but at Lincoln's suggestion the suspension was lifted.

With the country divided, Lincoln's press critics assailed him on a scale unsurpassed for its violence and vitriol. He was abused in print as "the Illinois ape ... a baboon ... a monster." One New York newspaper accused him of taking his presidential pay in gold, while rebel president Jefferson Davis was taking his in Confederate money, worth about a fourth of its face value. Yet, though he had no formal method of dealing with the press, Lincoln fully understood its role and dealt with newspapers and journalists on a more intimate basis than any of his predecessors.

As Lincoln's successor, Andrew Johnson was at a distinct disadvantage because of comparison with the Great Emancipator. Moreover, his public image suffered under the accusation that he was given to excessive drinking. The allegation—unfair, as it turned out—stemmed from his inauguration as vice president when because of an illness he drank some whiskey and water, which caused him to speak incoherently and act strangely.

During his presidency Johnson was constantly embroiled in controversy over his Reconstruction policies and efforts to remove him by impeachment. His practice of granting exclusive newspaper interviews was a means to reach out to the people. As part of an interview with Col. A. K. McClure of the *Franklin Repository*, Johnson was quoted as saying he wanted the South back "with all of its manhood," even though he was aware it might lead to "a sad breach between the President and the Congress." [50]

The Senate acquitted Johnson of wrongdoing by one vote—a fact etched in history—but to American journalists he is remembered for establishing presidential interviews as a regular practice.

Gen. Ulysses S. Grant was a hero to the nation because of his triumphant military campaigns in the Civil War, but as a president he was a failure, who because of his generous nature and political naiveté presided over an administration riddled with corruption. Newspapers for the first time engaged in what became known as investigative reporting, prompting Grant to declare he was "the subject of abuse and slander scarcely ever equaled in political history."

During his two terms in office, Grant had virtually no direct dealings with the press, partly because he was uncommunicative by nature and partly because of bad advice from aides and allies. This contributed to the poor press he received, giving vent to the haze of scandal that clouded his tenure as president.

The Press as Watchdog

By the time William McKinley was elected, the press had assumed its role as the people's watchdog over governmental affairs. McKinley allowed reporters to wait in an anteroom for interviews with visitors following important White House meetings. Also, his staff routinely gave reporters the president's speaking schedule and advance copies of his speeches. However, McKinley himself remained distant from the press and any direct contact was left largely to chance.

The first American president to fully appreciate the influence of the press in society and public affairs and to cultivate journalits for personal and political purposes was Theodore Roosevelt. The genesis of the White House press corps took shape during his administration. He courted publicity and reaped political currency by casting himself as a "trustbuster." But when crusading journals sought to expose the monopolistic and unprincipled activities of some of these same trusts, he branded them as "muckrakers"—a term intended as derogatory but which came to be descriptive of a respected journalistic function.

TR's dynamic personality, rhetorical flair, sense of the dramatic, and instinctive gravitation toward the camera made him a favorite subject of the press. He was an unswerving advocate of an unfettered press, but he frequently took issue with newspaper accounts and was sensitive to criticism. Above all, he insisted that the relationship should be on his own terms.

On his first day as president, he called in a group of wire service reporters and laid down a set of ground rules that would give them unprecedented access to the White House but leave him in control of what was published. He demanded that information given in confidence remain in confidence. Anyone who broke the rule would be barred from the White House and denied access to legitimate news. "If you ever hint where you got [the story]," he warned, "I'll say you are a damn liar." [51]

Roosevelt arbitrarily divided reporters between insiders and outsiders, the former comprised of those whose stories reflected favorably on his administration. He was able to impose such a dictum because the idea of professional journalistic standards was still in its infancy and the adversary relationship between press and government had not yet evolved. Nevertheless, he was responsible for bringing White House press relations into the modern era.

But it was not until Woodrow Wilson that the ad hoc interrelationship between the press and the president set-

tled into an institutionalized format. Continuing Theodore Roosevelt's custom of frequent meetings with the press, Wilson opened them to all reporters and initiated the first formal news conferences, at which reporters were required to submit their questions in written form.

Wilson's relations with the press soon deteriorated, however, because of what he considered excessive prying into his private life and a breach of confidence by some reporters concerning an "off-the-record" account by the president on conditions in Mexico. Soon thereafter, the White House Correspondents Association was formed to set guidelines for presidential news conferences and establish standards of professional conduct. Following World War I Wilson embarked on a publicity campaign to gain public support for his "Fourteen Points" treaty proposals, but he failed in the attempt.

Franklin Roosevelt, through the force of his personality, his keen sense of what made news, and his profound appreciation of the value of public opinion, exerted a great impact on White House press relations. During his record tenure as president, he was the central figure in a national economic recovery effort and a global war, providing him with a stage from which he dominated the news.

In his initial meeting with the press as president, he announced he was dispensing with written questions and introducing a new working relationship with White House correspondents. Labeling his sessions with reporters as "delightful family conferences," he said White House information would be presented in any of four different categories: (1) occasional direct quotations permitted only through written authorization from the White House; (2) press conference comments attributed to the president "without direct quotations"; (3) background information to be used in stories without reference to the White House; (4) off-the-record remarks not to be repeated. He additionally appointed the White House's first official press secretary, Stephen T. Early. [52]

During his more than twelve years in office, FDR invited reporters into the Oval Office for news conferences on 998 occasions, usually on Tuesdays and Fridays. They met in an informal setting, with the president seated behind his desk encircled by members of the White House press corps. Almost always he seemed eager to take on his inquisitors, was well informed and lavish in his comments. Seldom did the reporters leave without a story. Though generally good-humored, he would not infrequently chastise reporters whom he felt had inaccurately or unjustly misrepresented the administration's position. Once he suggested that a reporter stand in the corner with a dunce cap on his head. No matter what the situation, he was always in command.

FDR was equally a master at speaking over the radio to inform the American people of his policies and decisions and to appeal to them for support. His "fireside chats"—as they were called—became a familiar part of the American scene and, as such, have never been quite duplicated in terms of national interest.

The Television Era

The emergence of mass communications technology in the post-Roosevelt era, with its emphasis on imagery and symbolism and the new refinements in public relations techniques, further compelled presidents to be skillful communicators and establish an effective relationship with an increasingly pervasive media. As a visual medium, television created instant impressions and required presidents to operate more in the open. As they soon learned, this could be both a curse and a blessing.

Mainly because of his popularity as a war hero, few presidents enjoyed more favorable treatment at the hands of the press than General Eisenhower. While it was generally believed that "Ike" was indifferent to publicity and his relations with the news media, revisionist studies indicate that he was intensely preoccupied with public relations. In personal letters, he noted that his public image helped him carry out his role as a military leader.

Prominent among the network of businessmen who gathered around Eisenhower and persuaded him to run for president in 1952 were several professional public relations consultants. During his campaign they served as his media advisers and developed his political commercials. Among them was actor and television producer Robert Montgomery, who instructed Eisenhower on the mechanics of delivering speeches and how to perform on television.[53]

In 1960 the nation was stunned when it was disclosed that the Soviets had shot down a U.S. reconnaissance plane manned by Francis Gary Powers. At first, the Eisenhower White House reported that the plane was on a weather surveillance mission. But when the Soviets announced they had captured Powers and that the airplane was virtually intact, the White House changed its story and admitted that the U-2 was a "spy plane" on an espionage mission. Media critic A. J. Liebling contended the exposure marked the "beginning of wisdom" in the media's attitude toward the government.

Eisenhower was the first president to hold a televised news conference, but before the film was shown to the public it was edited by his press secretary, James C. Hagerty, to delete segments that might reflect unfavorably on the president or be confusing to viewers because of his garbled syntax in speaking.

The first "live" TV presidential news conference was held by his successor, Kennedy, whose youth, good looks, and disarming wit were ideally adaptable to television. Kennedy was generally popular with the White House press. He had briefly worked as a reporter before turning to politics and counted some well-established Washington journalists as his friends and confidants, including columnist Charles Bartlett and Benjamin C. Bradlee, who became executive editor of the *Washington Post*.

Before the 1961 Bay of Pigs assault in Cuba by U.S.-backed anti-Castro forces, Kennedy took the unusual step of prevailing upon the *New York Times* to tone down a story on the imminent invasion for the sake of national security. Following the ill-fated attack, Kennedy expressed regret he had persuaded the *Times* to modify its story, because advance disclosure of the operation might have spared the country a disaster.

Among modern presidents, few experienced worse press relations than Richard Nixon. His evident distaste of the "establishment" press, and its distrust of him, permeated his administration and nurtured a conspiratorial state of mind among his aides. This mind-set incited the Nixon White House to include several journalists on its "enemies' list." The blackballing further contributed to the Watergate coverup, for which ten presidential aides were convicted and jailed after the groundbreaking work of reporters such as the *Washington Post*'s Bob Woodward and Carl Bernstein.

Notwithstanding his grasp of politics, his knowledge and understanding of foreign policy, and his familiarity with governmental affairs, Nixon was an anomaly in the

Franklin D. Roosevelt Library

The forceful FDR transformed presidential press relations. He held 998 Oval Office news conferences during his twelve years in office.

Eisenhower was the first president to hold a televised news conference. But before the film was shown to the public, it was edited by his press secretary.

new media age. He became president when a high premium was being placed on charisma, yet his public image was that of a stiff, plastic figure. Television tended to underline his personal defects. Yet, possibly because of this incompatibility with the media, he was particularly conscious of its effect on public opinion. He consequently sought to remedy the situation through organizational initiatives. During his presidency, the White House's press/public relations operation was vastly enlarged. A White House communications office was established to deal with reporters and broadcasters outside of Washington; an office of public liaison was set up to deal with interest groups; and a news summary unit was created to monitor the print and electronic media.

The hostility between the Washington press and the Nixon White House reached a peak in the Watergate scandal, ultimately ending in the president's resignation and his replacement by Gerald R. Ford.

Seldom has a president taken office on such cordial terms with the news media as Ford. In his inaugural address, he pledged that his would be an administration of "openness and candor." Because of his constant contact with the press during his quarter of a century in Congress, Ford knew many journalists by name and enjoyed a personal association with many of them. His rapport with the news media was strengthened when he appointed Jerald F. terHorst, Washington bureau chief of the *Detroit News*, as White House press secretary.

Ford's "honeymoon" with the press ended abruptly, however, one month after he took office and pardoned former president Nixon, sparing him any trial in connection with Watergate. Ford's credibility additionally came into question because he had earlier indicated that he was opposed to a pardon for the time being.

The unexpected pardon also prompted terHorst to resign, because, as he said, he disagreed in principle with the action and was not informed of it in advance. From that point on, Ford's relations with the Washington news media proceeded along conventional lines.

Jimmy Carter, who rose to the presidency as a virtually unknown former governor of Georgia, was in a large measure indebted to the national news media for the highly favorable treatment he received during his 1976 campaign. Early in his administration, he indicated a deep appreciation of the balance between the press and the president and their respective roles, stating, "If I can stay close to the people of this country and not disappoint them, I think I have a chance to be a great president." [54]

His walk down Pennsylvania Avenue hand-in-hand with his wife as they returned to the White House following his inauguration caught the spirit of his campaign, as did his decision to wear a sweater during one of his first televised talks to the nation.

Generally, Carter's attitude toward the press was one of correctness and cordiality. There was none of the cloying affection sometimes displayed by Lyndon Johnson or, at the other extreme, any of the embittered antipathy inherent in Nixon's relations with the press. Early on, Carter pledged to hold press conferences every other week. And on alternate weeks, out-of-town editors and broadcasters were invited to the White House. Carter also employed a number of unconventional techniques to communicate with the electorate, including fireside chats, participation in town meetings, overnight stays at the homes of private citizens, and a regional televised question-and-answer session with Southern California residents.

Before the end of his first year in the White House, however, Carter's relations with the press began to cool, mainly because of his persistent defense of his good friend Bert Lance, director of the Office of Management and Budget, whose private banking practices were being questioned and who subsequently resigned under a cloud. Presumably disillusioned by the course of events, Carter became noticeably more reserved toward the press and with time his news conferences became less frequent.

The "Great Communicator"

Ronald Reagan's ascendancy to the White House was largely viewed as the natural culmination of the dominance of American politics by image-makers, television consultants, pollsters, speech writers, and other specialists who transformed campaigning into a form of media theater. No president in modern history, other than perhaps Franklin Roosevelt, was more successful in the presentation of himself than Reagan, a former Hollywood actor and television host. His long career before the cameras, his buoyant personality, and affable temperament ideally equipped him for the on-stage existence that contemporary presidents must endure.

Referred to as the "Great Communicator," Reagan had a natural knack for synthesizing and clearly defining complex issues, as well as leavening weighty topics with humor. After being wounded in a 1981 assassination attempt, he quipped to his wife, Nancy, "I forgot to duck."

The high priority given to public relations and press communications in the Reagan White House was reflected in its hierarchical structure. Among the senior advisers were Michael K. Deaver, longtime friend and professional public relations executive who served as deputy White House chief of staff, David R. Gergen, assistant to the president for communications, and Richard Wirthlin, the president's special pollster and public opinion analyst.

Reagan's press and public relations advisers were especially adept at orchestrating media events and staging the president in highly visible situations, while at the same time protecting him from inquisitive reporters. "Photo opportunities" were routinely available, but formal press conferences were few and far between.

Ironically, even as he was being perceived as the Great Communicator, Reagan's administration was intent on rigid management of the news and stemming the free flow of information. Measures to regulate government information included the widespread use of lie detector tests to trace news leaks by government employees and contractors with high-level security clearance; discretionary upgrading of classified information by federal agencies for an indefinite period, as well as the reclassification of information already in the public domain; a requirement that government officials possessing top security clearance sign statements forcing them for the rest of their lives to submit for official, prepublication review all articles and books they write for public consumption; a tightening of exemptions allowed under the Freedom of Information Act; and vigorous enforcement of the 1952 McCarran-Walter Act, prohibiting writers, artists, and political figures from entering the United States because of their views and associations.

Reagan enjoyed a fairly high level of popularity during most of his two terms in office. A crack in his credibility developed, however, with the disclosure in 1987 of the Iran arms sales/contra funding affair. Reagan insisted the secret operation was conducted without his knowledge or approval and blamed the news media for sensationalizing the incident.

Presidential Attitudes toward the News Media

As John F. Kennedy neatly phrased it when he said that he was reading the press more and enjoying it less, all presidents inevitably become frustrated in their dealings with the Fourth Estate.

Thomas Jefferson complained that "newspapers, for the most part, present only the caricature of disaffected minds. Indeed, the abuses of freedom of the press have been carried to a length never before known or borne by any civilized nation." These harsh comments underscore presidential ambivalence toward the press, for earlier it was Jefferson who had written that "were it left to me to decide whether we should have a government without newspapers or newspapers without a government, I should not hesitate to prefer the latter." [55]

It was said of Abraham Lincoln that "in his dealings with the press he knew how to be as wise as a serpent and as gentle as a dove, yet it cannot be said that he truckled to it, collectively or individually." [56]

Lincoln's skill in dealing with the press and his awareness of public opinion was evident in a letter he wrote to

Washington Post

The *Washington Post's* Bob Woodward, left, and Carl Bernstein, right, broke many of the Watergate stories that led to President Nixon's eventual resignation.

New York Tribune editor Horace Greeley, an early advocate of emancipation, in which the president stated, "My paramount object in this struggle is to save the Union, and it is not either to save or destroy slavery. If I could save the Union without freeing any slave, I would do it; and if I could save it by freeing some and leaving others alone, I would also do that. What I do about slavery and the colored race, I do because I believe it helps to save the Union. . . ." [57]

Actually, Lincoln had long been thinking about freeing the slaves but wanted a military triumph to make the emancipation effective. On September 19, 1862, following the battle of Antietam, Lincoln issued his famous proclamation.

Ironically, the newspapers virtually ignored Lincoln's epic address at Gettysburg. Instead, they favored a lengthy speech by Edward Everett, an eminent orator of the time. The *Cincinnati Gazette* published Everett's speech in full, while noting, "President Lincoln made a few remarks. . . ."

Ulysses S. Grant, who rode to the White House on his heroic exploits in the Civil War, proved to be a better soldier than politician. Because of his political naiveté and trusting manner, his two terms as president were marked by wholesale corruption at the highest levels of government. During this same period, the press began to develop its investigative function, thus shedding light on the unethical and illegal practices that plagued Grant's tenure in the White House.

The newspapers, with great relish, disclosed that he had appointed forty-eight of his relatives to government positions, that he was the beneficiary of lavish gifts—including three houses—from his wealthy friends, and that his sister's husband was involved in a conspiracy to rig the gold market.

With rare exceptions Grant had no official relations with the press. In his second inaugural address he declared that he had been "the subject of abuse and slander scarcely ever equaled in political history."

During Grant's second term it was learned that high administration officials had accepted stock for helping dishonest promoters of the Union Pacific Railway. The War Department was rocked by a scandal, involving the president's own brother Orvil, in which bribes had been taken by political appointees. Subsequently, the *St. Louis Democrat* exposed a conspiracy of revenue officials to defraud the government of tax money in what became known as the "Whiskey Ring" scandal. By the time he left office Grant was a broken and disillusioned man. He lived only long enough to write a widely acclaimed autobiography.

"Keyhole Journalism"

Grover Cleveland's relations with the press were tense and often stormy throughout his years in the White House. He particularly resented what he contended were misrepresentations and sensationalist innuendos and consequently kept reporters at a distance.

The course was set soon after his nomination in July 1884 when the *Buffalo Telegraph* reported that Cleveland was the father of an illegitimate son, then ten years old. His political opponents thereupon took up the cry:

Ma, Ma, Where's my pa?
Gone to the White House
Ha, Ha, Ha

Upon assuming the presidency in March 1885, Cleveland mostly dealt with White House correspondents through his secretaries. His marriage to the young Frances Folsom fifteen months later further distanced Cleveland from reporters who practiced the so-called "keyhole journalism." *(See box, A President's Wedding, p. 56.)*

Another incident in Cleveland's presidency is significant because it was the precursor of attempts by succeeding presidents to conceal or disguise actions and developments that they believed might be detrimental to their administration and the national welfare. Shortly into his second term, a malignant growth was found in the president's mouth. In an effort to avert a panic over the president's health in view of mounting economic instability, an operation was secretly performed aboard a friend's yacht.

UPI/Bettmann Newsphotos

Like FDR and JFK, Ronald Reagan was extremely adept at presenting himself through the media. His long career before the cameras and his affable temperament ideally equipped him for the on-stage existence that contemporary presidents must endure.

Most of Cleveland's upper left jaw was removed, incapacitating him for a period of time. But it was two months before the press learned the bare outlines of the story and twenty years before the complete facts were disclosed.

Theodore Roosevelt, who created the modern model of White House press relations and was probably the most prolific writer among U.S. presidents, offered his views on the responsibilities and functions of the press in an address before the Milwaukee Press Club in September 1910.

> The newspaper men—publishers, editors, reporters—are just as much public servants as are the men in the government service themselves, whether those men be elected or appointed officers.
>
> The highest type of newspaper man ought to try to put his business above all other business. The editor, who stands as a judge in a community, should be one of the men to whom you would expect to look up, because his function as an editor makes him a more important man than the average merchant, the average business man, the average professional man can be. He wields great influence; and he cannot escape the responsibility of it. If he wields it well, honor is his beyond the honor that comes to the average man who does well; if he wields ill, shame should be his beyond the shame that comes to the average man who does ill. . . .

Because Roosevelt understood the role of the press in public affairs, he was especially sensitive to it. He harbored a bitter antipathy toward Joseph Pulitzer's *New York World* ever since one of its correspondents, famed author Stephen Crane, wrote an unflattering account of his celebrated charge up San Juan Hill during the Spanish-American War. And when the *World* in 1908 exposed the involvement of several of his associates in the financing of the Panama Canal, Roosevelt tried to get Pulitzer indicted and thrown in jail.[58]

Woodrow Wilson set out in his presidency to establish a working relationship with the press, and at one of his early news conferences more than two hundred reporters crowded the Oval Office. But he soon became irritated with White House reporters for what he felt was an unjustified intrusion into his personal life and private family affairs, notably those involving his three daughters. An academic by training, he tended to give the impression that journalists were beneath his intellectual level.

As David Lawrence, one of the few Washington correspondents to gain Wilson's confidence, observed, "Mr. Wilson's quarrel with the press was not personal but impersonal. He disagreed with the methods of American journalism. . . ."[59]

"Making News and Being News"

While Franklin D. Roosevelt is acclaimed as a nonpareil in dealing with the press, he sometimes displayed an overbearing self-confidence in his attitude toward reporters. Often, he would tell them in an apparent attempt to influence their reports, "If I were writing this story, here is how I would write it," or, "If I were writing the heading on this story, here is how I would headline it."[60]

On more than one occasion, FDR complained directly to newspaper publishers about reporters whom he felt had misrepresented his views and even sought to have them transferred, among them Arthur Krock, Washington bureau chief of the *New York Times* and one of the most eminent journalists in Washington. "I am all in favor of chloroforming for certain newspaper men," he wrote a friend. As a mark of displeasure, he once presented a *New York Daily News* reporter with a German Iron Cross.[61]

In a reference to *Time* cofounder Henry R. Luce, Roosevelt declared, "Beginning with the first number of *Time*, I discovered that one secret of their financial success is a deliberate policy of either exaggeration or distortion. Pay no attention to them—I don't."[62]

However, as historian Arthur M. Schlesinger, Jr., noted, "By the brilliant but simple trick of making news and being news, Roosevelt outwitted the general hostility of the publishers and converted the press into one of the most effective channels of his public leadership."[63]

The end of World War II marked the beginning of a new era in relations between the White House and the press. Television and jet air travel allowed presidents to engage in frequent, direct communication with the American public, and thus they were less dependent on the Washington press corps to convey their views.

At the same time, however, the advent of the mass media brought with it a raised consciousness among journalists concerning their responsibilities and professional standards. Hence, the adversary relationship between the White House and the press became more intense and more public. Furthermore, the new technology and the growth of the Washington press corps produced a new breed of journalist less concerned with custom and tradition.

Harry S Truman became president upon FDR's death and announced he would continue his predecessor's press policies. Truman, however, possessed neither the skill nor the personality to match Roosevelt, and before long his feisty, occasionally irascible nature worked its way into his dealings with the press. He once said he was "saving up four or five good, hard punches on the nose" for reporters who, he felt, had been unfair to him. On another occasion, when White House reporters complained about an exclusive interview he had given to *New York Times* correspondent Arthur Krock, Truman replied, "I'll give interviews to anybody I damn please."

In a display of paternal outrage, the feisty Missourian sent off an angry letter to Paul Hume, music critic of the *Washington Post*, for his "lousy review" of a concert given by the president's daughter, Margaret, in December 1950. The president declared that Hume sounded "like a frustrated old man who never made a success" and that if he ever met Hume the critic would need "a new nose and plenty of beefsteak."[64]

Later, President Kennedy, in a fit of pique over stories critical of his administration, canceled his subscription to the *New York Herald Tribune*. Lyndon B. Johnson, called by Walter Lippmann "a pathologically secretive man," was appalled by what he considered the perfidy of the press and took every criticism of his administration as a personal blow. He once exclaimed, "You guys. All you guys in the media. All of politics has changed because of you. You've broken all the machines and the ties between us and Congress and the city machines. You've given us a new kind of people . . . Teddy, Tunney [Sen. Edward M. Kennedy, D-Mass., and John V. Tunney, D-Calif., House 1965-1971, Senate 1971-1977]. They're your creatures, your puppets. . . . They're all yours. Your product."[65]

Richard Nixon's perennial war with the news media was evident in personal White House files made available to the public in 1987 by the National Archives. In a series of memorandums to his chief of staff, H. R. Haldeman, and his press secretary, Ronald L. Ziegler, Nixon ordered that

A President's Wedding

The already-tense relations between Grover Cleveland and the press worsened early in his presidency when it became known that he was planning to marry Frances Folsom, the young and comely daughter of his late law partner. With unprecedented vigor the newspapers pursued the betrothal story, embellishing the smallest detail, some more imaginative than factual. At one point Cleveland, who wanted a quiet wedding, declared, "I regret that the President of the United States does not have the same rights and privileges as an ordinary citizen." [1]

Critics condemned the press for resorting to "keyhole journalism" because of the aggressively intrusive manner in which it covered the presidential wedding and honeymoon. Although such reporting would later become commonplace and be perceived as part of the burden of being president, Cleveland and his bride were victims of an emerging type of journalism, characterized by its assertiveness and penchant for intimate detail.

Speaking at the 250th anniversary celebration of Harvard College in 1886, about five months after the June 2 wedding, President Cleveland emotionally criticized newspapers that had engaged in this practice:

> No public officer should desire to check the utmost freedom of criticism as to all official acts; but every right-thinking man must concede that the President of the United States should not be put beyond the protection which American love of fair play and decency accords to every American citizen. This trait of our national character would not encourage, if their extent were fully appreciated, the silly mean and cowardly lies that every day are found in the columns of certain newspapers, which violate every instinct of American manliness, and in ghoulish glee desecrate every sacred relation of public life. . . . [2]

1. James E. Pollard, *The Presidents and the Press* (New York: Octagon Books, 1973), 504.
2. Ibid., 512.

certain reporters and columnists who had written unfavorable stories about him be cut off from White House access and their calls not be returned.

He noted in a June 1, 1971, memo that he had attended the annual White House Correspondents Dinner at Ziegler's suggestion, only to find at his next press conference that "The reporters were considerably more bad-mannered and vicious than usual. This bears out my theory that treating them with considerably more contempt is in the long run a more productive policy."

Shortly after the press conference and memo, Nixon, who had been angered by the *New York Times'* publication of the Pentagon Papers, the secret government history of the Vietnam War, directed Haldeman to see to it that "under absolutely no circumstances is anyone on the White House staff, on any subject, to respond to an inquiry from the *New York Times* unless and until I give express permission—and I do not expect to give such permission in the foreseeable future." [66]

Yet, notwithstanding Nixon's distrust of the press, he seemed, as his White House domestic policy adviser, John Ehrlichman, observed, "to believe there was no national issue that was not susceptible to public relations treatment."

In his White House memoirs, Ehrlichman wrote that "During the years I worked for him, Nixon was usually capable of a passionless and penetrating analysis of his press opportunities. He was a talented media manipulator. I often watched him successfully plan how he or his spokesmen would dominate the evening news, capture the headlines and right-side columns of the front page of *The Washington Post* or the lead story in *Time* or *Newsweek*. Richard Nixon could think like an editor." [67] Yet, it would be the news media that would eventually help bring down the Nixon presidency because of its Watergate-related transgressions.

Throughout his single term as president, Jimmy Carter's relationship with the Washington press was one of strained formality: neither side seemed to fully accept the other and consequently each kept its guard up. Carter's attitude was implicit in a remark he made in a memorable interview with *Playboy* magazine (November 1976) during his first presidential campaign: "Issues? The local media are interested, all right, but the national news media have absolutely no interest in issues at all. . . . What they're looking for is a 47-second argument between me and another candidate, or something like that. There's absolutely nobody in the back of this plane [the press section] who would ask an issue question unless he thought he could trick me into some crazy statement."

After leaving office, Carter maintained that his two greatest disappointments as president were the inertia of Congress and the "irresponsibility" of the press. He also referred to the national news media as "one of the blights of most presidents' existences, including to a high degree my own." [68]

Ronald Reagan, the first president to serve two full terms since Eisenhower, generally received benign treatment at the hands of the press. It is widely believed that his conviviality and jaunty optimism, as well as his actor's sense of the right gesture and his personal popularity, blunted the news media's innate skepticism. The press regularly reported his misstatements and verbal gaffes, but these reports made no dent in the president's popular standing.

Beneath the picture of congeniality and openness that he publicly presented, Reagan preferred to deal with the press in elaborately controlled settings. There was none of the give-and-take that characterized FDR's regular meetings with reporters. Despite his famous communications skills, Reagan held infrequent news conferences, fewer than any of his recent predecessors. *(See Table 2.)*

Instead, his media advisers arranged "photo opportunities," allowing constricted access to the president while showing him in a theatrical setting. Furthermore, background briefings with White House aides were carefully monitored and news leaks, a particular obsession with Reagan, severely condemned. Accordingly, imagery and the artful use of public relations reached unprecedented heights in the Reagan White House.

Emergence of Modern White House Press Corps

Theodore Roosevelt's generosity in allowing reporters to set up working quarters in the White House symbolized the emergence of the press as an institution in government affairs. Journalists have been based at the White House ever since, observing, reporting, analyzing, photographing, and eventually televising virtually every action as well as many private moments involving the occupant.

With the growth of the so-called "imperial presidency" and the introduction of television, members of the modern White House press corps have become, in effect, an elite subspecies of Washington journalism. They are, notwithstanding the traditional independence of the press, part of the monarchical white House entourage. They work within the heady environment of the White House—their creature comforts catered to and their professional prerequisites swiftly satisfied. They travel (at their employers' expense), occasionally play tennis with, and generally socialize with the presidential household.

In a speech at the 1975 White House Correspondents' Association dinner, President Ford embraced the members as part of the "White House family." He said,

> We work together. We laugh together. We exchange ideas, facts and speculation. We interact We cannot function without each other. This is the stuff that families are made of. And like all families, we have disagreements. We take in and assimilate individual attitudes, concerns, information, interests. Then, we shine the spotlight of our unique perceptions on each problem, each new challenge.[69]

Once but a handful—all could comfortably stand alongside FDR's desk in the Oval Office—the White House reporters have multiplied into a sizable legion. The increase in their numbers supports the perception of innate power. In 1955, when President Eisenhower left for a vacation in Denver, he was accompanied by twenty-two reporters. Thirty years later, more than one hundred fifty members of the news media trailed along whenever President Reagan left on a trip outside of Washington. Almost two thousand applied for press accreditation when Reagan traveled to Moscow in May 1988 for the fourth summit meeting with Soviet leader Mikhail Gorbachev.

From fewer than a hundred correspondents in the 1860s, the Washington press corps has grown to more than 2,500 newspaper, 1,025 magazine, and 2,400 radio-television reporters accredited in 1989 to the congressional media galleries.[70]

"Regulars" and Part-timers

The nucleus of the White House press corps is comprised of sixty to seventy-five journalists, referred to as the "regulars." They cover the White House and the activities of the president on a day-to-day basis. Their members represent just about every form of the mass media—major dailies, television and cable networks, wire services, national news magazines, specialized journals, trade publications, and foreign news organizations.

The regulars, for the most part, are confined to the West Wing press area. Each is provided with a private working cubicle in the basement operations section.

In addition, there are numerous "irregulars" who cover the White House only part time or whose interests are on particular issues or institutional aspects of the presidency. All must obtain Secret Service security clearance to receive a White House press card.

The White House "beat" is generally considered to be a coveted assignment because of its high visibility. Print reporters are ensured almost daily, bylined stories, and television correspondents are consistently seen on the evening newscasts. Surveys show that an average of four items on the nightly news shows deal directly or indirectly with the White House. Journalistic careers thus can be enhanced by this assignment.

Not unexpectedly, the various news organizations adopt their own internal systems in assigning reporters to the White House. Some newspapers simply allow the reporter who covered the victorious candidate in the campaign to follow the new president to the White House. Others replace their White House correspondents from time to time in search of a fresh perspective. Still others change their White House reporters with each new administration. Some, like United Press International, may leave them there indefinitely.

Overall, White House regulars are made up of a motley cast of journalists, differing widely in talent, personality, background, audience, and professional objectives. While there is inevitable turnover among them, there is also a hard core of veterans who provide continuity and institutional memory extending from one administration to another.

Regardless, all are subject to the flow of news, the rhythm of the White House operations, and the sitting president's attitude toward the news media. Accordingly, political scientists Michael B. Grossman and Martha J. Kumar, in their study of presidential press relations, refer to White House reporters as members of "Milton's Army," from the line in John Milton's *On His Blindness* that states, "They also serve who only stand and waite."[71]

Presidents and their aides must also deal with other members of the Washington press community, many of whom are highly vocal and nationally known and, hence, influential in varying degrees. Notable among them are syndicated columnists, television news anchors and commentators, and Washington bureau chiefs.

Once considered journalism's royal elite, columnists still enjoy an exalted position, but in recent years their status has somewhat declined because of competition from nonprofessionals, technical experts, and academics who have access to expanded editorial pages in the major newspapers. No longer perceived as "Renaissance men" in an increasingly complex world, the most prominent among them are recognized as specialists in particular areas or the voice of a distinct ideology. Television, however, has elevated many columnists to national stardom.

Playing to the Cameras

TV anchors and network commentators exercise an inordinate impact on public opinion because of their visibility and celebrity status. The bitter confrontation that ensued when CBS anchorman Dan Rather pressed Vice President George Bush concerning his role in the Iran-contra affair was considered one of the signal events of the 1988 presidential campaign.

Contemporary White House press aides openly acknowledge that their primary concern is television coverage of the president and his administration. In his White House memoirs, Donald T. Regan emphasized the role of Michael Deaver, President Reagan's public relations adviser and deputy chief of staff:

It was Deaver's job to advise the President on image, and image was what he talked about nearly all the time. It was Deaver who identified the story of the day at the eight o'clock staff meeting and coordinated the plans for dealing with it, Deaver who created and approved photo opportunities, Deaver who alerted the President to the snares being laid by the press that day. Deaver was a master of his craft. He saw—designed—each Presidential action as a one-minute or two-minute spot on the evening network news, or a picture on page one of the *Washington Post* or the *New York Times*, and conceived every Presidential appearance in terms of camera angles.[72]

Noting the dramatic change in routine White House coverage because of the importance and physical presence of television operations, former *Time* magazine White House correspondent Laurence I. Barrett observed that

Not a single television camera was present in the Oval Office when Lyndon Johnson held his first "impromptu" press conference soon after Kennedy's death. Today at least five TV camera crews and twelve to fifteen broadcast correspondents are present whenever the President is in the White House. The appetite for footage adaptable for evening news spots of 60 to 120 seconds or longer pieces on the morning shows is insatiable. The competition among network correspondents when they do their "standups" on the White House lawn is keener than the rivalry among soccer teams in Latin countries.[73]

The editorial decisions of Washington bureau chiefs and other media executives are of paramount interest to the White House because they determine what stories will be covered, who will cover them, and the extent of the play given them. The bureau chiefs further speak for their news organizations and are frequently called on to deal with officials on matters such as the establishment of reporter "pools," negotiating arrangements for travel with government executives, settling on media facilities at certain events such as national political conventions, and providing air time for presidential press conferences and speeches.

In sum, columnists, TV news personalities, and bureau chiefs are important to the White House because of the space and air time they can provide, the size and caliber of the audience they reach, their capacity to help frame the news agenda, their explanations of why particular events occurred, and their interpretations of the issues. Above all, the modern White House is aware that public impressions are largely filtered through the media. In another sense, the media act as the intermediary between the public and the government.

Daily Routine

The high point of the White House reporter's normal day is the prenoon briefing at which the presidential press secretary, sometimes assisted by other administration officials—and on rare occasions the president personally—delivers announcements and takes questions. The raw material for most of the day's White House stories are gleaned here.

Earlier in the morning, at about nine o'clock, the press secretary will have met with a select group of twenty or so regulars to update the previous days' stories and review the president's schedule, so that the media will be alerted as to what to anticipate. This early meeting sets the press direction for the rest of the day—barring unexpected developments. Also, information released at that time is sent out by the wire services and provides the basis for the day's first stories on radio and television.

More often than not the 11:30 briefing, which attracts a larger audience of regulars and other journalists, turns into a highly charged sparring match, as the reporters try to goad the press secretary, standing on a dais at one end of the press room, into saying more than the secretary is able or willing to say.

Information offered by the presidential assistants—involving, for example, the president's position on a policy issue, a new appointment, a scheduled trip, the White House's response to congressional action—generally provides White House reporters with the gist of their news stories for that day. Only rarely are the daily briefings televised. Invariably, they cover a broad range of subjects from the trivial to the highly complex. Increasingly, the tenor of the questions has centered on the personal life of the president and his family. When Donald Regan disclosed in his book, *For the Record*, that Nancy Reagan, the president's wife, used the services of an astrologer to help guide her husband in making decisions, reporters responded with seventy questions on the disclosure at a single briefing.

It is widely contended that White House reporters are the object of excessive indulgence. During the Ford years, author-journalist Richard Reeves characterized the White House press operations as "an adult day-care center" run by a press secretary whose job was to keep the reporters "occupied, dumb and happy." Indeed, on any major issue, an abundance of information is made available to reporters through briefings, interviews, press releases, special backgrounders, and possibly a session with the president. This is referred to as "handout journalism" by critics.

Good reporters, some of the best of whom are assigned to the White House, go beyond what they are given and seek other sources to flesh out their stories and offer a balanced picture.

A tableau of the White House press room during the LBJ era was offered by press secretary George Christian:

The reporters who covered Johnson on a regular basis were as much a part of the White House as the employees who worked there. The White House was their office, even if only a cubbyhole in the crowded press room off the West Lobby. Many of them never went to their own bureaus except to pick up their paychecks. From nine o'clock or so in the morning until the press secretary told them the business of the day was finished—which might be four-thirty in the evening or midnight—they lived in the environs of the West Lobby. Some had the habit of napping on the stuffed chairs and sofas in the lobby, which was the main entrance to the working West Wing of the White House. On occasion, the lobby took on the appearance of a genteel flop house.[74]

Since then, changes wrought by the Vietnam War and the Watergate scandal have sharpened the adversary relationship between the press and government. White House press/public relations operations have been significantly enlarged and refined in an attempt to exert greater management of the news. Members of the news media are physically quartered in the White House, but for all intents and purposes they are hermetically sealed off from the rest of the building. Vital decisions may be made only a few feet from the press room without its occupants being remotely aware of them.

Emblematic of the change in the relationship was the refurbishing of the White House press room. Early in the Reagan administration, rows of theater seats were installed in the open area of the press room. Metal plaques engraved with the names of the news organizations were attached to the seats, reserving them for their reporters during briefings. White House aides maintained that the purpose was to inject some order into the sometimes chaotic briefing sessions.

Be that as it may, the informal, if sometimes unruly yet democratic exchange that previously existed gave way to a regimented forum that permitted White House press aides to exercise greater control over the proceedings. Few, if any, of the White House regulars criticized the change; they were, after all, guaranteed reserved seats at the briefings. And the appropriately engraved metal plaque was recognized as a new status symbol.

The President's Press Secretary

Next to the president, the White House press secretary is one of the most visible officials in the U.S. government. With the growth of the presidency and big government, the advent of mass communications techniques, and the focal position of the United States in world affairs, the White House press secretary has become a household name, better known than most cabinet secretaries and all but a few members of Congress. The press secretary is never far from the president's side, is privy to most White House decisions, and is mentioned in the media virtually every day. Thus, modern presidential press secretaries have themselves become figures of national standing. *(See Table 3.)*

Among the roles the press secretary plays, other than that of principal conduit of news and messages from the president and major administration agencies to the press, are that of creator and protector of the presidential image, caterer to representatives of the print and broadcast media, and adviser in the art of communications, as, for example, the timing of the release of information, who should release it, and the form in which it is presented. The secretary is also administrator of the White House press-public relations section and coordinator of the administration's entire public affairs operations.

Still another less recognized function: because of the job's closeness to members of the news media, the secretary is able to pick up public opinion trends and issues of paramount concern to various constituencies. Far more than any other subordinate, the press secretary speaks publicly for the president, to the extent that anyone can. As George E. Reedy, onetime press secretary to President Johnson observed, "The press secretary is an echo of the president." [75]

Practically every word the press secretary utters is heard around the world and instantly dissected for its meaning and significance regarding administration policies and intentions. Hence, as noted by Larry Speakes, former press spokesman for President Reagan, "U.S. policy is . . . made from my podium." [76]

Every White House press secretary is fully aware, and is constantly reminded, that the first and overriding obligation is not to the press but to the president, at whose pleasure the secretary serves. The chief task of the press aide is to illuminate the presidency in the best possible light and attract popular support for the president's policies and programs. Accordingly, truth becomes less of a moral imperative than a commodity in the political marketplace.

In a real sense, a press secretary complements and is an extension of the president. Some have been so closely identified with a president that they seemed to be bodily projections of him, such as James C. Hagerty and Dwight Eisenhower, Pierre Salinger and John Kennedy, Ronald L. Ziegler and Richard Nixon, Jody Powell and Jimmy Carter. Press secretaries are never wholly their own persons. To serve effectively, they must assume the president's principles and philosophy.

Describing his role, Ronald H. Nessen, President Ford's press secretary, said, ". . . I always try to answer a question as the president would answer it if he were there. I think that is the most valuable service that a press secretary can perform—to be an accurate reflector of the president's own views." [77]

In addition, presidential press secretaries are burdened with administrative and personnel duties. Depending on their closeness to the president, they may participate in policy decisions.

Informal Press Relations

During the nineteenth century, several presidents sought advice on press relations in an informal, unstructured manner from friends and aides. The novelist Nathaniel Hawthorne, for example, performed such a service for his friend, President Franklin Pierce.[78]

Throughout Abraham Lincoln's presidency, his private secretary, John G. Nicolay, acted as his liaison with the press. Ever protective of the president, the faithful and tenacious Nicolay was an innovator in attempts to influence the press. He sent letters to newspapers complaining of what he considered unfair treatment of the president. On one occasion, he personally dressed down Horace Greeley, of the *New York Tribune*, for a "villainous, unfair, and untrue" editorial. The rebuked Greeley allowed Nicolay space in his newspaper to respond.

Since it was impossible for the president, whose time was monopolized by the war, to review the newspapers himself, Nicolay, along with another young White House aide, John Hay, began drafting brief summaries of important news stories—a practice that survives to this day. (Hay, in his early twenties at the time, would later become a leading novelist and outstanding secretary of state under Presidents McKinley and Theodore Roosevelt.)

As one writer noted, "Lincoln was no more immune to newspaper criticism than any other president, and he came to rely on Nicolay as his watchdog of the press." [79]

Subsequent presidents retained aides who served in a nonprescribed capacity as their contacts with the press. Grover Cleveland enlisted the services of Daniel Lamont, an Albany, New York, newspaper editor, and later Theodore Roosevelt relied on William Loeb, Jr., his secretary who became a role model for future White House chiefs of staff, to handle his press relations. Loeb employed a carrot-and-stick approach in dealing with reporters: those who wrote stories about the president perceived to be "fair" were given full cooperation of the White House, those critical of the administration were denied access and banished to outer darkness.

The evolution of presidential press relations made rapid strides with the dawn of the twentieth century. Joseph P. Tumulty, a secretary who had been with Woodrow Wilson since his days as New Jersey governor, coordinated the president's schedule and doubled as his adviser on press matters. Tumulty, who is credited with being one of the first presidential aides to appreciate the use of public relations in governmental affairs, often was obliged to smooth things with reporters when Wilson would express his distrust of them. During his first year in the White House, Wilson gave serious thought to creating a federal "publicity bureau" whose primary purpose would be to release "real facts" about the government to counter false impressions in the press. The idea, however, never got beyond the talking stage.[80]

Succeeding presidents Harding and Coolidge generally dealt with the press through an assistant who had other duties. Although radio had become a popular medium in the 1920s, the print journals were still the dominant purveyor of news and formulator of public opinion. The usual practice extending through the Hoover era was to require White House reporters to submit their questions in writing.

Modern Concept of the Office

The first White House aide formally designated as "press secretary" with the full-time job of handling reporters was George Akerson, one of three new presidential secretaries authorized by Congress when Herbert Hoover entered office.[81]

A popular man-about-town, Akerson had to abdicate some of his turf to another Hoover aide, Lawrence Richey. A mysterious presence in the Hoover White House, Richey served in various roles as the president's bodyguard, troubleshooter, plugger of news leaks, and reporters' nemesis. Richey reportedly prepared a "black list" of journalists who had "turned against" the Hoover administration—a device duplicated forty years later with Nixon's "enemies list." Akerson resigned before the end of Hoover's term.

The modern concept of the presidential press secretary dates from President Franklin Roosevelt's appointment of Stephen T. Early. A longtime Associated Press reporter, he is generally considered the first such aide to have a sense of presidential press relations. It was during his tenure that the press secretary function became permanently established.

Early would usually hold an informal briefing session with FDR to review the day's news developments before the president met with reporters at his 10:30 A.M. press conferences. The press secretary would then escort the reporters into the Oval Office where FDR would hold court. Marvin H. McIntyre, the president's appointments secretary, generally sat in on the sessions.

Early and McIntyre enjoyed the confidence of the press corps, but there was never any doubt that FDR was the supreme master at orchestrating White House media relations. He eliminated the awkward practice of having reporters submit questions in advance, and his use of radio to reach millions of Americans opened up a new chapter in presidential public relations.

Although always in FDR's shadow, Early was the first White House press secretary whose name became familiar to the public. Columnist Raymond Clapper once described him as "one of the most important voices in Government." [82]

In the course of his presidency, Truman was served by three press secretaries—Charles Ross, Joseph Short, and Roger Tubby. Each of the three men came from a journalistic background, solidifying a tradition of appointing professional journalists as White House press secretary.

The pattern for modern White House media operations was set by James C. Hagerty, former *New York Times* political reporter who served as press secretary throughout President Eisenhower's eight years in office—a period that coincided with the development of television as a political tool. Hagerty, who enjoyed Eisenhower's confidence and the respect of members of the press, was highly effective. His organizational and operational techniques established a prototype for succeeding White House press secretaries.

Hagerty's total effort as Eisenhower's press secretary was to protect the president and discourage the publication or broadcast of any views contrary to administration policy. He not only supervised White House press operations but also coordinated the executive agencies' news releases and counseled cabinet secretaries concerning their public relations. As a former reporter, he was adept at anticipating the needs of the working press. In this regard, one writer observed,

> Ninety percent of a Press Secretary's job is concerned not with policy but with endless routine: seeing that speeches and press releases are issued well in advance; arranging the press corps' travel plans on presidential trips; finding out what the President gave the First Lady for Christmas, and so forth. On such things, Hagerty was unbeatable. . . . Hagerty knows just what makes a good still picture, the exact amount of lighting for television, exactly when to break up a press conference in order to make deadlines for home editions on the East Coast.[83]

Hagerty's talent was particulary evident on the three occasions Eisenhower became ill, in 1955 when he suffered a heart attack in Denver, the following year when he underwent an ileitis operation, and in 1957 when he had a stroke. Hagerty's candor and penchant for detail set an example that future White House press secretaries would follow in releasing news and information about presidential illnesses.

Under Hagerty's direction, Eisenhower became the first president to allow edited telecasts of his news conferences. The natural progression of full-dress, live presidential press conferences occurred shortly afterward in the Kennedy administration. Pierre Salinger, Kennedy's press secretary and former reporter for the *San Francisco Chronicle* and *Collier's* magazine, was a firm believer that the job required extensive journalistic experience. Equally important in Salinger's case was his gregarious nature and ability to get along with reporters while maintaining his loyalty to the president. Salinger's personality ideally complemented the natural charm and dry wit of President Kennedy.

With the increasing emphasis on media politics, the White House press/public relations operations has burgeoned into one of the largest divisions of the presidential complex. The number of people in the White House press office alone rose from a mere handful in the Kennedy era to almost fifty in the Nixon years and in each succeeding administration.

In addition to the press office, the modern White House includes an Office of Communications, which deals with overall media relations; a news summary unit that monitors the print and electronic media for stories of interest to the White House; a pollster to measure public opinion and popular attitudes; a press advance detail that handles the logistics for members of the media during presidential trips; special radio-TV advisers and technicians; a photography staff; and an Office of Media Liaison that serves as the White House contact for news organizations outside of Washington. Working closely with the press operations is the White House Office of Public Liaison, which deals with special interest groups. Also, some of the various units of the Executive Office of the President have their own press relations officers, including the Office of Management and Budget, Council of Economic Advisers, and the National Security Council.

Dealing with Crises

During President Kennedy's relatively brief but eventful period of office, Press Secretary Pierre Salinger had to deal with the Bay of Pigs operation, the Berlin crisis of 1961, the Cuban missile crisis, and numerous domestic civil rights demonstrations, including the Birmingham riots of 1963.

Lyndon Johnson's obsessiveness with news coverage and his public image, as well as his demanding personality, created incessant problems for each of the three press secretaries who served under him—George Reedy, Bill Moyers, and George Christian. Johnson never fully understood the adversary role of the press, a conviction reaffirmed in his view by the Vietnam War coverage. Contemporary observers contended that Johnson, who kept three TV monitors in his office, attempted to be his own press secretary. His depictions of events were often at cross purposes with press reports, serving to further impair his relationship with the news media.

Throughout much of his political career, Richard Nixon's relations with the media were marred by barely concealed antagonism. Upon gaining the presidency, he restructured and expanded the press operations with the intent of centralizing the dissemination of White House news and controlling the flow of information. Appointed as presidential press secretary was Ronald Ziegler, who had joined the Nixon campaign from a Los Angeles advertising firm. Herbert Klein, a longtime Nixon political aide, was named director of the newly created Office of Communications, which was designed to circumvent the Washington press corps and deal directly with editors and broadcasters outside the capital.

From the beginning, it was apparent that Ziegler, who initially held the second-rank title of "press assistant," was not part of the senior Nixon staff and stood "outside the loop" of the White House decision-making apparatus, thus severely diminishing his effectiveness.

Eventually, the Watergate scandal strained Nixon's relationship with the press to the breaking point. A poisoned atmosphere permeated the White House press room as Ziegler and reporters clashed in inflammatory exchanges. Ziegler's occasional references to previous White House statements and explanations as being "inoperative" added to the hostility and, soon enough, he gradually relinquished the daily press briefings to the assistant press secretary, Gerald L. Warren. Several years after he left the White House, Ziegler conceded at a press symposium that much of the information that he gave about

Table 1 Presidential Press Secretaries, 1929-1989

Press secretary	President	Years	Background
George Akerson	Hoover	1929-31	reporter
Theodore G. Joslin	Hoover	1931-33	AP reporter
Stephen T. Early	Roosevelt	1933-45	AP, UPI reporter
Charles Ross	Truman	1945-50	reporter
Joseph H. Short	Truman	1950-52	reporter
Roger Tubby	Truman	1952-53	journalist
James C. Hagerty	Eisenhower	1953-61	reporter
Pierre E. Salinger	Kennedy	1961-63	investigative writer
Pierre E. Salinger	Johnson	1963-64	investigative writer
George Reedy	Johnson	1964-65	UPI reporter
Bill Moyers	Johnson	1965-67	associate director of Peace Corps
George Christian	Johnson	1967-69	reporter
Ronald L. Ziegler	Nixon	1969-74	advertising
Jerald F. terHorst	Ford	1974	bureau chief, newspaper
Ron H. Nessen	Ford	1974-77	journalist
Jody L. Powell	Carter	1977-81	advertising
James Brady[a]	Reagan	1981-89	Reagan campaign aide
Larry Speakes	Reagan	1981-87	reporter
Marlin Fitzwater	Reagan	1987-89	government information aide
Marlin Fitzwater	Bush	1989-	government information aide

a. Although Brady was severely wounded in the 1981 presidential assassination attempt, his title remained press secretary until 1989. Speakes's title was assistant to the president and principal deputy press secretary, while Fitzwater's was assistant to the president for press relations. He became White House press secretary in the Bush administration.

Watergate was incorrect "because I was not told what the facts were." [84]

President Ford's selection of Jerald terHorst as his press secretary temporarily restored peace in the White House press room. But after terHorst resigned in protest of the Nixon pardon, his successor, Nessen, experienced credibility problems. Reporters suspected that Nessen, a former NBC correspondent, was not privy to the White House inner councils.

Jimmy Carter's press secretary, Jody Powell, was perfectly suited for the position. A fellow Georgian, he had been a confidant, aide, and adviser to Carter for about ten years. White House reporters were keenly aware that Powell had the complete confidence of the president and that he had unrestricted access to Carter and accurately reflected his views. While Powell's easy manner and sense of humor made him popular with members of the press, they also recognized his unswerving partisanship as a Carter loyalist. As a result, he was seen as much as the president's chief salesman, image maker, and public defender as his official voice.

Powell was put to his most severe test during the 444 days of the Iranian hostage crisis, which dominated the final months of the Carter administration. With each evening TV newscast the networks played a drumbeat on the

Jimmy Carter Library

Jody Powell, left, fell within the tradition of press secretaries who reflected their president's personalities. A fellow Georgian, Powell had been a confidant, aide, and adviser to Jimmy Carter for about ten years.

increasing number of days that the fifty-two hostages had been held, keeping the issue alive in the public's mind. Seldom a day passed that Powell was not asked about the situation.

Because of the need for secrecy to protect the lives of the hostages, Powell was forced to grapple with a question that inevitably confronts most presidential spokesmen: should the government lie when national security is at stake? Powell concurred with Pentagon spokesman Arthur Sylvester's declaration in 1963 that under certain circumstances "government does have the right to lie." In his White House memoirs Powell wrote that when the welfare of the nation requires it, "government has not only the right but a positive obligation to lie." [85]

Powell was directly faced with the issue when asked by Jack Nelson, Washington bureau chief of the *Los Angeles Times*, whether the Carter administration was planning a military operation to rescue the hostages. Powell had been informed by the president himself that such an attempt was imminent. Yet, he denied there were any rescue mission plans, stressing instead the White House's "cover" story that it was considering a naval blockade or the mining of Iranian harbors—options that had already been ruled out.

Two days later, the hostage rescue attempt ended in disaster. Although troubled by the moral dilemma, Powell observed, "It is ludicrous to argue that soliders may be sent off to fight and die, but a spokesman may not, under any circumstances, be asked to lie to make sure that the casualties are fewer and not in vain." [86]

In Carter's own words, the hostage crisis had "cast a pall" over his administration, raising questions of his leadership and eventually contributing to his reelection defeat in 1980. [87]

Larry Speakes was propelled into the position of President Reagan's chief spokesman through a tragic accident of history. On March 30, 1981, slightly more than two months after his inauguration, Reagan was seriously wounded by bullets fired by John W. Hinckley, Jr., a troubled young man. White House press secretary James Brady, a member of the presidential party leaving a Washington hotel following a Reagan speech, was also hit, suffering a severe head wound. Brady in the ensuing confusion was at first reported to have been killed. He eventually recovered but, while retaining the title of White House press secretary, never actively resumed the duties.

Speakes, a public relations consultant who had worked as a White House press aide in the Nixon and Ford administrations, was immediately thrust into the job. For almost the next six months, he served as Reagan's chief spokesman with the title of principal deputy press secretary.

For most of his time in the position, Speakes, at his own admission, "was excluded from a number of key meetings" and not until the near end of his tenure was he admitted as a member of the White House inner circle. [88]

Speakes's exclusion from the inner circle resulted in an embarrassment for him in October 1983 when CBS White House correspondent Bill Plante asked about a report that U.S. forces were poised to invade the Caribbean island of Grenada, where a bloody military coup was taking place. Speakes replied he would check on it and passed the inquiry on to Rear Adm. John M. Poindexter, deputy director of the National Security Council and later a central figure in the clandestine Iran-contra affair. "Preposterous," Poindexter replied—the exact word Speakes used when he got back to Plante. Twelve hours later, U.S. military forces attacked Grenada. [89]

Ironically, Speakes received his greatest amount of national publicity after he left the White House. In *Speaking Out*, a book on his White House experience, he acknowledged that on at least two occasions he fabricated quotes attributed to the president—once in September 1983 following the Soviet Union's shooting down of Korean Air Lines Flight 007, killing 269 people, and in November 1985 during the Geneva summit between Reagan and Soviet leader Mikhail Gorbachev. In the latter instance, Speakes reported to the press that the president had said to Gorbachev, "There is much that divides us, but I believe the world breathes easier because we are talking here together."

The comment was picked up by the U.S. and international media and heard around the world—yet Reagan had never made such a statement. The disclosure by Speakes in his book more than two years later created a furor in the press and at the White House, where his successor, Marlin Fitzwater, denounced the improvisation as a "damn outrage." Shortly afterward, Speakes was forced to resign from his job as a vice president for communications with a New York brokerage firm.

Presidents' Techniques of Managing the News

The success of modern-day presidents depends in a large measure on the artful use of persuasion and their skills as communicators to mobilize a national coalition and gain popular support. Just as the press needs the White House to carry out its function as the collector, relayer, and interpreter of news and information, so the White House needs the press to spread its message.

Not unexpectedly, presidents want news of their administration presented in a favorable light and editorial opinions and commentaries couched in terms compatible with official policy lines. This helps account for the elaborately orchestrated attempts by incumbent administrations to manage the news and shape its content.

To an immeasurable degree—for good and bad—the business of government is public relations. Seeded throughout the federal landscape, from the White House to the gargantuan cabinet departments to the mini-agencies cloistered in bureaucratic depths, is a huge, amorphous network of employees whose chief mission is to package and dispense information about government policies, services, and programs at one level and to promote them on another. The former is essentially an educational function; the latter is primarily political in nature. It is this dichotomy that has traditionally bred confusion and suspicion about federal public affairs operations.

At least part of the problem is that the line between the need to inform as a public service and the desire to solicit public support for political objectives has never been satisfactorily delineated. Moreover, it has never been established as to how many federal employees are engaged in what is broadly construed as government public relations—preferably referred to in the bureaucracy as public affairs or public information—or what the total costs are, mainly because of misleading job titles and budgets that camouflage the outlays.

Unofficial estimates place the number of government employees involved in some facet of public relations in excess of 25,000 and the cost at about a billion dollars a year. Indeed, no governmental warren is too small to have a public affairs officer, including the U.S. Marine Band.

Each day this vast, interlocking federal information machine spews forth millions of words, pictures, statistics, magazines, advisories, books, and films. It arranges tours, sets up exhibits, sponsors aerial events, schedules speakers, offers press interviews and news briefings, transmits radio programs around the world, and produces telecasts beamed abroad by orbiting satellites. The objective, simply put, is the selling of the government.

It is generally conceded, particularly in an age of mass communications and sophisticated image making, that the flow and quality of information that emanates from Washington are vital ingredients in the democratic process. As amply documented, the government can withhold information, classify it, distort it, or, on occasion, even lie. But more important is what the government chooses to report and reveal and the manner in which it is done.

For the most part, presidents assess communications in terms of helping or hindering them in the pursuit of their goals. Prohibited by the First Amendment from controlling or censoring the press, they seek to manage and manipulate it, or circumvent it through resources at their command.

At times, in their zeal to protect their administrations, they have resorted to untruths, half-truths, and deceptions, including the Eisenhower administration's misleading account of the U-2 incident, the attempt by the Johnson administration to conceal the escalation of U.S. military involvement in the Vietnam War, the Nixon White House's blatant efforts to cover up and delude the public and press throughout the Watergate scandal, and the secrecy im-

Marlin Fitzwater succeeded Larry Speakes as head of press relations in 1987. When Speakes later published memoirs disclosing White House operations, Fitzwater denounced the book's revelations as a "damn outrage."

Bill Fitz-Patrick, The White House

posed by Reagan administration officials in the Iran arms sale/contra aid episode.

Such questionable tactics are aberrations in the affairs of government. In the main, the White House attempts to manage the news by utilizing conventional techniques that have evolved over the years and are constantly being refined in step with advancements in communications technology.

Prominent among these techniques are daily press briefings, background briefings, formal televised press conferences, exclusive interviews, the issuance of news releases and handouts, photo opportunities, impromptu question-and-answer sessions, and public announcements.

The Daily Briefing

The most common and possibly the most effective tactic in White House news management involves the daily briefing conducted by the presidential press secretary. The customary practice among modern press secretaries has been to hold a news briefing each day, shortly before noon, thereby giving the television correspondents plenty of time to film "visuals" and put together their stories for the evening newscasts.

Almost always, the press secretary, standing at a podium in the White House press room before rows of seated reporters, opens the briefing with a series of announcements concerning the president and the administration. The announcements, for example, may concern the president's position on pending legislation, an innovative policy proposal, the introduction of a new administration program, a high-level government appointment, or a planned presidential trip. In so doing, the White House, in effect, sets the news agenda for the day because of presidents' dominance in American politics and the insatiable demand for news about them and their activities. As a result, news organizations are virtually compelled to publish and broadcast what the press secretary reports at the daily briefing. In a sense, members of the press are "captive" to the White House.

When it suits its objectives, the White House may provide special "backgrounder" briefings for reporters, generally to explain and elaborate on administration initiatives. These sessions may take any one of several forms. They may be: "on the record," meaning that the remarks may be quoted and the source identified; "on background," in which the source cannot be identified, except by status, as, for example, "an administration official"; on "deep background," under which attribution of any sort is prohibited; and "off the record," in which information given to reporters may not be included in their stories and is mainly provided for their guidance. Briefing sources may range from the president personally, to cabinet secretaries, White House aides, press officers, and policy specialists.

Regularly scheduled daily briefings are also held by the State Department and at least twice weekly by the Defense Department. Other departments and agencies hold them in response to events and developments or as the need requires.

While backgrounders may furnish reporters with useful information, they are especially beneficial to the administration. By evading direct quotation, officials may speak out on sensitive policy issues without being directly accountable for their words. It ensures them greater flexibility in getting their message across to the public or, if the case may be, to special constituencies, Congress, and foreign governments.

Backgrounders may also be used to send up "trial balloons" to gauge public reaction to prospective administration proposals, to mute speculation about presidential plans, to disseminate self-serving propaganda or "disinformation," to inflate the administration's public image, and to scotch rumors. As an example of the latter, President Carter once invited the Washington bureau chiefs of the *New York Times* and *Los Angeles Times* to his office to deny published reports that Vice President Walter F. Mondale was being excluded from his inner circle of advisers.[90]

Reporters are aware that they are being "used" in such instances, but are usually willing to go along with protecting the identities of their sources since they receive more information complying with the system than they would without it. It is the White House, however, that determines in line with its own self interest what information will be released, when, how, and to whom.

Programmed Events

Stage-managing, using the tricks and techniques of the theater, have become a staple of the White House. President Reagan, a former actor and TV show host, was particularly adept at such presentations under the direction of aide Michael Deaver, the former California public relations consultant and longtime friend and confidant of the Reagans. There were widely publicized scenes scripted by Deaver of President Reagan delivering a speech high above the steep cliffs of Pointe du Hoc, France, on the fortieth anniversary of the Normandy invasion as veterans of the historic assault looked on, and of Reagan, standing at the Korean Demilitarized Zone, dramatically peering through field glasses into Communist North Korea. In such scenes, conceived for their visual impact, members of the press are cast as extras in a public relations spectacle.

Sometimes in an attempt to convert an illusion out of reality, the White House will try to put a "spin" on what actually occurred. As a notable example, following the breakdown of the October 1986 Reykjavík summit between Reagan and Soviet leader Mikhail Gorbachev, White House chief of staff Donald Regan told the president's advisers, "This summit must not be seen or portrayed as a defeat. We've got to turn any such perception around, starting now." [91]

Shortly afterward Regan told a *New York Times* reporter that "Some of us are like a shovel brigade that follow a parade down Main street cleaning up. We took Reykjavík and turned what was really a sour situation into something that turned out pretty well." [92]

Access to the president and principal aides, other than through programmed media events, is a White House reporter's ultimate objective. During the Eisenhower administration almost all news and information was channeled through the White House press office. Subsequent administrations loosened the system, making White House officials sometimes available to the press—but always under the control of the president and staff. Because reporters do not have easy access to the presidential inner circle, they are more often than not compelled to go along with the official account of events.

Because of the expanding role of the media, modern presidents have increasingly granted exclusive interviews to selective reporters, usually those from major news organizations and those known to be sympathetic toward the administration. It has further become customary for presidents to grant private interviews to Washington-based foreign correspondents from countries they are scheduled to visit. In so doing, they set the stage for their visits and define their objectives and expectations on their own terms.

White House officials have come to appreciate that small, private sessions with members of the media allow them to have more influence over the tone and content of stories than they do in heavily attended press conferences. Furthermore, they find that it is a way to build media support.

As might be expected, however, those reporters excluded from private meetings with the president are likely to vent their displeasure. This occurred when Franklin Roosevelt granted his exclusive interview to the *New York Times'* Arthur Krock. FDR pledged to an angry White House press corps that he would never do it again—and he did not.

The granting of exclusive interviews is widely recognized as the president's privilege, and though there may be costs involved they are usually less than the benefits received, because the president almost always holds some trump cards in relations with the press.

Managing the news has reached such a stage of refinement that Reagan White House staff aides would meet each morning and decide what they wanted to be "the story of the day" to advance the president's interests. As one television correspondent observed, "Then they let the press in at presidential appointments or gatherings that lend themselves to that 'story' and keep the press away from those that don't. This forces television into a choice of airing the pictures and words they let us see and hear or not having any White House pictures that day. We can always put on a story without them, but pictures are our main commodity—and the [White House] staff knows it." [93]

Means of Evasion

A classic example of how the White House can mislead the press occurred in 1985 when President Reagan, who had only recently undergone intestinal surgery, appeared with a small bandage on the side of his nose. Press Secretary Larry Speakes was asked by reporters if a biopsy had been performed to check for cancer. Evading their questions, Speakes simply reported that a patch of skin had been scraped for testing. Later that day, the White House released a statement saying that a small area of skin on the right side of the president's nose had been "aggravated by the adhesive tape used while the president was in the hospital. It was submitted for routine studies for infection, and it was determined no further treatment was necessary."

However, it was soon learned that a biopsy had been performed and that it showed the president had skin cancer, which was correctable by mild surgery. Mrs. Reagan, nonetheless, ordered that the news be constricted and that the word "cancer" not be used in the press releases. A few days later, President Reagan himself publicly revealed the whole truth.

A relatively recent development in White House media operations is the "photo opportunity." Formalized in the Carter White House, a photo opportunity, as implied, is simply giving photographers a few minutes to take pictures at a special White House event, or, as more often the case, at the beginning of a meeting between the president and a distinguished visitor. The undisguised purpose is to provide the White House with visual exposure in a controlled environment.

Reporters, however, began to accompany the photographers and took advantage of the chance to ask the president questions, often unrelated to the event. Because of several embarrassing misstatements by President Reagan on such occasions, the White House moved to limit the practice by permitting only a representative "pool" of reporters to attend photo opportunities.

Recent administrations have further employed rather disingenuous methods of managing the press. It became the customary practice, for example, of the Reagan White House to discourage reporters from shouting questions to the president as he left for his Camp David retreat by having the pilot turn up the motors of the presidential helicopter. Frequently, Reagan would indicate to the reporters that he could not hear them above the roar of the engines. That saved the president from engaging in risky dialogue with the media, leaving them merely with pictures of him waving as he boarded the helicopter.

Another White House technique involves "stonewalling" by the president's press secretary or other administration officials. The term applies to the refusal to satisfy inquiries, generally by responding with "no comment," or by giving misleading answers, or by clouding the issue through obfuscation. It came into common political usage during the Watergate scandal as a tactic employed by Nixon press secretary Ronald Ziegler and others in the administration.

It is not unusual for a White House press secretary to avoid making mistakes, or lying, or having to plead ignorance by sidestepping reporters' questions with "no comment." In his book on the Reagan White House, Larry Speakes declared, "There are 10,000 ways of saying 'no comment.'" [94]

White House press managers also routinely release bad news on late Friday nights when media organizations are minimally staffed. Another advantage is that the news is likely to draw less public attention over the weekend. Still another ploy is to have someone other than the president announce bad news, thus separating him from public reaction.

With the increasing popularity of TV talk shows and public service programs, White House press officers have become casting directors or booking agents. They deliberately pursue a strategy of carefully selecting—or rejecting—administration officials who will appear on the shows. This ensures them a measure of control over the television outlets. They may further impose certain conditions: that the administration representative will be guaranteed a set amount of air time, for example, or they may exact a promise that no unfriendly opponent will appear on the same program.

Presidents, meanwhile, have additional resources at their command to circumvent the news media and get their message across without its being filtered through reporters. These include speeches to organized interest groups; national television appearances in connection with critical events; regularly scheduled radio addresses; constitutionally mandated reports, such as those on the State of the Union and the nation's economy; and the public release of administration documents and publications.

Presidential Showcase: The Televised News Conference

With the possible exception of the presidential debates, the televised news conference affords Americans the best opportunity to see their president in the act of thinking and speaking. It takes viewers onto the scene, where they can assess the performance and derive a sense of where the chief executive hopes to lead the country.

Traditionally, press conferences have been a mutually beneficial device employed by presidents to disclose their plans and policies and explain their decisions, and by reporters to gain information and insights into governmental decision making—and the person in charge of that process.

Students of government further note that the question-and-answer sessions are analogous to the British parliamentary system in which the prime minister regularly faces interrogation by members of the House of Commons, and thus they offer one of the few institutionalized opportunities to hold the president accountable.

As observed in a 1975 National News Council study, "Presidents aren't compelled to explain themselves to anybody—not to their own party, nor to the opposition (as in Great Britain), nor least of all to the press." Yet, presidential news conferences have become such an ingrained part of the political process that they almost seem to be "as much a part of government as voting . . . one of the few visible examples of democracy in action." [95]

Though they are unmentioned in the Constitution and not required by statute, any move by a president to abandon them would be taken at great political risk.

Presidential press conferences, as currently conceived, began their genesis in Woodrow Wilson's administration. At the outset of his presidency he held weekly question-and-answer sessions open to all correspondents. Before long, however, Wilson, who maintained a condescending attitude toward reporters, became disenchanted with what he viewed as breaches by the press. In one instance, an off-the-record account he had given of conditions in Mexico appeared on the first page of several newspapers. Eventually, his weekly press sessions were dropped.

Since Wilson, presidents have used news conference techniques in their own way, according to the manner most comfortable to them and in conformity with their attitudes toward the press and their communications skills. Warren Harding, Calvin Coolidge, and Herbert Hoover each insisted that reporters' questions be written and submitted in advance. The practice began when Harding, unprepared for a question concerning a diplomatic treaty, gave an erroneous interpretation of it.

Coolidge added new stringencies: reporters were not only prohibited from quoting him, but they could not even say that they saw the president or report any White House news as coming from an official. Upon taking office, Hoover announced that he was liberalizing press regulations. But none of the promised reforms were instituted. Instead, Hoover further exacerbated White House press relations when he repeatedly refused to answer a great majority of the questions and began favoring sympathetic reporters with choice stories.

It was not until the presidency of Franklin Roosevelt that reporters were allowed to ask spontaneous questions and the news conference became an institutionalized part of the White House public affairs operations. Roosevelt had a particular knack of preparing reporters for controversial decisions by educating them in advance with confidential background information, thus averting unnecessary surprises and gaining their endorsement because they understood the reasons behind his actions.

Harry Truman and Dwight Eisenhower held regular news conferences, but neither was able to master the process. Truman tended to give snappy, off-the-cuff answers and seemed unable to envision how his words would look in print or how they might be interpreted.[96]

Eisenhower usually gave the impression that news conferences were a presidential burden that had to be tolerated. His natural inclination to garble syntax and use tortuous sentence structures was a constant vexation for White House reporters. But Eisenhower relaxed the rule against direct presidential quotation, and he was the first president to permit his press conferences to be taped and edited for TV viewing.

His successor, John Kennedy, introduced live, televised news conferences. His youth, good looks, and comfortable rapport with members of the news media were ideally suited for television. At the first live telecast of a presidential news conference, in January 1961, Kennedy attracted 418 correspondents and an extraordinarily large audience of 65 million viewers.

Where Kennedy's polished persona came across perfectly on television, Lyndon Johnson's mercurial personality, so effective in face-to-face encounters, seemed wooden on the screen. He disliked formal TV press conferences, preferring impromptu meetings with reporters in his office or in rambling walks around the White House Rose Garden. Yet, he continued to hold regular news conferences because he recognized that a president had an obligation to the public to be seen and heard.

Richard Nixon, whose relationship with the press throughout his political career was marked by overt and mutual hostility, held an average of less than one press conference every two months during his presidency. He and his White House aides were more intent on staging events that would appear on prime-time network television than on exposing him to the reporters' sharp-edged questions.

Although Nixon did not come across well on television, he did have a firm grasp of policy and governmental issues—in contrast to Reagan, who projected a likable image but was not effective at communicating issues. It was universally agreed that Reagan was considerably more adept at delivering prepared messages and speeches than at impromptu responding to reporters' questions at formal press conferences.

Gerald Ford, like Lyndon Johnson, preferred informal news conferences that were announced briefly in advance of the meetings—the advantage being that reporters had less time to prepare difficult questions.

Upon taking office, Jimmy Carter pledged to hold press conferences twice a month. But by the time he left the White House Carter, like other modern presidents, was holding them only about once every two months. For all of his use of symbolic gestures, Carter always kept the press at arm's length, leaving the impression that to him it was one more entrenched Washington interest group with which he had to deal.

The President's Advantages

Basically, the president controls the press conferences, notwithstanding the sometimes persecutorial tone of the reporters' questions. "It's his news conference, not the media's," observed George Reedy, President Johnson's former press secretary.[97]

The president decides when a press conference will be held, he sets the ground rules, he selects the reporters who will ask questions, and he alone decides what information will be divulged. In an extreme case, during the 1973-1974 Watergate investigation, Nixon went five months without a press conference and, at one stretch, fourteen months without a televised meeting with reporters.

Toward the close of his presidency, Eisenhower was asked by a reporter if he felt that the press had been fair to him in their questions. Hinting at the decided advantage that presidents hold in their relationship with the press, Eisenhower replied, "Well, when you come down to it, I don't see what [sic] a reporter could do much to a president, do you?"[98]

Sometimes, presidents may evade a question by making a quip or pleading inability to reply on grounds of national security. They may simply decline to answer some questions without giving a reason, or they may abruptly change the tone and direction of the questioning by calling on a reporter with a reputation for asking soft questions. Prior to a press conference, the president studies the conference room's seating arrangements to know where certain reporters will be located.

Reedy additionally noted that "the aura of the presidency" tends to inhibit reporters from becoming too aggressive, even though the unembellished directness of some questions may indicate otherwise. "Most [reporters] are not going to be disrespectful to the president," Reedy said. "After all, he symbolizes the United States."[99]

There are still other invisible advantages that the presidents enjoy. By scheduling long intervals between news conferences they can ensure a supply of superficial questions, because the reporters will have so much to cover. And when there is a major development, most questions center on it, which means little else is covered.

The vastly increased size of the press corps itself has had an impact on presidential news conferences. When White House reporters were able to gather around FDR's desk in an informal exchange on issues of the day, they were able to deeply explore his thinking and discover the reasons he made certain decisions. Members of today's massive press corps are fortunate if they are able to ask even one question, let alone delve deeply into the president's reasoning.

The ritualistic formula followed at press conferences also gives the president an edge. TV press conferences almost always last but one half-hour. Some presidents, such as Lyndon Johnson, invariably consume a good portion of that time with announcements at the start of the press conference, leaving reporters with less time to ask questions.

Moreover, some reporters are accorded special recognition. Tradition requires that the senior wire service reporter asks the first question. Almost always, the president then calls on easily recognizable TV correspondents who are in the front-row seats. Only an average of eighteen questions can be asked in a half-hour, which means most of the print press reporters are denied an opportunity to ask a question.

Formerly, reporters were allowed to ask only one question; but the Reagan White House, with the concurrence of the news media, instituted a new system that permitted reporters to ask a follow-up question. That, of course, took up additional time, further reducing reporters' chances of being allowed to query the president.

On cue, the wire service reporter who began the questioning ends the press conference with the familiar expression, "Thank you, Mr. President."

The biggest danger to presidents is that they will issue a misstatement or inadvertently report an untruth or make a mistake. They must be meticulous and cautious, yet informative and affable. A single word, an inflection of voice, or a raised eyebrow can send tremors throughout the world.

Truman, for example, committed a verbal gaffe when asked about the possible use of atomic weapons in the Korean War. His reply that such action was always under consideration served to alarm many foreign governments, including U.S. allies.

Similarly, President Reagan erred during a press conference when he said that no third country had been involved in clandestine U.S. arms sales to Iran. Within minutes afterward the White House issued a news release acknowledging that Israel had been involved in the transaction.

The Reporters' Role

For members of the news media, presidential press conferences offer a chance to assert themselves as the fourth branch of government under the limelight of national television. In the past, members of the media were recognized only as the supporting cast at these sessions. But Washington reporters today seek and have been accorded almost equal billing with the president within the theatrics of the news conferences. Their performance and the tenor of their questions hold nearly as much interest as the president's utterances from the spectators' view. At times, the two sides engage in a war of words, or a battle of semantics and a search for nuance.

Until recently most reporters were not identified when they stood to ask a question of the president, because the TV crews covering the conference could not know the faces of all the reporters in the room. But the networks have largely solved this problem, and the reporter's name is

Table 2 Presidential News Conferences with White House Correspondents, 1929-1988

President	Average number of press conferences per month	Total press conferences
Hoover (1929-1933)	5.6	268
Roosevelt (1933-1945)	6.9	998
Truman (1945-1953)	3.4	334
Eisenhower (1953-1961)	2.0	193
Kennedy (1961-1963)	1.9	64
Johnson (1963-1969)	2.2	135
Nixon (1969-1974)	0.5	37
Ford (1974-1977)	1.3	39
Carter (1977-1981)	1.2	59
Reagan (1981-1988)	0.4	46

Source: Harold W. Stanley and Richard G. Niemi, *Vital Statistics on American Politics* (Washington, D.C.: CQ Press, 1988), 50.

usually flashed on the screen, giving him or her a measure of star treatment. Ironically, in an earlier era, print reporters resented being involuntary participants in the television conferences. But before long they began vying to be seen on TV while asking the president a question. It afforded the mostly anonymous print reporters national TV exposure and was valued by many as a career boost.

Overall, the press's role at these events is rife with ambiguity. On the one hand, reporters are faulted for asking soft questions that presidents can exploit to their advantage; on the other hand, the journalists are accused of being rude and unnecessarily hostile.

Defenders of the press maintain that asking the president to explain, justify, and defend his policies is a critical function in a democracy. In recent years, however, the news conferences' format and function have radically changed, and there is a sense that they have declined in significance. With the increased use of television and other forms of mass communications, as well as jet travel, presidents are less dependent on the press to convey their views.

The new breed of TV correspondents is mainly interested in headline news and fifteen-second sound bites, completely revising the nature of what constitutes news. Furthermore, the news conferences have become elaborately staged events in which the visual image has become equally as important as the substance of the president's statements. For modern presidents, they have become an opportune vehicle for self-promotion, diverting criticism, and soothing political supporters.

Presidential press conferences, in essence, have become more confrontational than informational, more choreography and theater than legitimate news, more of an egocentric exhibition than an opportunity to probe presidents' intentions and assess their leadership.

Against that background, Larry Speakes, press secretary for President Reagan, declared,

The press conference in its present form may have outlived its usefulness, its usefulness to the presidency, its usefulness to the press and to the public.... What's wrong? The press conference is a theater. They're scripted. Reporters ask written questions to which a president gives a rehearsed answer. The spontaneity is lost. The press is not looking for information, they're out to make news. An "I gotcha" syndrome prevails. There is an attempt to entrap a president. How can we get him to say what he doesn't want to say? [100]

Speakes, nonetheless, conceded that the press conferences play "an important role in the relationship between the president and the press." In a real sense, they combine the most powerful office in the nation with the most powerful medium, providing the best chance for most Americans to see and hear the person at the helm of government.

Governmental Efforts to Control Information

With the growing recognition that information is power, the struggle between the news media and the government over the free flow of information and opinion has become a critical issue of the communications age.

Tension between the two institutions is endemic, largely because of their conflicting roles. The press is conditioned to challenge authority and act as a buffer against extraconstitutional and questionable governmental activities; the government, on the other hand, seeks to put its best face forward by controlling the terms of public debate. In furthering its objectives, the government may take measures to tighten control over the release of information about what it is doing or planning, often under the guise of national security.

On occasion, the government may attempt to delude the press through secrecy or deception or try to circumvent it entirely. Inevitably, the two institutions clash over the extent of the public's right to know what is being done in its name.

While presidential administrations have always sought to justify and embellish their actions through ingenious fabrications, the nation as a whole first became conscious of such tactics in the tumultuous decade of the 1960s—a period of social unrest at home and military adventures abroad.

Americans, it has been said, lost their innocence in 1960 when a United States U-2 spy plane was shot down over the Soviet Union. Its penetration of Soviet air space was a clear violation of national sovereignty, which the Eisenhower White House at first dismissed as a weather reconnaissance mission. In swift succession other incidents occurred in the realm of foreign affairs, a policy area where the president can act with minimal constraints. The disastrous 1961 Bay of Pigs invasion was feebly portrayed by the Kennedy administration as a unilateral expedition by rebel Cuban exiles. President Johnson asserted that U.S. Marines were sent into the Dominican Republic in April 1965 to save American lives, but it was widely suspected that the real reason was fear of a Communist takeover. As one author-journalist wrote, "Within days more than 24,000 U.S. troops had invaded the small Caribbean country; the President spent hours personally attempting to convince newsmen that this was justified because 'fifteen hundred innocent people were murdered and shot, and their heads cut off,' which turned out later to be pure myth." [101] Later U.S. military incursions in Vietnam, Laos, and Cambodia were shrouded in secrecy and subterfuge.

Distortions and misleading accounts by President Johnson concerning the escalation of the Vietnam War created what became known as LBJ's "credibility gap." A White House reporter wrote, "The credibility gap has left scars on the institution of the Presidency. It has impaired the image of the American government. It has been a factor in serious foreign policy failures. The problem of credibility, in its broadest sense, will remain after Lyndon Johnson leaves the White House." [102]

Not long afterward, an attempt by President Nixon to block release of the Pentagon Papers, which detailed the genesis of the Vietnam War, was widely viewed as a ploy to intimidate and control the press.

The faith of many Americans in their government was further shaken by the abuse of power and coverup revealed in the Watergate scandal leading to President Nixon's resignation, and later by the high-level deception and deceit that masked the Iran arms sales/contra funding affair in President Reagan's second term.

As early as 1973, an observer of the Washington scene contended,

> The American system is based not only upon formal checks and balances among the three branches of government, it depends also, and perhaps more importantly, on a delicate balance of confidence between the people and government. That balance of trust has been altered.
> By 1972 the politics of lying had changed the politics of America. In place of trust, there was widespread mistrust; in place of confidence, there was disbelief and doubt in the system and its leaders. [103]

During this same period, television was emerging as a pervasive purveyor of news and commentary; it graphically underscored high-level duplicities and exacerbated the adversary relationship between press and government. Thus, several related of issues were brought into play, including free speech guaranteed under the First Amendment, the media's role and responsibility, the need to ensure the nation's security, occasional conflicts between civil liberties and ideology, and the people's right to know as a basic element in the shaping of official policy in a democractic society.

Reagan Administration Actions

Ironically, although Ronald Reagan was universally hailed as the "Great Communicator," he presided over an administration that was criticized as being intent on stemming the free flow of information and muzzling the national news media.

From the beginning, the Reagan administration assumed an unprecedented narrow view of the First Amendment rights involving free speech and the unfettered flow of information. Accordingly, it consistently invoked measures to regulate the dissemination of government information, including:

~ The prohibition of a large number of foreign writers, artists, and political figures from entering the United States under the 1952 McCarran-Walter Act. Among them were Nobel Laureate Gabriel Garcia Marquez, the widow of former Chilean president Salvador Allende, and Canadian nature writer Farley Mowat.

~ A requirement that all government employees and contractors who had or had sought high-level security clearance, including political appointees but not elected officials, submit to lie detector tests. The purported purpose of the polygraphs was to guard against infiltration by spies and to trace leaks of information to the press.

~ An executive order signed by the president expanding the discretion of federal agencies to classify information for an indefinite period. The order additionally provided authority to reclassify information already in the public domain.

~ A decree under the Foreign Agents Registration Act that certain foreign documentary films—mainly those considered ideologically inconsistent with U.S. policy—be required to carry notices that they were "political propaganda" when shown in the United States. Among the targeted films were several involving nuclear war and acid rain, including three from Canada: the Academy Award-winning documentary, *If You Love This Planet*, as well as *Peace—A Conscious Choice* and *In Our Backyards—Uranimum Mining in the United States.*

~ A mandate that all government officials with access to high-level classified information sign statements requiring them during their lifetime to submit for official, prepublication review all articles and books they wrote for public consumption. A book by former CIA director Stansfield Turner, *Secrecy and Democracy, the CIA in Transition*, was delayed eighteen months before being cleared by censors who insisted on almost one hundred deletions on security grounds.

~ A directive that required two million civil servants to sign secrecy pledges not to reveal "classifiable information." Opponents, including federal employee unions and several members of Congress, challenged the order, maintaining it would have a chilling effect on the flow of information to Congress and the public. In related litigation, a federal district judge ruled that the use of the word "classifiable" without a clear definition was unconstitutional.

Other stratagems designed to constrict government information: CIA director William J. Casey, in an apparent attempt to inhibit the media, threatened to prosecute news organizations should they disclose classified data involving national security; the Justice Department subpoenaed video and audio tapes made by members of the news media of the June 1985 terrorist hijacking of TWA Flight 847 and the seventeen-day hostage crisis in Beirut; the National Aeronautics and Space Administration imposed a news blackout of the March 1986 explosion of the *Challenger* space shuttle; a pornography commission headed by Attorney General Edwin Meese III warned bookstores, drugstore chains, and other retailers they would be placed on a "blacklist" if they continued to sell "adult magazines"—action that a federal court subsequently held to be a violation of the First Amendment.

The 1983 Grenada invasion provoked one of the most highly publicized and contentious incidents involving the press and government. Reagan indicated that the purpose was to forestall "another Cuba" in the Caribbean by local, Cuban-trained Marxists who had earlier staged a military coup and executed the prime minister. The president further expressed concern about the several hundred American medical students studying there and contended that the United States was in fact responding to a formal request by the Organization of Eastern Caribbean States to help restore order and democracy on the island. Whether the latter reasons were valid or were designed to legitimize the neutralization of Grenada has become a matter of debate.

Breaking a long tradition dating back to the Civil War, reporters were barred from accompanying the assault troops and a news blackout was imposed. Coverage of the initial stages of the operation was selectively provided by the Defense Department's own news services, whose reports were marred by glaring omissions and serious inaccuracies. American military planes threatened to shoot any U.S. reporters who tried to reach the island on their own, even though some foreign newsmen were allowed to cover the invasion.

At the time, Reagan administration officials, discounting military precedent, said they were primarily concerned for the safety of the journalists. Later, Defense Secretary Caspar W. Weinberger defended their action as a means to maintain secrecy and help ensure the operation's success. Secretary of State George P. Shultz claimed the action was taken because "reporters are always against us, and so they're always seeking to report something that's going to screw things up." [104]

In the view of one journalist, "The administration seemed to want a news monopoly until it could shape public attitudes." [105]

At first, public opinion supported the news blackout. But by December, with disclosures of military foul-ups—including the bombing of a hospital—and the difficult time the U.S. forces had in overcoming a small band of Cuban defenders, public opinion polls showed that most Americans felt that the administration had erred in not letting reporters accompany the troops into Grenada. As a result of the furor, a joint military-press commission was set up, which proposed that a press pool go along on future military operations.

A "Right" to Lie?

Whether the government has the right to lie and resort to deception to camouflage its actions and decisions has long been an issue of ongoing debate. The debate went public in 1963 when Pentagon spokesman Arthur Sylvester declared in response to a reporter's question, "Yes, under certain circumstances I think government does have the right to lie."

In his White House memoirs Jody Powell, President Carter's press secretary, admitted that he had deceived the press on matters less serious than the Iran hostage rescue mission discussed earlier. He maintained that ". . . government has a legitimate right to secrecy in certain matters because the welfare of the nation requires it. In other cases, individuals, even public figures, have a certain right to privacy because common decency demands it." [106]

Powell admitted that on one occasion he "lied" in reply to a reporter's question about the personal life of a White House colleague and his family to avert "great pain and embarrassment for a number of perfectly innocent people. Beyond that, I could see no reason why the matter should be of public interest."

Occasionally, administration press relations officers are purposely kept in the dark about high-level plans and decisions. As Larry Speakes subsequently explained about his deception of reporters concerning the Grenada invasion plans: "I had been lied to, not the one who had been the liar." [107]

Carter press secretary Powell agreed with the Reagan administration's decision to deceive journalists rather than risk disclosing the Grenada invasion plans. In his book he quoted Britain's World War II prime minister, Winston Churchill, as saying in 1943 that " 'In wartime, truth is so precious that she should be attended by a bodyguard of lies.' " [108]

In some instances, presumably rare, the government has resorted to "dirty tricks" not to save lives but to promote its policies. It was disclosed in October 1986 that President Reagan approved a strategy of "disinformation" aimed at Libyan leader Muammar Qaddafi. A memo drafted by Poindexter, then Reagan's national security adviser, and obtained by the *Washington Post*, proposed that false information be leaked to the press with the objective of bringing down Qaddafi. It advocated a propaganda campaign that "combines real and illusionary events—through a disinformation program—with the basic goal of making Qaddafi think that there is a high degree of internal opposition to him within Libya, that his key trusted aides are disloyal, that the U.S. is about to move against him militarily." [109]

Earlier, as the recipient of an apparent leak, the *Wall Street Journal* reported on August 25 that Qaddafi "has begun new terrorist attacks" and that "the U.S. and Libya are on a collision course again." [110]

The disclosure stunned many Americans because "disinformation" was invariably associated with Soviet techniques for planting false information. Further, it exposed a side of the U.S. government that was seldom seen—one that it was not generally thought capable of heeding.

Poindexter asserted that the disinformation was not intended to mislead the American news media, but to keep Qaddafi off balance. Nevertheless, much of the U.S. press felt that the administration had sought to use and manipulate it by creating a phony crisis in the furtherance of its foreign policy vis-à-vis Qaddafi.

Freedom of Information Act

Acting quietly but effectively, the Reagan administration was able to tighten accessibility to government information by constrictions applied to the Freedom of Information Act. Passed by Congress in 1968, and amended in 1986, the FOIA was designed to make all but the most secret government documents available to the public, press, and academicians. Critics, including constitutional lawyers, journalists, scholars, and public interest advocates, maintained, however, that the administration subverted the act's intent.

It severely limited the scope of the act through several devices, including restrictions on the type and amount of government material made available, delaying responses to requests beyond the designated time limit, charging exorbitant fees for copies of documents, deleting—or blacking out—all but the most innocuous information, denying fee waivers for academic researchers and sometimes forcing them to pay tens of thousands of dollars for documents, thus compromising scholarly investigations.

Also, staff reductions in FOIA offices at the various federal departments and offices further made the procedure more cumbersome, discouraging use of the act. Even acknowledgment of requests filed under the act could take a year or more. And some documents dating back three decades or more have yet to be declassified.

In still another attempt at controlling information, recent administrations have taken increasingly harsh steps to plug news leaks, by requiring federal employees to take lie detector tests, threatening to fire "leakers," and reas-

signing them to less meaningful jobs. Ironically, incumbent administrations may themselves engage in authorized leaking—to promote their own interests—but inevitably they oppose leaks that serve to question their policies and decisions.

As a classic example, the Justice Department in 1985 prosecuted Samuel L. Morison, a Navy Department intelligence analyst, for selling satellite photos of a Soviet shipyard to the British magazine *Jane's Defense Weekly*. Morison was convicted of violating the Espionage Act of 1917—a rarely invoked law that had previously been used to prosecute people for aiding a foreign enemy, but not for leaking to the Western press. One study showed that at least 42 percent of senior federal officials had participated in leaks to reporters. [111]

Stages in White House-Press Relationship

Every modern president enters office promising to preside over an "open" administration, to offer all information necessary for the public to assess the administration's policies and performance, to make the chief executive accessible to the news media, and to hold frequent news conferences.

Following his 1968 election victory, Richard Nixon proclaimed that his administration would be "open to new ideas . . . open to the critics as well as those who support us." Jimmy Carter pledged "more accessibility to the press and public." He even considered opening cabinet meetings to the press.

George Bush promised to meet with members of the media more often than Ronald Reagan, who held fewer news conferences than any modern president. In the first week of his presidency, Bush invited two reporters (from the *New York Times* and the *Houston Post*) into the Oval Office for a brief interview and held a forty-three-minute news conference with the White House press corps.

Inevitably, however, promises remain unfulfilled, proposed policies are revised or rejected, presidential decisions are criticized, and the relationship between the White House and the news media evolves from early acceptance and cooperation to mutual tolerance, and, finally, to suspicion and thinly cloaked hostility.

As an example, Carter made a commitment to hold two news conferences a month. With time, however, he cut back on them, and by the end of his term he held them about once every six weeks. After leaving the White House, Carter recalled that he had been warned by knowledgeable Washington insiders that he "could not win a war with the press." [112]

At the heart of this predictable pattern is the media's natural tendency to want to know virtually everything that is going on inside the White House, and the White House's predisposition to manage the news and release only selective information—that which is favorable to the president and the administration.

In their study of the White House and the news media, political scientists Michael B. Grossman and Martha J. Kumar refer to the traditional stages in the relationship between the two institutions as "alliance," "competition," and "detachment." [113]

The initial phase coincides with the incoming president's so-called "honeymoon." During this brief period of good feelings, there are high expectations and a willingness to cooperate. Appropriately, the new president's first 100 days coincide with spring, a time of hope and rejuvenation in a confluence of politics and nature.

It is additionally a period when news flows from the White House in abundance concerning new appointments, fresh policies, and dramatic decisions. In that short spell, presidential character is defined, working habits are set, and the tone and direction of the administration are fixed. The changing of the guard is completed, and the president settles into his job and new home. Thus, the news media's thirst for news is gratified.

Sometimes, however, these euphoric early months are disrupted by unexpected developments, creating tension between the press and the president. Before the end of his first 100 days in office, tremors from the Bay of Pigs disaster shattered John Kennedy's "honeymoon." Gerald Ford's pardon of Richard Nixon, only thirty days days after succeeding him, cast a shadow over the remainder of his presidency. Similarly, the publicity generated during Carter's first year in office over alleged banking improprieties by Bert Lance, the president's good friend and budget director, before he had come to Washington inflicted inestimable damage on the new administration. As Jody Powell, Carter's press secretary, remarked, "There never was a honeymoon with the press, just a one-night stand."

At the other extreme, President Reagan, because of his personal popularity, was able to deflect media criticism throughout most of his two terms, except for doubts raised concerning his role in the Iran arms sales/contra funding episode. Ironically, during his first year in office he enjoyed a "second honeymoon" beginning March 30, 1981, when he survived an assassin's bullets. His good humor and courage, amplified by the real-life drama, made him a hero in the eyes of many Americans and served to disarm much of the press.

Normally, during the initial phase of a new presidency, White House aides, seeking maximum exposure, are readily accessible and are on friendly terms with reporters, eager for stories about the incoming administration. This is a time when the symbiotic relationship between the two sides is particularly evident. The president is likely to hold regularly scheduled news conferences, administration officials make themselves available for interviews, and news stories are more likely to be favorable to the administration.

Also, presidents tend to be more amenable to media requests and to give more private interviews in the beginning of their terms than in the latter stages. President Johnson, for example, met with reporters thirty-five times during his first thirteen months in office, while holding only sixteen press conferences during his second full year in the White House.

Not unnaturally, the second or "competitive" phase in president-press relations begins with political conflicts over issues and policies. Administration opponents openly voice their disenchantment and leak adverse information to the news media. Interest groups seek out the press to make known their displeasure with administration priorities.

The "free ride" or soft treatment given the president by the news media may change perceptibly. In retaliation, the White House closes regular avenues to press access and becomes more manipulative in its handling of news and information. Reporters deemed to be overly critical may find themselves cut off from administration sources.

During this period the adversary relationship blooms in full flower. Tempers often flare at the White House press secretary's daily news briefing. On one such occasion, Ron Nessen, President Ford's press secretary, deplored what he called the "poisoned atmosphere" in the White House press room. By now, the lines have been drawn between the White House and the news media, and each side warily eyes the other even as they are obliged to work side by side.

The detachment phase occurs at varying times among administrations but usually in the autumnal years of a presidential term. White House media advisers, convinced that press criticism subverts presidential decisions, try to keep reporters at arm's length. Press conferences are few and far apart. Requests for interviews are carefully reviewed, and frequently the White House insists on controlling which administration officials appear on TV talk shows.

Unlike the early months of the administration, the relationship is much more formal and structured. During the latter period of the Reagan presidency, reporters mostly had contact with him at "photo opportunities," when they would seize the moment to shout questions at him.

More and more, the president uses controlled channels to get his message across, including TV-radio addresses, news releases, public speeches to carefully selected groups, highly publicized trips, and meetings with other world leaders.

Notwithstanding the influence and pervasiveness of the American news media, it is generally conceded that the president—especially if he is a skilled communicator—enjoys the upper hand in dealing with the press. As Clinton Rossiter observed, "The President is the American people's one authentic trumpet, and he has no higher duty than to give a clear and certain sound." [114]

Notes

1. Bradley H. Patterson, Jr., *The Ring of Power* (New York: Basic Books, 1988).
2. Richard Rose, *The Postmodern President* (Chatham, N.J.: Chatham House, 1988).
3. Doris A. Graber, *Mass Media and American Politics*, 3d ed. (Washington, D.C.: CQ Press, 1989), 237-238.
4. *Responsibility and Freedom in the Press*, Report of Citizen's Choice, National Commission on Free and Responsible Media, 1985, 1.
5. Donald H. Johnston, *Journalism and the Media* (New York: Barnes & Noble Books, 1979), 45.
6. Joseph R. Dominick, *The Dynamics of Mass Communication*, 2d ed. (New York: Random House, 1987).
7. David L. Lange, Robert K. Baker, Sandra J. Ball, *Violence and the Media*, vol. xi, *A Report to the National Commission on the Causes and Prevention of Violence* (Washington, D.C.: Government Printing Office, 1969), 16.
8. Dominick, *Dynamics of Mass Communication*.
9. Leonard W. Levy, *Emergence of a Free Press* (New York: Oxford University Press, 1985), as quoted in the *Washington Times*, August 26, 1985.
10. Ibid.
11. James Q. Wilson, *American Government: Institutions and Policies* (Lexington, Mass.: D. C. Heath, 1986), 502.
12. Ibid.
13. Phillip Knightley, *The First Casualty: From the Crimea to Vietnam: The War Correspondent as Hero, Propagandist,*

and Myth Maker (New York: Harcourt Brace Jovanovich, 1975).

14. Ibid.
15. Edwin Emery and Michael Emery, *The Press and America: An Interpretive History of the Mass Media,* 4th ed. (New York: Prentice-Hall, 1978), 264-265.
16. Frank Luther Mott, *American Journalism* (New York: Macmillan, 1950), 519.
17. John K. Winkler, *W. R. Hearst: An American Phenomenon* (New York: Simon and Schuster, 1928).
18. W. A. Swanberg, *Citizen Hearst* (New York: Charles Scribner's Sons, 1961).
19. J. Herbert Altschull, *Agents of Power: The Role of the News Media in Human Affairs* (New York: Longman, 1984), 55.
20. Lange et al., *Violence and the Media,* 25.
21. Emery, *The Press and America,* 514-516.
22. Emmet John Hughes, *The Living Presidency* (New York: Coward, McCann, & Geohegan, 1972), 157.
23. Bruce D. Itule and Douglas A. Anderson, *News Writing and Reporting for Today's Media* (New York: Random House, 1987), 6.
24. Dominick, *Dynamics of Mass Communication,* 87.
25. Edward Jay Whetmore, *Mediamerica,* updated 3d ed. (Belmont, Calif.: Wadsworth Publishing, 1987).
26. Associated Press, "Permanent 'Fairness Doctrine' Vetoed," *Washington Post,* June 21, 1987.
27. Edward Bliss, Jr., and John M. Patterson, eds., *Writing News for Broadcast,* rev. 2d ed. (New York: Columbia University Press, 1978).
28. William L. Shirer, *Twentieth Century Journey: The Nightmare Years 1930-1940* (Boston: Little, Brown, 1984), 303.
29. Graber, *Mass Media and American Politics,* 44.
30. Michael Schrage, "Advertising on Software Could Be Coming to a PC Near You," *Washington Post,* March 9, 1987.
31. Sydney W. Head and Christopher H. Sterling, *Broadcasting in America,* 4th ed. (Boston: Houghton Mifflin, 1982), 532-537.
32. Graber, *Mass Media and American Politics,* 39.
33. Douglass Cater, *The Fourth Branch of Government* (New York: Vintage Books, 1965), 22.
34. James E. Pollard, *The Presidents and the Press* (New York: Octagon Books, 1973), 3.
35. Ibid., 16.
36. Ibid., 7.
37. Ibid., 15.
38. David H. Weaver and G. Cleveland Wilhoit, *The American Journalist* (Bloomington: Indiana University Press, 1986), 2.
39. Cater, *Fourth Branch of Government,* 78.
40. Federal Writers' Project of the Works Progress Administration, *Washington—City and Capital* (Washington, D.C.: Government Printing Ofice, 1937), 177.
41. Cater, *Fourth Branch of Government,* 76.
42. Knightley, *First Casualty,* 20.
43. J. Cutler Andrews, *The North Reports the Civil War* (Pittsburgh: University of Pittsburgh Press, 1955), as quoted in Knightley, *First Casualty,* 21.
44. Federal Writers' Project, *Washington—City and Capital,* 176.
45. Pollard, *Presidents and the Press,* 14.
46. Philip C. Dolce and George H. Skau, eds., *Power and the Presidency* (New York: Charles Scribner's Sons, 1976), 238.
47. Pollard, *Presidents and the Press,* 113.
48. Ibid., 187.
49. Arthur M. Schlesinger, Jr., *The Cycles of American History* (Boston: Houghton Mifflin, 1986), 333.
50. Pollard, *Presidents and the Press,* 414.
51. George Juergens, *News from the White House* (Chicago: University of Chicago Press, 1981), 17.
52. Samuel Kernell, *Going Public: New Strategies of Presidential Leadership* (Washington, D.C.: CQ Press, 1986), 63-64.
53. Fred I. Greenstein, *The Hidden-Hand Presidency* (New York: Basic Books, 1982).
54. Edward Walsh, "Carter Sees Chance to Be Great President," *Washington Post,* January 20, 1977, A24.
55. George C. Edwards III, *The Public Presidency: The Pursuit of Popular Support* (New York: St. Martin's Press, 1983), 106.
56. Pollard, *Presidents and the Press,* 390.
57. Ibid., *Presidents and the Press,* 355.
58. John W. Tebbel in Dolce and Skau, *Power and the Presidency,* 242.
59. Pollard, *Presidents and the Press,* 690.
60. Arthur Krock, *Memoirs—Sixty Years on the Firing Line* (New York: Funk and Wagnalls, 1968), 182.
61. Ted Morgan, *FDR: A Biography* (New York: Simon and Schuster, 1985), 561.
62. Arthur M. Schlesinger, Jr., *The Coming of the New Deal* (Boston: Houghton Mifflin, 1958), 565.
63. Ibid., 566.
64. James E. Pollard, *The Presidents and the Press: Truman to Johnson* (Washington, D.C.: Public Affairs Press, 1964), 38.
65. David Halbertstam, *The Powers that Be* (New York: Knopf, 1979), 6.
66. "Nixon's Notes Tell of an Early Distrust of the Press," *New York Times,* May 31, 1987.
67. John Ehrlichman, *Witness to Power: The Nixon Years* (New York: Simon and Schuster, 1982), 263-264.
68. Jimmy Carter, speech delivered at a presidential colloquium, Southern Methodist University, March 26, 1984.
69. *Public Papers of the Presidents, Gerald R. Ford, 1975, Book 1* (Washington, D.C.: Government Printing Office, 1977), 237-238.
70. According to superintendents of the House and Senate press, periodical, and radio-television galleries.
71. Michael B. Grossman and Martha J. Kumar, *Portraying the President: The White House and the News Media* (Baltimore: Johns Hopkins University Press, 1981), 36.
72. Donald T. Regan, *For the Record: From Wall Street to Washington* (New York: Harcourt Brace Jovanovich, 1988), 247-248.
73. Laurence I. Barrett, *Gambling With History: Reagan in the White House* (New York: Doubleday, 1983), 437.
74. George Christian, *The President Steps Down* (New York: Macmillan, 1970), 190.
75. Dom Bonafede, "Powell and the Press—A New Mood in the White House," *National Journal,* June 22, 1977, 980.
76. Larry Speakes with Robert Pack, *Speaking Out: The Reagan Presidency from Inside the White House* (New York: Charles Scribner's Sons, 1988), 168.
77. Dom Bonafede, "White House Report: Nessen Still Seeks 'Separate Peace' With Press," *National Journal,* October 11, 1975, 1411.
78. William C. Spragens, *From Spokesman to Press Secretary: White House Media Operations* (Lanham, Md.: University Press of America, 1980), 5, 34.
79. Michael Medved, *The Shadow Presidents* (New York: Times Books, 1979), 21.
80. Pollard, *Presidents and the Press,* 640.
81. Spragens, *From Spokesman to Press Secretary,* 88.
82. Pollard, *Presidents and the Press,* 784.
83. Patrick Anderson, *The President's Men* (New York: Doubleday, 1968).
84. Ronald L. Ziegler, remarks at the Presidential Press Secretaries' Forum, Gonzaga University, April 1, 1978.
85. Jody Powell, *The Other Side of the Story* (New York: William Morrow, 1984), 223.
86. Ibid., 233.
87. Jimmy Carter, *Keeping Faith: Memoirs of a President* (New York: Bantam Books, 1982), 4, 569.
88. Speakes, *Speaking Out,* 151, 168.
89. Ibid., 152.
90. Grossman and Kumar, *Portraying the President,* 168.
91. Regan, *For the Record,* 354.
92. Ibid., 336.
93. Sam Donaldson, *Hold On, Mr. President!* (New York: Ballantine Books, 1987), 158.

94. Speakes, *Speaking Out,* 156.
95. Lewis W. Wolfson, *A Report on the State of the Presidential Press Conference* (Washington, D.C.: National News Council, 1975), 5.
96. Richard A. Watson and Norman C. Thomas, *The Politics of the Presidency,* 2d ed. (Washington, D.C.: CQ Press, 1988), 173.
97. Dom Bonafede, "Thank You, Mr. President," *National Journal,* May 5, 1987, 1070.
98. Text of Eisenhower's January 18, 1961, news conference, his last as president, *Congressional Quarterly Weekly Report,* January 20, 1961, 101.
99. Bonafede, "Thank You, Mr. President," 1070.
100. Speech at National Press Club, Washington, D.C., January 30, 1987.
101. Godfrey Hodgson, *All Things to All Men* (New York: Simon and Schuster, 1980), 188-189.
102. James Deakin, *Lyndon Johnson's Credibility Gap* (Washington, D.C.: Public Affairs Press, 1968), 14.
103. David Wise, *The Politics of Lying* (New York: Random House, 1973), 18.
104. Hedrick Smith, *The Power Game: How Washington Works* (New York: Random House, 1988), 435.
105. Ibid.
106. Powell, *Other Side of the Story,* 223.
107. Speakes, *Speaking Out,* 153.
108. Powell, *Other Side of the Story,* 233.
109. Smith, *Power Game,* 447
110. Ibid.
111. Martin Linsky, *Impact: How the Press Affects Federal Policymaking* (New York: W. W. Norton, 1986), 172, 238.
112. Carter, *Keeping Faith,* 117.
113. Grossman and Kumar, *Portraying the President,* 273-274.
114. Clinton Rossiter, *The American Presidency,* rev. ed. (New York: New American Library, 1962).

Selected Bibliography

Cater, Douglass. *The Fourth Branch of Government.* New York: Vintage Books, 1965.
Dominick, Joseph R. *The Dynamics of Mass Communication.* 2d ed. New York: Random House, 1987.
Edwards, George C. III. *The Public Presidency: The Pursuit of Popular Support.* New York: St. Martin's Press, 1983.
Graber, Doris A. *Mass Media and American Politics.* 3d ed. Washington, D.C.: CQ Press, 1989.
Grossman, Michael B., and Martha J. Kumar. *Portraying the President: The White House and the News Media.* Baltimore: Johns Hopkins University Press, 1981.
Halberstam, David. *The Powers That Be.* New York: Knopf, 1979.
Hertsgaard, Mark. *On Bended Knee: Ronald Reagan and the Taming of the Press.* New York: Farrar, Straus, & Giroux, 1988.
Hughes, Emmet John. *The Living Presidency.* New York: Coward, McCann, & Geohegan, 1972.
Kalb, Marvin, and Frederick Mayer. *Reviving the Presidential News Conference: Report of the Harvard Commission on the Presidential News Conference.* Cambridge: Joan Shorenstein Barone Center on the Press, Politics, and Public Policy, John F. Kennedy School of Government, Harvard University, 1988.
Kernell, Samuel. *Going Public: New Strategies of Presidential Leadership.* Washington, D.C.: CQ Press, 1986.
Knightley. Phillip. *The First Casualty: From the Crimea to Vietnam: The War Correspondent as Hero, Propagandist, and Myth Maker.* New York: Harcourt Brace Jovanovich, 1975.
Patterson, Bradley H., Jr. *The Ring of Power.* New York: Basic Books, 1988.
Pollard, James E. *The Presidents and the Press.* New York: Octagon Books, 1973.
_____ . *The Presidents and the Press: Truman to Johnson.* Washington, D.C.: Public Affairs Press, 1964.
Rose, Richard. *The Postmodern President.* Chatham, N.J.: Chatham House, 1988.
Smith, Hedrick. *The Power Game: How Washington Works.* New York: Random House, 1988.
Speakes, Larry, with Robert Pack. *Speaking Out: The Reagan Presidency from Inside the White House.* New York: Charles Scribner's Sons, 1988.
Spear, Joseph C. *Presidents and the Press: The Nixon Legacy.* Cambridge: MIT Press, 1984.
Spragens, William C. *From Spokesman to Press Secretary: White House Media Operations.* Lanham, Md.: University Press of America, 1980.
Whetmore, Edward Jay. *Mediamerica.* Updated 3d ed. Belmont, Calif.: Wadsworth Publishing, 1987.
Wolfson, Lewis W. *A Report on the State of the Presidential Press Conference.* Washington, D.C.: National News Council, 1975.

Public Support and Opinion

Democratic processes—with their emphasis on measurement of popular support—have always been just one element of U.S. politics. Politics also involve bargaining among elite groups, negotiating with foreign countries, struggling over legal definitions, controlling public institutions such as schools and utilities, and managing major economic institutions.

Although public support is just one element of political strategy, it is an important one. As political scientist E. E. Schattschneider has argued, politicians always have tried to bolster their positions by claiming support from ever expanding segments of the population.[1] Since the nation's suffrage expanded to almost all citizens, politicians have turned to other ways to widen the "sphere" of politics. Public opinion polls offer one way to bolster claims of support. Demonstrations, letters, telegrams, telephone calls, and feedback from key party leaders, elected officials, and interest groups also indicate support.

Understanding the role of public opinion in the presidency requires first understanding the fundamental levels and sources of support for the presidency as an office, then determining the way specific presidents work with that support. All presidents enjoy a basic reserve of support because of the public's near-reverence of the office. But individual presidents experience a complex, constantly changing level of support for their programs and style of leadership.

The President's Relationship with the Public

The American public has deep psychological bonds to all of its presidents. Those bonds often strain as a result of specific events and the conflicting interests of the population, but they are a foundation for the president's oscillating relationship with the public.[2]

Schools, media, economic enterprises, voluntary associations, cultural events, and even religious institutions all teach Americans to respect and even revere the presidency, even when they find fault with the specific president on important issues. This fundamental support for the presidency creates a basic reserve of popular support for the

By Charles C. Euchner

occupants of the White House to develop backing for their specific programs and actions.

The presidency is revered largely because the chief executive is the most visible single figure in American life. All but a tiny segment of the population knows who the president is at a given moment—98 percent, according to one study, compared with 57 percent for one senator, 39 percent for the House member, and 31 percent for both senators. The president is well-known throughout the world. In a 1972 British poll, the president tied for first place among most-admired world political figures.[3]

As the only government official who represents the entire population, the president is unique in American politics. Other elected officials—members of Congress, governors, and local government officials—have parochial outlooks. The Supreme Court has a national constituency, but its members are appointed, and its role in American politics is obscure and usually limited to narrow legal argumentation. The president is the only person who can profess to speak for the "national interest" or the "general will" of the people.

The prestige of the presidency is enhanced by the president's role as head of state as well as the top government official. Other nations, such as Great Britain and Japan, give symbolic functions to a king or emperor, and leave the job of governing to someone else. But the president is the embodiment of the state in the United States. The emotional attachment that Americans give to the nation as a whole, therefore, is transferred also to the president.

The first political figure that children ever learn about is the president, and the president is depicted to the child as a uniquely benevolent, intelligent, and even-handed person. Early impressions are important. Although people grow up to be more skeptical of specific presidents, they retain the early lesson that the presidency is a special, important, stabilizing office usually deserving of awe.[4]

The "legacy of juvenile learning," to use the term of political scientist Fred I. Greenstein, is evident in the different attitudes of adults to the office of the presidency and the specific president in office. It is common for the president's backers in difficult times to ask for public support by referring to "the president" rather than the specific name of the president. Richard Nixon's 1972 campaign slogan was "Reelect the President" rather than "Reelect Richard Nixon."

The childhood lesson that the president is benign and

patriotic comes to the surface any time the nation faces a crisis. A military attack such as Pearl Harbor, a technological challenge such as the *Sputnik* launch, or national grieving over tragedies such as the assassination of John F. Kennedy cause the public to offer the president unquestioned, almost paternal loyalty for at least a short period.

Because the average citizen knows little about politics, the president is a symbol of the government. The president is covered in the media as a personality as well as a government official, so citizens develop a vicarious relationship with the president. Citizens identify with the president's personality as a shortcut to dealing with the complexities of the government. If citizens can develop "trust" for the president's personality, they can feel safe leaving the complexities of governing to the president.

Political scientist Murray Edelman, a leading student of the political uses of symbols and language, has written:

> Because it is apparently intolerable for men to admit the key role of accident, or ignorance, and of unplanned processes in their affairs, the leader serves a vital function by personifying or reifying the processes. As an individual, he can be blamed and given "responsibility" in a way that processes cannot. Incumbents of high public office therefore become objects of acclaim for the satisfied, scapegoats for the unsatisfied, and symbols of aspiration or of whatever is opposed.[5]

National Archives

The single most visible figure in American life, the president is covered by the media as both personality and government official.

The public has a tendency to "project" its own desires on the president—in other words, to interpret the president's actions to fit with the way it would like the president to be. Psychologists speak of citizens reducing "cognitive dissonance," or avoiding unpleasant facts or interpretations that might undercut a preferred view of the world. The citizen's desire to believe in the strength and stability of the system causes this identification with the president. This process becomes evident when the president uses vague language to appeal to groups with different goals. Even when the president's actions have clear winners and losers, both groups often interpret those actions in a way that makes them coincide with their own desires.

Psychological needs for strong leadership contribute to a steady base of presidential support. A study has confirmed the following proposition: "Persons having great needs for strong guidance, regimen, and a well-ordered society will probably score more highly on measures of general support for the president than individuals who do not have such needs."[6]

The president not only has a basic reserve of support based on widespread respect for the office. The president also can rely on the makeup of public opinion remaining somewhat constant in terms of social class, region, race, education, and residence in urban or rural areas. Since the president operates in a federal system, putting together majorities of support across the country is less important than putting together coalitions of support from the nation's different regions and groups.

The president usually can count on the South and West to be more conservative than the rest of the country, and city-dwellers to be more liberal than suburbanites or residents of rural areas. Educated people tend to be among the more independent citizens, with a "show me" attitude toward politicians on the day's leading issues. Paradoxically, many educated people take cues more readily from political parties. Ethnic and religious groups also display consistency in the way they approach certain issues.

Americans tend to be less ideological and more pragmatic than citizens of other countries. Surveys show that most Americans place themselves in the "moderate" middle part of the political spectrum. The U.S. system has a great deal of consensus on issues ranging from individual rights to the most preferable economic system. Presidents and other public officials who veer too far away from the American mainstream do so at their own risk.[7]

Measuring Support before Polls

In the years before polling became a regular part of politics and government, the measures of public support were rough and sporadic. The unscientific nature of public support fits with the original desires of the Founders. The drafters of the Constitution were wary of the constant pressures that public sentiments would have on the government's operation. The Constitution thereby contains limits to the influence of public opinion, such as indirect election of the president and Senate, the "checks and balances" between branches of government, a divided legislature, an independent judiciary appointed for life, and a federal system of national and state governments.

Institutions usually mediated public opinion in the nation's first century. As former corporate executive Chester Barnard has noted, to gauge public opinion nineteenth-century legislators "read the local newspapers, toured their districts, and talked with voters, received letters from the home state, and entertained delegations which claimed to speak for large and important blocks of voters." [8]

Party and Other Organizations

Until about World War II, state and local party organizations provided the most regular and reliable information about political attitudes. Party leaders were in touch with voters about issues ranging from trade to internal improvements. Attitudes about political matters were revealed by local party meetings, as well as by outside efforts of reform organizations and petition drives. If the issue persisted, officials at higher levels often began to pay attention.

Much of the reform impulse in national politics around the turn of the century came from the activities of parties and reform organizations in states and cities.

As states and localities passed reform legislation for the organization of city government and the regulation of business, national leaders began to shift their way of doing business. Woodrow Wilson's legislative program can be seen as a response to the demands of reform organizations in the states. Franklin D. Roosevelt kept a regular watch on party organizations in cities such as New York, Chicago, Philadelphia, and Detroit.

Party organizations not only offered a rough barometer of popular opinion but also stabilized opinion. Political figures could be more certain of their popular standing with active citizens since party membership demanded some commitment. Polls measure the opinions of uncommitted as well as committed citizens. As political scientist Theodore J. Lowi has written: "The moorings of the voters are now so loose that, regardless of any partisan consistency displayed in local elections (which is lessening too), their relationship to the presidency is highly personal." [9]

The rise of third parties in the pre-polling years offered a dramatic demonstration of changes in public opinion. When the two major parties did not address developing political issues, additional parties developed to give voice to those concerns. Public opinion found expression in third parties on issues such as slavery, agriculture policy, monetary policy, women's rights, and labor relations.

Interest groups and other elected officials have long been vehicles for transmitting opinion information to the president. The Kennedy administration kept a finger on the pulse of the civil rights movement through contacts with leaders of the National Association for the Advancement of Colored People and other organizations. Presidents regularly visit economic leaders in groups such as the Chamber of Commerce and the Business Roundtable.

Public Demonstrations

Public events—such as demonstrations, parades, and riots—have always provided the president and other government leaders with dramatic expressions of public opinion. With the development of more regular and "scientific" means for measuring public opinion, public spectacles have declined in importance. [10]

Protests and demonstrations have served as a means of expressing public opinion throughout U.S. history on issues such as slavery, tariffs, women's rights, ethnic and religious divisions, Prohibition, wars, abuses of monopolies, capital-labor disputes, problems of agriculture, the death penalty, civil rights, welfare rights, school busing, abortion, education, and drug abuse. Despite the dominance of polls as expressions of public opinion, demonstrations have been used since the 1960s to express opinions on civil rights, abortion, and involvement in war.

Demonstrations expressed public opinion most vividly during the 1880s and 1890s when farmers, workers, and owners of small businesses took to the streets to demand government regulation of corporations and basic protections and assistance programs. The protest movements of that period were instrumental in forming populist organizations and campaigns as well as in structuring the countermovements of the progressives and conservatives. [11]

Protest is a way of expressing opinions more for people who either do not have the ballot or find the ballot to be an empty gesture. Political scientist Benjamin Ginsberg has found that nations with regular voting procedures do not experience demonstrations when economic conditions change for the worse; the citizens of nations with more sporadic voting procedures, such as Latin American countries, must take to the streets to express their opinions. [12] The findings suggest that formal procedures for expressing opinion preclude spontaneous development and expression of opinion.

Studies show that lower-income people are more likely to take part in demonstrations than they are to vote. Underrepresented in voting booths and many surveys, these people go to the streets to express their opinions about a wide range of issues. [13]

Newspapers

Until the Civil War, newspapers were partisan sheets designed not so much to deliver news as to persuade or agitate a fiercely partisan audience. The fortunes of a newspaper—especially the size of its circulation, advertising, and the reaction it got from elites and the general public—provided a rough barometer of the public mood. Newspapers also indicated party strength since they depended on the parties for advertising and readership. The newspapers' indications of party strength provided clues about the popularity of presidents. Newspapers were important in shaping as well as measuring public opinion. James Bryce, the noted British analyst of American politics, wrote of readers' acceptance of partisan newspaper versions of events: "They could not be at the trouble of sifting the evidence." [14]

With the newspaper boom of the late nineteenth century, newspapers dropped their blatant partisan ties. Readership of the New York *World*, the nation's first mass-circulation newpaper, rose from 15,000 to 1.5 million between 1883 and 1898. [15] Because newspapers were cheap and geared toward the general public, they reached every class of people. Many cities had a dozen or more newspapers with distinct readerships. The news pages, letter columns, and advertising space all provided clues about the tenor and trend of popular opinion.

Letter Writing

One of the more regular forms of expression is to write letters to the president and other public officials. [16]

In the nation's early years, letter writing was a practice used mostly by economic and educational elites. As the nation expanded its notion of democracy, and as the government extended its reach during times of crisis, the letter-writing population grew to include not only elites but the whole literate public. Then, with the growth of mass communications, the letter became a regular tool of instantaneous public opinion pressure.

The first major letter-writing campaign persuaded George Washington to seek a second term as president in 1792.

Like other forms of political activity, letter-writing booms during periods of national crisis. During periods of "normalcy" before the New Deal, the number of letters written per 10,000 literate adults ranged from 4.7 in 1900 during William McKinley's administration to 11.8 during Herbert C. Hoover's administration before the 1929 economic crash. The letter-writing rate increased during the crises of the Civil War (44 letters per 10,000 literate adults) and World War I (47). A major—and permanent—change came with the public presidency of Franklin D. Roosevelt. Roosevelt's mail rate reached 160 during the Great Depression and fell to 111 during the calm of the late 1930s.

Letter writing still influences both large- and small-scale policy initiatives. As might be expected, however, letter writing has been part of the larger process of technologically sophisticated politics. Computers have become a large part of this once intimate form of communication.

Until recent years, most letters were the work of persons acting on their own initiative. According to one study, less than 10 percent of Franklin Roosevelt's third-term mail could be linked to interest groups: "Mail is very often a means through which unorganized and transitory interests make themselves heard." [17]

Headline events are most likely to spur letter writing. State of the Union addresses, presidential speeches on television, press conferences, congressional hearings, wars and other military events, major appointments, Supreme Court decisions, international summits or meetings, and political scandals spark mass letter writing. The top letter-writing events in recent years include the Vietnam War, the Watergate scandal, the energy crisis, the Iran-contra affair, the appointment of Robert H. Bork to the Supreme Court, events in the Middle East, relations with the Soviet Union, and the testimony of White House aide Lt. Col. Oliver North before a congressional committee.

Many letter-writing campaigns result from the public urging of prominent officials during controversial political events. Sen. Joseph R. McCarthy of Wisconsin, for example, initiated a deluge of letters to President Dwight D. Eisenhower urging that the United States cut ties with countries doing business with the People's Republic of China. Members of Congress who regularly correspond with voters urge constituents to write letters to the president on key issues.

The president, too, sometimes calls for letters to the White House and to Congress to indicate support for presidential policies. Full-time White House staffers read and keep track of letters the president receives to determine the general flow of opinion.

Interest groups have begun to play a more prominent role in spurring letter writing. National organizations and grass-roots organizations often circulate postcards and letters on specific issues for supporters to sign and send to the White House and Congress. Interest groups also print advertisements in newspapers urging a barrage of letters to elected officials. Interest groups with vast memberships are capable of managing letter-writing blitzkriegs to the president, to members of Congress, and to state officials. Those letters often get brief consideration because it is easy for the recipients to see that they are not spontaneous. But they do reinforce the sense of vulnerability of some elected officials.

Even though polls have replaced letters as the regular means for assessing public opinion, letters can provide clues about concerns that are submerged in the restricted format of surveys. In 1954, for example, the Democratic National Committee received a number of letters from people concerned about the effects of inflation on pensions. It was the first indication that inflation was a prime concern among the elderly. Letters can draw attention to issues that pollsters do not include in their surveys.

Besides giving the president a means of measuring public opinion, letter writing provides a way of pressuring other politicians in Washington. The power of letters was vividly underscored when both President Reagan and Rep. Daniel Rostenkowski (D-Ill.) appealed to television audiences to write to them about tax reform issues. The president and congressional leaders both used letters to bolster their arguments during the tax reform procedures.

Telephone Calls and Telegrams

For immediate reaction to political events, telephone calls and telegrams have replaced letters and augmented the increasing use of overnight polls.

Telegrams provide a tangible if biased indication of support. White House officials refer to the volume of positive telegrams to bolster their credibility during crises such as Watergate, Vietnam, the explosion of the space shuttle *Challenger,* and the congressional hearings over the Reagan administration's secret dealings with Iran.

Richard Nixon survived a major crisis as a candidate for vice president in 1952 when he appealed on television for telegrams expressing support. Nixon's "Checkers speech" produced, according to Nixon's own reckoning, between one million and two million telegrams and permitted him to stay on the Republican ticket despite the controversy over the propriety of a fund for his personal expenses.

During the Iran-contra affair in 1987, White House officials and backers pointed to the thousands of telegrams sent to fired National Security Council aide Oliver North as a sign of outward support. North brought bags of the telegrams to the congressional hearings, giving both himself and the White House a boost during the administration's greatest crisis.

During the Iran-contra affair, Reagan referred to the deluge of supportive telephone calls he received. "After my speech, some 84 percent of those people who called in supported me," Reagan said. "It was the biggest outpouring of calls they've ever had. The letters coming in are in my favor." [18]

Development of Formal Surveys and Polling

Presidents and other political figures have used surveys since the early nineteenth century, but only since the development of sophisticated systems of communications and analysis have surveys and polls become a major part of White House efforts to measure and shape public opinion.

Polling data are often sketchy and contradictory, but they at least reduce the uncertainty under which the president operates. As President Reagan's pollster, Richard Wirthlin, suggested, polling is "the science of ABC—almost being certain." [19]

The first poll in the United States was a straw poll of presidential candidates John Quincy Adams and Andrew Jackson that appeared in the *Harrisburg Pennsylvanian* in 1824. With the rise of mass circulation newspapers in the 1880s, polls became regular features. Papers such as the *New York Herald Tribune, Los Angeles Times,* and *St. Louis Republic* all published regular poll results. A 1936 survey of *Literary Digest* readers, which predicted that Alfred Landon would defeat Franklin Roosevelt for the presidency, both damaged polling's credibility and helped pave the way for more sophisticated surveys. The *Digest's* huge mistake—Roosevelt won by a landslide—could be attributed to the built-in bias of the magazine's predominantly Republican, well-to-do readership.

The founder of modern polling was George Gallup, whose surveys helped his mother-in-law win election as secretary of state in Iowa in 1932. Gallup wrote a doctoral thesis on sampling techniques and in 1935, with Elmo Roper and Archibald Crossley, founded the independent Gallup Poll, which was the leader in scientific polling for decades. Gallup was a key figure in giving polling its scientific credentials by using large, representative sample sizes and carefully worded questions.

Franklin Roosevelt was the first president to use polling data regularly to interpret the public's reactions to the political and policy actions of the administration. As U.S. involvement in World War II became more likely in the late 1930s, Roosevelt got advice from Gallup on how to frame his rhetoric on possible U.S. involvement. Around the same time, Princeton University professor Hadley Cantril conducted surveys to determine the supply and demand of housing and consumer goods as well as public attitudes about the war. Cantril later polled members of the military about their housing and supply conditions during the war.

In 1946, New York lawyer and congressional candidate Jacob K. Javits was believed to be the first candidate for a public office to commission a private political poll.[20] Harry S Truman in 1948 and Dwight Eisenhower in 1952 used polls to develop campaign appeals. With regular information about voter attitudes, elections and governing became more and more intertwined. John F. Kennedy hired pollster Louis Harris two years before his successful 1960 presidential campaign to gauge support and develop strategy.

Polls gradually developed into a daily part of government action and the flow of news and academic analysis. Dozens of newspapers and magazines, television and radio stations, government agencies, business firms, universities, and private organizations commission surveys of political and social attitudes and habits. Surveys are so pervasive that pollsters now ask survey questions about polling itself.[21]

By 1962, virtually all gubernatorial candidates, two-thirds of all Senate candidates, and half the winning candidates for the House of Representatives commissioned polls sometime during their campaigns.

Lyndon B. Johnson was the first president to hire a pollster to the White House staff, Hadley Cantril's son Albert. The administration also consulted the pollster Oliver Quayle regularly. Throughout his term, Johnson kept a steady stream of polling data from every state. Academics working at Johnson's presidential library in Austin have found dozens of memorandums and poll results among Johnson's papers.

When faced with growing opposition to the Vietnam War, Johnson constantly referred to polls that suggested a majority of Americans favoring the administration's war policies. Johnson rejected arguments that most of the nation was uninformed and that those who were knowledgable about the war opposed it. When polls showed a majority of Americans opposing the war effort, Johnson moved toward a decision against seeking a second full term.

Nixon's public-relations campaigns were based on the idea of the "silent majority," which the president claimed backed his administration's policies on Vietnam, civil rights, crime, regulation, social programs and budget priorities, and the Watergate affair. The lack of widespread opposition to his policies, Nixon argued, could be interpreted to be approval. Nixon's argument, in effect, gave as much weight to people with no strong feelings or knowledge as those with well-informed, strong views.

Nixon regularly used polls to formulate policy statements to go over the heads of Congress and interest groups. When polls showed that he was personally popular with blue-collar workers, Nixon decided to ignore the opposition of labor union leadership on issues such as wage and price controls.

Current Public Opinion Efforts

Polls became pervasive in U.S. politics in the 1970s. In 1972, no newspapers conducted their own polls; they relied on private polling organizations. By the end of the decade, most major news organizations conducted their own regular surveys, which became an important part of determining which stories were "news." Polling also became a permanent part of the White House staff with the elections of Jimmy Carter in 1976 and Ronald Reagan in 1980.

Carter's Use of Polls

Carter became president with no Washington experience and an uncertain ideology; he therefore did not have a strong sense of his role in the government. His campaign was successful partly because of the work of Patrick Caddell, a pollster who was one of the top architects of the campaign agenda. Caddell gave Carter regular advice in the White House.[22] Polling data were a regular part of decision making in the Carter White House. Carter often relied on polls to tell him what an ideological "compass" told presidents such as Ronald Reagan.

Perhaps the most significant moment of Carter's presidency was the nationally televised speech he delivered about the country's moral lassitude. During a gas shortage in the summer of 1979, Carter planned to deliver a speech to promote a variety of energy conservation and development initiatives. While working on the address, however, he decided that it would fail to move a public that had already heard four such speeches. Caddell gave Carter polling data and a memorandum recommending a shift in emphasis. Carter's decision to act on the data was one of his presidency's fateful moments.

Caddell's data suggested that the public would react

cynically to another call for new energy conservation. The memorandum said that the public had become "completely inured" to warnings about the energy crisis, and would not make sacrifices because of cynicism about both the government and the oil industry.[23] Caddell argued that the breakdown of faith in U.S. institutions could be overcome only with a dramatic call for common cause and sacrifice. Caddell had made that argument to Carter at least since the 1976 campaign.[24]

Carter's speech—which analyzed a "crisis of confidence" in the American public—originally was well received. But a series of cabinet firings, which Carter acknowledged handling "very poorly," created an atmosphere of crisis not in the nation as much as in the administration.[25] The "malaise" speech, as it came to be known, became a source of ridicule rather than national unity.

Reagan's Use of Polls

Despite widespread criticism of Carter's reliance on polls, Reagan brought campaign pollster Richard Wirthlin with him to the White House in 1981. Reagan was able to have the best of both worlds with in-house polling. While consistently touching on a wide range of common themes, he steered specific public debates according to information supplied by specific polling data. Richard Beal, an associate of Wirthlin, was given a White House job sifting through polling data. White House communications director David Gergen, a founder of the magazine *Public Opinion,* was another influential aide. Annual funding from the Republican National Committee (RNC) of about $900,000 allowed Wirthlin's firm, Decision Making Information, to conduct the most extensive and expensive polls ever undertaken on behalf of a president. Wirthlin was a paid staffer, and in the early Reagan years his firm got paid separately by the RNC for conducting research.

Wirthlin's surveys and regular "tracking" polls—in which changes in a sample of opinion are followed daily—affected administration policy in several areas. Reagan's "honeymoon" poll results persuaded the president to seek dramatic tax and budget legislation in early 1981. Later data, as well as an outcry from legislative leaders and interest groups, persuaded Reagan to drop plans for wholesale changes in Social Security. When the 1982 economic slump threatened big midterm election losses, polling data showed widespread support for giving the administration's tax policies a chance but disturbing declines in support from blue-collar voters. In 1982, Reagan agreed to budget and tax compromises with Congress when polls revealed big drops in the percentage of the public urging the administration to "continue as is." [26] Polling data also guided administration actions on the nomination of Sandra Day O'Connor to the Supreme Court, U.S. involvement in the Lebanese civil war, Reagan's visit to the Bitburg cemetery in West Germany, and tax reform.

Wirthlin's most extensive polling took place in early 1987, when the administration struggled to control the effects of disclosures that the White House had secretly sold arms to Iran in exchange for help in releasing American hostages in Lebanon and that profits from these sales went to help rebels against the government of Nicaragua. During the first six or seven weeks of the year, Wirthlin conducted constant rounds of interviews with a total of twenty-five thousand people—more than most pollsters interview in an entire year.[27]

The Reagan administration, attentive every day to poll results, orchestrated a number of dramatic events that provided surges of support. Foreign summits, Oval Office speeches, military attacks on Libya and Grenada, emotional public appearances after such tragedies as the truck-bombing of the marine barracks in Lebanon and the space shuttle *Challenger* explosion, and strongly worded statements after terrorist attacks and the Soviet attack on the Korean Air Lines plane all provided "rally points" for Reagan.

No president uses polls to determine major policy stances. But polls give the president information about what issues to highlight and downplay. Polls showing public alarm over the truck-bombing of the marine barracks in Lebanon in 1983, for example, alerted the administration

Pete Souza, The White House

Despite criticism of Carter's reliance on polls, Reagan brought campaign pollster Richard Wirthlin with him to the White House in 1981. Wirthlin's surveys and regular tracking polls affected administration policy in several areas.

to the need to shore up public support. Many critics also charge that the U.S. invasion of the tiny island of Grenada two days after the Lebanon bombing was designed to divert public attention from the disaster. As a result of the poll data, Reagan also gave a major television address to increase his support.

Political scientist Philip Converse puts the use of polls into perspective:

> Acquiring relevent public opinion data is not unlike the riverboat captain buying the latest mapping of sandbar configurations before embarking on a voyage. Few politicians consult poll data to find out what they should be thinking on the issues, or to carry out errands. But they have very little interest in flouting the will of their constituency in any tendentious, head-on way. Such data give them a sense of what postures to emphasize and avoid.[28]

Cycles of Presidential Popularity

Presidential popularity tends to decline throughout the four-year term in office, with temporary increases after important international events and at the beginning of a reelection campaign or at the end of the term.

Since 1945, the Gallup Poll has surveyed Americans about once a month to determine popular support for the president. The identical question—"Do you approve or disapprove of the way [the incumbent] is handling his job as president?"—has produced a unique series of data about presidents' relations with the public. The data suggest the limits of presidential leadership via appeals to public opinion.

Every president enjoys a honeymoon period in which the nation gives the new chief executive broad, general support.[29] The administration's early days are considered the best time for a president to pass difficult legislation, such as Carter's energy program or Reagan's tax- and budget-cutting packages. Presidential popularity averages about 69 percent in the first year in office. The approval ratings are much higher early in the year. After their third month in office, Truman received a rating of 89 percent, and Kennedy received a rating of 83 percent. Lyndon Johnson had a rating of 80 percent after his second month, and Gerald R. Ford and Carter had early 71 percent ratings.[30]

Political scientist Samuel Kernell has argued that a president's popularity throughout his term is partly determined by the results of previous polls.[31] Poll results do not vary much from month to month—mostly because only a small segment of the population is likely to veer very far from its orientations, but also because of the public's inertia and use of previous polls to judge the president. Presidents therefore have a strong base of support at the beginning of their term. The key question for the president is how quickly the support will decline.

Since the beginning of the Gallup survey, public approval of the president has ranged from a low of 14 percent under Carter to a high of 87 percent under Truman.[32] The approval rating for Nixon during the final days of perhaps the greatest crisis of the modern presidency—the Watergate affair, which led to Nixon's resignation August 9, 1974—was 23 percent.

The oscillation of support within an administration was greatest during the Truman presidency. Truman's support varied by as much as 64 percentage points, from a low of 23 percent to a high of 87 percent. Eisenhower had the most consistent support. In his first term, approval scores were almost always between 60 and 80 percent, and in the second term the scores were almost always between 50 and 70 percent.

The average level of support for presidents has varied widely, too. Kennedy received the highest average rate of support, 70.5 percent, during his shortened presidency. Other average levels of support are: Eisenhower (64.8), Johnson (56.3), Nixon (48.7), Ford (46.8), Carter (50.1), and Reagan (52.7).

Patterns of Support

Studies by political scientists John E. Mueller and James A. Stimson suggest that public support of the president follows regular patterns, no matter who is president and what policies the president pursues. Mueller argues that the president's popularity declines steadily, in a straight line, after the first several months in office.[33] Stimson argues that popularity ratings follow the form of a parabola, a curve that slowly declines before flattening out and then rising slightly late in the term.[34] Stimson writes: "The president, in this theory, is largely a passive observer of his downsliding popularity." [35]

Both Mueller and Stimson agree that the trend is interrupted—but only temporarily—by "rally points" such as U.S. military involvement overseas, the release of economic news, assassination attempts, and campaign activities. Such events can give a president a spurt of approval above the point on the overall line of decline. But even if a president benefits from public attention to highly visible news, the basic trend of decline is immutable.[36]

Mueller simply states that after an average approval rating of 69 percent early in the term, the president's rating will fall about 6 percentage points each year. Because of a "coalition of minorities" effect—in which groups aggrieved by administration policies slowly but steadily build an antiadministration coalition—presidential popularity ratings form a line in steady decline on a chart. Different presidents decline in popularity at different rates.

Stimson disagrees with Mueller mainly about the dynamic aspects of public opinion. A president's popularity at a given point cannot be considered an isolated judgment of the president, Stimson argues. Instead, one month's approval rating feeds into and influences the next. Rather than simply reflecting accumulation of grievances, as Mueller argues, the decline in popularity is the result of the public's psychological relationship with the president.

Because the public is usually inattentive to politics, it does not know much about presidents. But in the media excitement and soaring rhetoric of a new president, the public develops high expectations of the president. The two factors—inattentiveness and high expectations—are a dangerous combination for presidents. Political scientist Thomas Cronin has written:

> The significance of the textbook presidency is that the whole is greater than the sum of the parts. It presents a cumulative presidential image, a legacy of past glories and impressive performances ... which endows the White House with a singular mystique and almost magical qualities. According to this image ... only men of the caliber of Lincoln, the Roosevelts, or Wilson can seize the chalice of opportunity, create the vision, and rally the American public around that vision.[37]

The public, in effect, wants the president to reach the promised land but it does not appreciate the rockiness of the terrain.

The public's response, Stimson argues, is not just a steady decline of support but a deep disappointment. That deep disappointment is reflected in a fast decline of support. The decline then bottoms out and rises slightly at the end of the term, both because of the public's desire to correct its overreaction and the president's return to more simplistic rhetoric as the reelection campaign approaches.

President Reagan's first-term surge in popularity was unusual. After approval ratings similar to Carter's and Nixon's, Reagan's support surged in his third and fourth years. A January 1983 poll put Reagan's popularity at 35 percent; by his second inauguration, it was almost 62 percent. Scholars attribute the surge to favorable economic trends, such as lower inflation and interest rates, and to adept use of public events to rally the nation around the president's leadership. Another cause also might be the nation's desire for a leader in which it could place faith. After the assassination of President Kennedy and the failed presidencies of Johnson, Nixon, Ford, and Carter, the public may have decided to believe in Reagan's leadership just to give the nation stability it had lacked since the 1950s.

Second-term presidents are generally less popular than first-term presidents. Eisenhower, Johnson, Nixon, and Reagan all had lower support scores after their second inauguration. Johnson and Nixon were driven from the White House at least partly by depressed opinion scores.[38]

The second-term decline has several explanations. First, the president is a "lame duck," without the prospect of a bold reelection campaign to inspire supporters. The public, Congress, and key bureaucrats expect to be involved with national politics after the president's departure, which makes the president's position on long-term issues less and less relevent. Second, problems are more difficult to explain away with reference to the mistakes of the previous president. Reagan constantly referred to the "mess" left him by Carter, but the public was less willing to blame Carter the longer Reagan was in office. Third, the best members of the administration often leave office soon after the president's reelection, creating the aura of a provisional and "second-string" team less deserving of respect. The president also loses top political operatives as they go to work for other politicians who will be involved in public life after the president leaves office. Finally, other politicians, who want to develop an independent base and perhaps succeed the president, try to develop their own political messages distinct from that of the president, reducing the reinforcement that the president's message receives.

Steadiness during the Cycles

Throughout the cycles of presidential approval, the public offers a steady level of support and opposition to the president. Many groups are constantly for or against the president, while "swing" groups fluctuate greatly and cause the ups and downs of presidential approval.

Different segments of the population react to public events according to their education, income, gender, and political involvement.

The president usually can depend on support from citizens who are members of the same party and opposition from members of the opposing party. The groups expressing support for the Vietnam War switched with Republican Richard Nixon's move into the White House and Lyndon Johnson's move out, that is, Republicans generally opposed the war under Johnson but supported it under Nixon.

Unless the president deeply offends the basic tenets of party, he usually can count on party identifiers for support. Many of those people actually will be registered with the party, and others will just "lean" toward the party—and rely on the party for cues—on most issues.[39]

Besides these "partisans," the president must also deal with a set of "believers," a small minority of the population with fully developed ideological stances on a wide range of economic, social, and political issues. Believers are committed to a cause, such as the security of Israel, free-market values, or a U.S. struggle to "contain" Soviet geopolitical threats. They also have "psychological predispositions" on issues ranging from military activity to community values. Presidents can count on consistent behavior by believers, just as they can count on consistent behavior by partisans. But the consistency depends on the issue rather than the political affiliation.

Another group—the "followers"—is willing to follow the president's lead on a wide range of issues, especially foreign affairs, simply because the president is the president. This group often associates its support for the president with patriotism—a "my president, right or wrong" attitude.

The battle for public opinion, then, centers on the opinions of the less aligned, more independent citizens. The opinions of people with greater status and involvement fluctuate and polarize more than those of the rest of the population. If they identify with a party, these citizens react to the "cues" of party politics and current events more than people of lower status. But if they are part of the growing number of independents, they react primarily to the constantly shifting set of news events. Because better educated people tend to read newspapers more regularly, they respond to the fluctuations of news more than the rest of the population. If they know that a president is struggling with Congress or the Soviets, for example, a better-informed citizen may alter previously positive feelings about the president. The better-informed citizen has constantly changing "good" and "bad" political news that she or he uses to judge the president.[40]

Why Support Declines

No matter whether the Mueller or Stimson models best depict the trends of approval, it is clear that presidential approval usually declines throughout a term of office. There are several explanations for the decline:

~ Inevitable disappointment after high expectations. Presidential campaigns are exercises in popular education and excitement. As the nation prepares to select its next leader, the candidates attempt to depict the positive changes that would occur in their administration as dramatically as possible.[41]

The public—usually inattentive to politics—gradually gets to know prospective presidents and develops personal attachments to the personalities of the leading contenders. As the media explore the candidates' personal background, voters get an intimate view of the persons who might lead the next government.

When the president takes office, the public has unrealistic expectations of what might be accomplished. When the public begins to see the president's weaknesses, it views the president less and less favorably. Even when it supports the president's stances and policies on specific issues, the public might be critical because of the president's inability to achieve all that was promised. Even when the president is able to deliver on a specific program, support among certain groups might decline because the program yields less impressive results than were expected.

~ Accumulation of grievances. When taking the oath of office for the first time, the president has not yet damaged the material fortunes of any segment of society. Even the most skeptical observers—such as business leaders under a Democratic administration or labor leaders under a Republican administration—are willing to suspend judgment of the new chief executive. Their hope is that their skepticism can be used to move the president closer to their own way of thinking.

As the president submits federal budgets, adopts legislative programs, and uses the "bully pulpit" to promote various social causes, different groups develop specific grievances with the administration. Any public policy decision helps some groups at the expense of others. Even defense and economic policies—which, the president argues, benefit all members of society—have clear winners and losers.

As the president builds a record, some groups develop into consistent winners and others into consistent losers. As the president becomes involved in more and more policy areas, the number of groups affected negatively by policy decisions increases. Even if a group receives some benefits as well as losses because of the administration's policies, the group's support for the president likely will decline because of unhappiness with the losses.

Mueller calls the accumulation of grievances the "coalition of minorities effect." The premise of Mueller's study is that groups that are dissatisfied with government policy are more likely to organize than groups that are satisfied with the government.[42]

Political scientist Richard A. Brody has linked presidential popularity to the amount of "good" and "bad" news the public receives in the media. Brody's model posits that the public keeps a running score of the news about politics and the economy and rewards presidents who have presided over periods full of good news—regardless of their role in creating that news.[43] Still, presidential popularity will decline.

~ Manipulation of the political calendar for electoral advantage. When first taking office, the president has one overriding goal: creating the best possible circumstances for a reelection campaign four years later. Secondary goals include passage of important policies and improvement of the president's party strength in Congress and state governments.

These goals demand different kinds of presidential popularity at different points in the nation's electoral cycles. The president will try to time the administration's policies and pronouncements to produce the support necessary for the crucial electoral and policy-making decisions.

Most presidents, for example, are willing to see their popularity decline after the first year in office. The first year is usually the best time for achieving budgetary and other legislative goals, which require high levels of popularity. After a couple years of lower levels of support—during which the White House might pursue policy goals through regulation and more modest or bipartisan legislative action—the president seeks to boost public support in time for the reelection campaign.

~ Persisting problems. Major national problems—many of which give the president broad support when first exposed publicly—develop into liabilities for the president if they are not resolved quickly.

The Korean War, Vietnam War, Watergate, Iran hostage crisis, fears about drug trafficking and abuse, and American involvement in the Lebanese civil war all gained the president broad public support when they first came to the public's attention. But after those problems remained unsolved for one or more years, the public became disenchanted and turned against the president.

Jimmy Carter's experience with Iran is a dramatic example. When Iranian students stormed the American embassy in Tehran and took fifty-two Americans hostage on November 4, 1979, Carter's popularity jumped dramatically. Carter's approval rating was 14 percent on October 30; the approval rating was 38 percent on November 13, and almost 58 percent the next January 22. As the crisis dragged into the summer months, Carter's popularity ratings dipped into the low 30s.

~ Evidence of a breach of faith. Because of their highly personal relationship with the president, Americans are more likely to lose confidence in the chief executive over a personal moral failing, such as lying, than over ineffective, dangerous, or even immoral policies.

President Nixon's slide in public opinion did not come with revelations that his administration had undertaken questionable activities, such as illegally bombing Cambodia during the Vietnam War, destabilizing the Marxist regime of Chilean leader Salvador Allende, and presiding over a number of unethical campaign practices. The slide came instead with revelations that he had consistently covered up such activities.

Controversial Reagan administration policies in Central America, the Middle East, Iran, and South Africa did not cause Reagan as much trouble as the public's concern that he may have lied about his activities. When former White House aide Oliver North acknowledged and even bragged about breaking the law (shredding government documents, lying to Congress, diverting government funds to Nicaraguan rebels), the White House experienced a surge of support.

Issues Affecting Presidential Popularity

The relative importance of foreign affairs and domestic politics to presidential popularity is difficult to determine. In foreign affairs, the public is quick to unite behind the president because the source of concern is external. But domestic policy usually involves internal divisions, so public support is less monolithic.

Domestic Affairs

Referring to the election adage that people vote according to "pocketbook issues," some students of public opinion maintain that a president is only as popular as the economic conditions allow. During periods of high unemployment or high inflation, the president's popularity is bound to suffer. As the nation's most visible public figure, the president bears the brunt of voter anxiety about the economic health of the country. Likewise, presidents benefit when economic conditions are bright.

The experience of twentieth-century presidents lends some support to the pocketbook interpretation of presidential popularity. The most dramatic example of a president suffering from poor economic conditions was Herbert Hoover, president when the Great Crash of October 1929 plunged the nation into its most severe depression. The popularity of Hoover's successor, Franklin Roosevelt, appeared to decline at the end of his second term when the nation experienced another economic downturn. Historian David Green has argued that the failure of the New Deal to produce prosperity forced Roosevelt to shift political tactics by 1938. To distract the nation from the economic slump, Roosevelt launched public campaigns against "reactionaries" at home and fascists abroad.[44]

Eisenhower's popularity ratings—the steadiest ever recorded for a president—declined when the nation entered a deep recession in 1958. The first poll of the year gave Eisenhower a 60 percent approval rate; by the time of the midterm congressional elections, it was down to 52 percent. Eisenhower also had the highest disapproval scores of his two terms during 1958—as high as 36 percent. More important, Eisenhower's Republicans were thrashed in the congressional campaign, losing forty-seven House seats and fifteen Senate seats.

The 1970s were a particularly difficult time for the U.S. economy, with, at various times, double-digit inflation and unemployment rates, a trebling of energy prices, high interest rates, and unprecedented trade and budget deficits. The conditions led one president, Richard Nixon, to make drastic changes in the U.S. and world monetary systems and to impose wage and price controls for the first time in peacetime.

The presidents during the economic stagnation struggled to maintain a moderate level of popularity. Johnson, Nixon, Ford, Carter, and Reagan all suffered in the polls during perilous economic times. As political scientist Kristen R. Monroe has argued, economic factors such as unemployment and inflation may have both an immediate and a cumulative effect. The public has a "lagged response" to inflation. A single monthly increase in inflation will have a political effect for as many as eleven months. Monroe has written: "The lagged impact suggests that the public has a long memory. The public is not easily distracted by sudden declines in inflation which directly precede an election."[45]

Pocketbook issues besides the nation's economic condition also affect presidential popularity. Tax rates, the strength of social welfare programs, and perceptions of government efficiency all affect the public's sense of economic well-being and, perhaps, its view of the president's performance. Studies show that economic problems are more likely to damage a president's popularity than economic well-being is likely to boost the president's standing.[46]

Other domestic events affect presidential popularity as well. Domestic disturbances such as the urban riots of the 1960s, controversial issues like busing and abortion, protests over the deployment of nuclear weapons, presidential appointments, and domestic scandals all tend to damage the president's popularity.

Political scientist Theodore J. Lowi has argued that "pocketbook" and other domestic issues do not provide the popularity boost that most presidents seek. Instead, a series of foreign policy events often is the only thing that can help a president regain popularity.[47] For example, most analysts attribute President Reagan's strong rebound from low poll ratings during his first term to improvements in the economy. One study states that the rise in Reagan's approval rating from 35 percent to 61 percent "seems to have been caused almost entirely by changes in economic conditions in the country."[48]

Lowi maintains, however, that the economic improvements took place too gradually and affected people in too minor a way to produce Reagan's dramatic turnaround. Indeed, Reagan's ratings on specific economic issues—such as inflation, budget deficits, and efforts to get the country out of the recession and to help groups in economic distress—were very negative. Lowi points to other evidence against the pocketbook explanation for presidential popularity. Economic conditions improved in both 1968 and 1976 but did not help Presidents Johnson and Ford, whose high negative ratings and intense public opposition prevented both from winning reelection.

The Foreign Policy Explanation

Reagan experienced impressive improvements in his approval rating after foreign policy events with which he associated publicly, such as the bombing of the U.S. embassy in Lebanon, the Soviet attack on the Korean Air Lines plane, the redeployment of marines in Lebanon, changes of leadership in the Soviet Union, and the invasion of Grenada.

As Lowi has suggested, foreign policy events of short duration help a president's public standing, even if the event was not considered a "success" for the president. Domestic politics have a less certain effect on ratings. Economic news is considered the most useful domestic event for a president, but many experts question how much it can help a president's overall standing. Other domestic events are more divisive, since they almost always produce clear losers as well as winners.

That president's tendency to get more involved with foreign policy as the term progresses may be an indicator of the public's inclination to "rally 'round the flag." Other reasons for greater presidential involvement in foreign policy exist, such as the greater experience and expertise that the administration acquires over time. But the steady decline in approval ratings gives the president reason to take actions that provide at least temporary surges of support.

The public's willingness to back a president in times of international crisis is almost complete. President John Kennedy marveled at his public support after an event that he acknowledged to be a complete failure, the aborted invasion of Cuba and attempted overthrow of Fidel Castro at the Bay of Pigs. Kennedy's public approval rating jumped from 73 to 83 percent after the disaster, with only 5 percent giving negative views. A Democratic fund raiser in Chicago produced an overwhelming show of support for Kennedy.

Kennedy and other presidents have experienced surges of support after other major foreign policy events, whether or not they could be considered "successes." Kennedy's own foreign policy crises included the Cuban missile crisis, the construction of the Berlin Wall to separate the eastern and western parts of Berlin, the Kennedy-Khrushchev showdown at Vienna, and the assassination of South Vietnamese president Ngo Dinh Diem, as well as the Bay of Pigs disaster.

Incidents producing gains in the president's approval rating include: the Gulf of Tonkin crisis (Johnson); early bombing of North Vietnam and Cambodia (Nixon); the *Mayaguez* incident and the fall of Saigon (Ford); the tak-

Table 1 Effect of Foreign Policy Events on Presidential Popularity, 1939-1975

Date and type of event	Incumbent	Specific event	Popularity Before	Popularity After	Change	Duration in months
Wars and military crises						
1941/12	Roosevelt	Pearl Harbor	72	84	+12	8
1962/10	Kennedy	Cuban missile crisis	61	73	+12	8
1975/5	Ford	*Mayaguez* incident	40	51	+11	8
1950/6	Truman	North Korea invades South Korea	37	46	+9	5
1961/7	Kennedy	Berlin crisis	71	79	+8	12
1966/6	Johnson	Extension of bombing, Hanoi	48	56	+8	2
1967/6	Johnson	War in the Middle East	44	52	+8	1
1958/7	Eisenhower	Troops sent to Lebanon	52	58	+6	3
1965/4	Johnson	Troops to Dominican Republic	64	70	+6	3
1939/8	Roosevelt	War starts in Europe	57	61	+4	—
1970/4	Nixon	Troops to Cambodia	56	59	+3	2
1948/4	Truman	Berlin blockade	36	39	+3	1
1965/2	Johnson	Bombing North Vietnam	68	69	+1	1
1971/1	Nixon	Expansion of war to Laos	56	49	−7	14
Peace and reconciliations						
1973/2	Nixon	Vietnam settlement	51	67	+16	2
1954/7	Eisenhower	Indochina truce signed	64	75	+11	2
1951/6	Truman	Korean talk begins	25	29	+4	5
1968/4	Johnson	Partial bombing halt	42	46	+4	5
1953/7	Eisenhower	Korean truce signed	71	74	+3	2
1974/5	Nixon	Middle East ceasefire	25	28	+3	1
1963/10	Kennedy	Test ban treaty signed	56	58	+2	1
1968/10	Johnson	Full bombing halt	42	43	+1	1
Summit conferences						
1959/12	Eisenhower	Good-will tour to Europe	67	76	+9	1
1972/5	Nixon	Trip to Russia	53	62	+9	2
1970/10	Nixon	Trip to Europe	51	58	+7	2
1959/9	Eisenhower	Camp David	61	66	+5	7
1975/11	Ford	Trip to China	41	46	+5	1
1955/7	Eisenhower	Geneva summit	72	76	+4	2
1972/2	Nixon	Trip to China	52	56	+4	1
1973/6	Nixon	Brezhnev visit	44	43	−1	1
1974/7	Nixon	Trip to Russia	26	24	−2	1
1961/6	Kennedy	Summit with Khrushchev	74	71	−3	1
Policy initiatives						
1947/3	Truman	Truman Doctrine announced	48	60	+12	9
1969/10	Nixon	Vietnamization speech	56	67	+11	1
1953/11	Eisenhower	UN speech on atom	58	66	+8	6
1961/2	Kennedy	Peace Corps	72	78	+6	6
1948/4	Truman	Marshall Plan announced	36	39	+3	1
1941/6	Roosevelt	Lend-lease program	73	73	0	0
International setbacks						
1973/12	Nixon	Vietnam talks break off	59	51	−8	1
1968/1	Johnson	Tet offensive-*Pueblo*	48	41	−7	5
1975/4	Ford	Cambodia falls	44	39	−5	2
1951/4	Truman	MacArthur recalled	28	24	−4	2
1960/5	Eisenhower	Japan trip canceled	65	61	−4	1
1950/11	Truman	China intervenes	39	36	−3	7
1951/8	Truman	Korean talks break off	31	30	−1	1
1957/10	Eisenhower	*Sputnik* launched	57	60	+3	1
1960/5	Eisenhower	U-2 incident	62	65	+3	1

Source: Jong R. Lee, "Rallying around the Flag: Foreign Policy Events and Presidential Popularity," *Presidential Studies Quarterly* 7 (Fall 1977): 254-255; and Center for the Study of the Presidency, New York, N.Y.

The Great Communicator: Reagan after Grenada, 1983

Reagan was falling in public esteem immediately after the deaths of 241 marines in Beirut on October 23, 1983, and the invasion of the Caribbean island of Grenada on October 25. His response, on October 27, came in the form of a masterful television address to the nation that immediately boosted his ratings and had a chilling effect on critics. (These findings are from national *Washington Post/ABC News* opinion polls the evening before and the evening after the address.)

Q: Would you say the United States is trying to do too much with its armed forces overseas, or not?

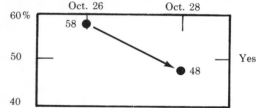

Q: Do you approve of the way Reagan is handling the situation in Lebanon?

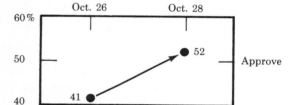

Q: Would you say you approve or disapprove of the invasion of Grenada by U.S. troops?

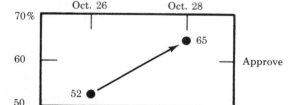

Q: Do you approve or disapprove of the way Ronald Reagan is handling his job as president?

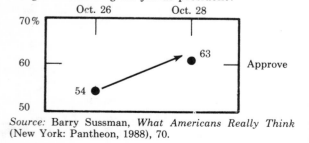

Source: Barry Sussman, *What Americans Really Think* (New York: Pantheon, 1988), 70.

ing of American hostages at the U.S. embassy in Iran and the Soviet invasion of Afghanistan (Carter); and the bombing of a discotheque in Berlin, terrorist attacks in Europe, the attack on a Korean Air Lines plane that strayed into Soviet territory, the Grenada invasion, the U.S. bombing of Libya, and the U.S. response to crises in the Philippines and Haiti (Reagan).[49]

It might be incorrect to ascribe paramount importance to either domestic or foreign policy issues for presidential popularity; both policy areas can increase or decrease the president's range of options. Domestic concerns perhaps provide a more durable base of popularity. Foreign policy events, by contrast, provide a dramatic but fleeting opportunity for the president to build popularity.

Effects of Opinion on Public Debate

Especially since the dawn of the media age, the president's popularity has been an important tool for attaining public policy goals. Presidents use information about their level of public support to persuade Congress to go along with their proposals for foreign and domestic policies.

Especially on issues on which the public has not formed strong opinions, presidents can shape public opinion simply by speaking out on an issue. The public's deep-seated desire to support its president gives the president opportunities for moving the population. A number of surveys have determined that the public is more willing to support an initiative if it knows the president proposed or backed the measure. One researcher, Corey Rosen, for example, found different samples showing different levels of support for proposals when respondents are either told or not told that the president backs the proposals.[50] The identification of the proposal with the president served to "personify" the policy and brought support in line with public approval of the president.

Political scientist Lee Sigelman used one sample to determine that public support for the policy rises when respondents are told of the president's position. Sigelman found the public less willing to go along with the president's policies as the president's position became more "radical."[51] The latter finding suggests that the president's prestige depends to a great extent on a strong base of public respect for the president's office. That respect is one of the nation's fundamental values. As presidents move away from the nation's other fundamental values with "radical" proposals, they might lose the public's automatic support.

History offers additional evidence for the academic findings of Rosen and Sigelman. Public support for President Truman's proposed aid to Greece and Turkey—which was not a prominent issue at the time—rose dramatically after Truman's speech of 1947 on the matter.[52] Support for bombing Hanoi and Haiphong increased from 50 to 80 percent after the bombing there began in 1966.[53] Before Lyndon Johnson announced a halt to bombing of North Vietnam on March 31, 1968, only 40 percent of the public opposed bombing the enemy. In early April, polls showed that 64 percent approved the bombing halt.

Samuel Kernell has argued that "going public" has at least partly replaced negotiation with other powerful actors in Washington as a means of achieving policy goals. By referring to the public's general support for the president and its support for specific policies, the White House takes the initiative away from Congress. Congress is given the choice of supporting the president's agenda or facing the wrath of voters back home.[54] Congress almost always gives the president the initiative, especially on foreign policy.[55]

Influencing Capitol Hill

The link between presidential approval ratings and support of the White House on Capitol Hill is not clear. Political scientist Richard E. Neustadt has argued that high approval ratings and poll support for specific policies help the president persuade Congress to support key policy proposals.[56] But the record of postwar presidents suggests that the link is indirect and that other factors enter into the calculation of Congress and other actors to follow the president.

One reason Congress pays attention to presidential popularity is that many members of Congress have no other regular barometer of the public mood. The president is the dominant figure in national politics, and when the public reacts to administration stands, members of Congress gain a sense of public opinion. Another reason is that the public generally expects Congress to cooperate with the president.[57]

Political scientist George C. Edwards III analyzed the president-Congress link with a statistical analysis of congressional roll-call votes and presidential popularity polls. Constituents expect their representatives to cooperate with the president, and Congress members respond to the general desires of their major supporters back home. "In effect, congressmen choose which groups within their constituencies they will represent. These groups will generally be part of their successful electoral coalitions. In addition, it is these groups with whom the congressmen are likely to communicate most frequently."[58]

Edwards found that congressional support for the president was strongest with "secure" Congress members and on foreign policy issues. Not surprisingly, Edwards found, partisanship played a role in the responses of both the Congress members and their constituents. Edwards argued that the president should "attempt to influence congressmen indirectly by strengthening his support among the American people."[59] Such a strategy, however, is limited by partisan and other considerations.

Statistical analysis by political scientist Harvey G. Zeidenstein concluded that a president's public support affects the willingness of Congress to go along with the president on key votes. Of all the congressional votes on which presidents from Eisenhower to Carter expressed a preference, 27 percent can be explained by the president's public approval ratings. The explanatory power of presidential ratings increases to 46 percent when the Eisenhower administration is removed from the sample.[60]

Eisenhower's popularity, unlike that of his successors, did not greatly influence congressional action. The Eisenhower exception helps to explain the limits of the link between presidential popularity and congressional support. Other factors were clearly more important in Eisenhower's congressional support, such as his rocky relations with his own party in Congress, an absence of divisive public issues, moderate legislative proposals, and a willingness to allow Congress to act without presidential prodding.[61]

If a president decides to use high approval ratings as a tool in working with Congress, the result could be greater acceptance of White House initiatives. Eisenhower apparently was not as inclined as other presidents to risk his personal support on specific programs. Eisenhower might have been concerned that identifying with one side in a controversial matter would give the other side reason to reduce its support for him.

There are many examples of the link of popularity and congressional action. Congress went along with President Reagan's budget, tax, and military policies during the height of his popularity but started to distance itself from Reagan when he struggled. Congress cut off funds for the Vietnam War as President Nixon's popularity plunged.

Public Opinion

The regularity of polling operations on every conceivable issue gives the president and other political figures the opportunity to shape public opinion and react to it.

Pollsters gather information daily about the ways all kinds of citizens think on a variety of issues, including many hypothetical situations. Polling data include combinations of conditions to which the polling subject can respond. The president can anticipate the way the population—and specific groups of the population—will react to large and small initiatives on any issue imaginable. By analyzing polling data, the president can know, for example, what the Jewish population thinks about the administration's policies in Lebanon and other parts of the Middle East and what it thinks about different approaches to the broad problems as well as the minor elements of the situation.

With the inevitable decline in popularity, the president is inclined to take dramatic, public actions to improve poll ratings. Presidential leadership then "tilts" toward dramatic actions designed to bolster approval ratings rather than concerted effort and cooperation with other government officials to deal with complex problems.

George Gallup relates the public's desire for strong leadership to the president's sometimes feverish activity to boost ratings:

> I would say that any sharp drop in popularity is likely to come from the president's inaction in the face of an important crisis. Inaction hurts a president more than anything else. A president can take some action, even a wrong one, and not lose his popularity.... People tend to judge a man by his goals, what he's trying to do, and not necessarily by what he accomplishes or how well he succeeds. People used to tell us over and over again about all the things that Roosevelt did wrong and then they would say, "I'm all for him, though, because his heart is in the right place; he's trying."[62]

Recent events appear to support Gallup's statement: Nixon's trips to the Soviet Union and China in 1974 during the height of the Watergate controversy, Ford's military action against Cambodia after the attack on the *Mayaguez,* Carter's dramatic actions after the Soviet invasion of Afghanistan and the Iranian seizure of hostages, and Reagan's Grenada and Libya attacks.

Implications of Polling

Changes in public opinion measurement have produced a fundamental alteration in the way groups press political demands and political leaders respond to those problems. Scholars have disagreed about whether a system with constant polling promotes or damages democracy.

Some argue that regular polling makes political leaders responsive to the wishes of the electorate more than infrequent elections ever could. Gallup, one of the pioneers of modern polling, maintains that elected officials can be expected to do a better job if they have "an accurate measure of the wishes, aspirations, and needs of different groups within the general public."[63] Behavior in office that is influenced by polls is a kind of rolling election campaign, with officials constantly on the lookout for ways to please and avoid displeasing the public.

Proponents of polling stress the "scientific" nature of findings and the increasingly sophisticated views of the political landscape that well-done polls offer. If gathered comprehensively, proponents say, polls can offer a more complete picture of politics than any other single tool.

Others disagree. Political scientist Benjamin Ginsberg argues that polls have the effect of stifling public expressions rather than measuring them in a neutral manner for voter-conscious political leaders.

The regular assessment of a wide variety of public attitudes—where a diverse range of issues is assessed according to the many demographic characteristics of survey respondents—enables the government to "manage" demands rather than dealing with the complex problems that produce political demands. By determining which groups in society would object to certain governmental actions, the government is able to adapt its policies and presentation of those policies to avoid conflict. Many issues, then, never receive the full public discussion that they might if the public pulse were not so regularly tested.

Ginsberg cites a federal conservation program that surveys found to have aroused opposition in southern communities. Rather than canceling the program or negotiating with citizens, administrators used polling data to pinpoint the public's most nagging concerns and use propaganda to dispell those concerns.

> Opinion surveys provided officials with more or less reliable information about current popular sentiment, offered a guide to the character of the public relations efforts that might usefully be made, and served as means of measuring the effect of "information programs" on a target population. In essence, polling allowed officials a better opportunity to anticipate, regulate, and manipulate popular attitudes.[64]

Presidents Carter and Reagan employed full-time White House pollsters who monitored the vagaries of public opinion among all imaginable demographic groups. Other parts of the federal government—from executive departments and agencies to Congress—also use polls regularly to monitor and shape public opinion. To the extent that such polling allows public officials to head off a full discussion of major issues, critics argue, democracy is thwarted.

Ginsberg also is concerned about the way polling shapes the expression of public opinion. He has argued that poll data channel political expression into formulations provided by the pollster that discourage group political action. Besides allowing government officials to manage public opinion, polls have four possible negative effects on democratic expression.

First, polling eliminates the cost of expressing an opinion, which reduces the influence of the people most concerned and knowledgable about various issues. Polls tally the preferences of cross-sections of the population that include people who do not know or care about issues. The respondent's knowledge and the issue's salience are usually ignored. "Polls, in effect, submerge individuals with strongly held views in a more apathetic mass public."[65]

Second, polls shift the concern of public debate from behavior to attitudes. Where expressions of opinion previously took the form of demonstrations that required some kind of public interaction, polls simply tally the isolated responses of survey subjects. Polls give the government the opportunity to shape opinion before it can enjoy full debate, thereby reducing public engagement.

Third, polls shift politics from the group to the individual. Before polls, citizens needed to band together to express their desires and demands. Such a requirement served to build political institutions such as parties, unions, neighborhood groups, and farmer cooperatives. Active involvement in such groups has declined as public officials have turned to polls for information about public opinion.

Fourth, polls shift political expression from assertions to responses. Survey subjects can react only to the agenda of the poll-taker; they rarely make an independent assertion. The subjects that respondents—and therefore, the public—can discuss is thereby limited to the interests of pollsters.

Notes

1. E. E. Schattschneider, *The Semisovereign People* (New York: Holt, Rinehart, and Winston, 1960).
2. This discussion relies mostly on the following studies by Fred I. Greenstein: "Popular Images of the President," *American Journal of Psychiatry* 122, no. 5 (November 1965): 523-529; "The Benevolent Leader: Children's Images of Presidential Authority," *American Political Science Review* 54 (December 1960): 934-943; "College Student Reactions to the Assassination of President Kennedy," in *Communication in Crisis*, ed. B. Greenberg and E. Parker (Stanford, Calif.: Stanford University Press, 1965); and "What the President Means to Americans," in *Choosing the President*, ed. James David Barber (Englewood Cliffs, N.J.: Prentice-Hall, 1974), 121-147. See also Roberta S. Sigel, "Image of the American Presidency, Part II of An Exploration into Popular Views of Presidential Power," *Midwest Journal of Political Science* 10 (February 1966): 123-137.
3. Greenstein, "What the President Means to Americans," 125, 128-129.
4. The respect for the presidency is not uniformly strong. Groups that are left out of the mainstream of economic and political life, such as blacks and Appalachian whites, respond less favorably to mention of the presidency and specific presidents.
5. Murray Edelman, *The Symbolic Uses of Politics* (Urbana: University of Illinois Press, 1985), 78.
6. Samuel Kernell, Peter W. Sperlich, and Aaron Wildavsky, "Public Support for Presidents," in *Perspectives on the Presidency*, ed. Aaron Wildavsky (Boston: Little, Brown, 1975), 150, 158-164.
7. For examinations of consensus in U.S. politics, see Louis Hartz, *The Liberal Tradition in America* (New York: Harcourt, Brace, Jovanovich, 1955); Daniel Boorstin, *The Genius of American Democracy* (Chicago: University of Chicago Press, 1958); Daniel Bell, *The End of Ideology* (Glencoe, Ill.: Free Press, 1960); and Samuel H. Beer, "In Search of a New Political Philosophy," in *The New American Political System*, ed. Anthony King (Washington, D.C.: American Enterprise Institute, 1978), 5-44.
8. Benjamin Ginsberg, *The Captive Public* (New York: Basic Books, 1986), 61.

9. Theodore J. Lowi, *The End of Liberalism* (New York: Norton, 1979), 91.

10. Michael Lipsky, "Protest as a Political Resource," *American Political Science Review* 62 (December 1968): 1144-1158.

11. Richard A. Cloward and Frances Fox Piven, "Toward a Class-Based Realignment of American Politics: A Movement Strategy," *Social Policy* (Winter 1983): 8.

12. Ginsberg, *Captive Public*, 56-57.

13. See Frances Fox Piven and Richard A. Cloward, *Regulating the Poor* (New York: Random House, 1972), and *Poor People's Movements* (New York: Random House, 1979).

14. Quoted in Michael E. McGerr, *The Decline of Popular Politics* (New York: Oxford University Press, 1986), 22.

15. Daniel Boorstin, *The Americans: The Democratic Experience* (New York: Random House, 1973), 403.

16. Leila Sussman, "Dear Mr. President," in *Readings in American Public Opinion*, ed. Edward E. Walker et al. (New York: American Book Company, 1968).

17. Barry Sussman, *What Americans Really Think* (New York: Pantheon Books, 1988), 336.

18. Ibid., 226.

19. James R. Beniger and Robert J. Guiffra, Jr., "Public Opinion Polling: Command and Control in Presidential Campaigns," in *Presidential Selection*, ed. Alexander Heard and Michael Nelson (Durham, N.C.: Duke University Press, 1987), 189.

20. Larry J. Sabato, *The Rise of Political Consultants* (New York: Basic Books, 1981), 105.

21. Herbert Asher, *Polling and the Public* (Washington, D.C.: CQ Press, 1988), 13.

22. For a critique of Caddell's conception of politics and polling, see Sidney Blumenthal, "Mr. Smith Goes to Washington," *The New Republic*, February 6, 1984, 17-20.

23. Jimmy Carter, *Keeping Faith* (New York: Bantam Books, 1982), 114.

24. Sabato, *Rise of Political Consultants*, 74-75.

25. Carter, *Keeping Faith*, 123.

26. Laurence I. Barrett, *Gambling with History* (New York: Doubleday, 1983), 351-352.

27. Sussman, *What Americans Really Think*, 35-36.

28. Philip E. Converse, "Changing Conceptions of Public Opinion in the Political Process," *Public Opinion Quarterly* 51 (1987): 22.

29. Some scholars argue that the honeymoon is no longer something a new president can rely upon. See Karen S. Johnson, "The Honeymoon Period: Fact or Fiction," *Journalism Quarterly* 62 (Winter 1985): 869-876.

30. Gary King and Lyn Ragsdale, *The Elusive Executive: Discovering Statistical Patterns in the Presidency* (Washington, D.C.: CQ Press, 1988), 295-307.

31. Political scientist Theodore J. Lowi has argued that the honeymoon, the period in which presidents try "sincerely to succeed according to their oath and their promises," is the only opportunity for the president to achieve major policy gains—and that period is shortening. See Lowi, *The Personal President*, (Ithaca, N.Y.: Cornell University Press, 1985), 7-11.

32. King and Ragsdale, *The Elusive Executive*, 292-293.

33. See John E. Mueller, *War, Presidents, and Public Opinion* (New York: Wiley, 1973). Mueller's shorter works include "Presidential Popularity from Truman to Johnson," *American Political Science Review* 64 (March 1970): 18-34; and "Trends in Popular Support for the Wars in Korea and Vietnam," *American Political Science Review* 65 (June 1971): 358-375.

34. James A. Stimson, "Public Support for American Presidents: A Cyclical Model," *Public Opinion Quarterly* 40 (Spring 1976): 1-21.

35. Ibid., 10.

36. See the works by Mueller and Jong R. Lee, "Rallying Around the Flag: Foreign-Policy Events and Presidential Popularity," *Presidential Studies Quarterly* 7 (Fall 1977): 252-256.

37. Thomas E. Cronin, *The State of the Presidency* (Boston: Little, Brown, 1980), 84.

38. King and Ragsdale, 296-307.

39. This discussion relies on John E. Mueller, "Public Opinion and the President," in *The Presidency Reappraised*, ed. Rexford G. Tugwell and Thomas E. Cronin (New York: Praeger, 1974), 133-147. It should be emphasized that the categories overlap; for example, a citizen can have elements of both the partisan and the follower.

40. See ibid. and Richard A. Brody and Benjamin I. Page, "The Impact of Events on Presidential Popularity: The Johnson and Nixon Administrations," in *Perspectives on the Presidency*, ed. Wildavsky, esp. 145: "Foreign events reach people through news reports, [while] some domestic events, like real personal income, may be perceived without mediation."

41. Eric B. Herzik and Mary L. Dodson have suggested that the "climate of expectations" has more to do with the president's personal appeal than with programmatic plans ("The President and Public Expectations: A Research Note," *Presidential Studies Quarterly* 12 [Spring 1982], 168-173).

42. Mueller, "Presidential Popularity," 20-21.

43. Richard A. Brody, "Public Evaluations and Expectations and the Future of the Presidency," in *Problems and Prospects of Presidential Leadership in the 1980's*, ed. James Sterling Young (New York: University Press of America, 1982), 45-49. See also Stanley Kelley, *Interpreting Elections* (Princeton, N.J.: Princeton University Press, 1983), for a similar view of how voters make judgments.

44. David Green, *Shaping Political Consciousness* (New York: Oxford University Press, 1988), 126-134.

45. Kristen R. Monroe, "Inflation and Presidential Popularity," *Presidential Studies Quarterly* 9 (Summer 1979): 339. See also Kristen R. Monroe, "Economic Influences on Presidential Popularity," *Public Opinion Quarterly* (1978): 360-370. Kim Ezra Sheinbaum and Ervin Sheinbaum, "Public Perceptions of Presidential Economic Performance: From Johnson to Carter," *Presidential Studies Quarterly* 12 (Summer 1982): 421-427, find a strong link between prosperity and popularity. Henry C. Kenski, in "The Impact of Economic Conditions on Presidential Popularity," *Journal of Politics* 39 (1977): 764-773, argues that high unemployment and inflation rates affect Republican and Democratic presidents differently.

46. Henry C. Kenski, "The Impact of Unemployment on Presidential Popularity from Eisenhower to Nixon," *Presidential Studies Quarterly* 7 (Spring-Summer 1977): 114-126.

47. Lowi's analysis of the spurts in presidential popularity is part of his overall critique of the public presidency. See Lowi, *The Personal President*.

48. Thomas Ferguson and Joel Rogers, *Right Turn* (New York: Hill and Wang, 1986), 26.

49. See Mueller, *War, Presidents, and Public Opinion*.

50. Corey Rosen, "A Test of Presidential Leadership of Public Opinion: The Split Ballot Technique," *Polity* 6 (1972): 282-290.

51. Lee Sigelman, "Gauging the Public Response to Presidential Leadership," *Presidential Studies Quarterly* 10 (Summer 1980): 427-433.

52. Samuel Kernell, "The Truman Doctrine Speech: A Case Study of the Dynamics of Presidential Opinion Leadership," *Social Science History* 1 (Fall 1976): 20-45.

53. See Mueller, *War, Presidents, and Public Opinion*.

54. Samuel Kernell, *Going Public: New Strategies of Presidential Leadership* (Washington, D.C.: CQ Press, 1986).

55. Mueller, "Public Opinion and the President," 141.

56. Richard E. Neustadt, *Presidential Power* (New York: Wiley, 1980), 64-73.

57. See George C. Edwards III, "Presidential Influence in the House: Presidential Prestige as a Source of Presidential Power," *American Political Science Review* 70 (March 1976): 101-113.

58. Edwards, "Presidential Influence in the House, " 107.

59. Ibid., 113.

60. Harvey G. Zeidenstein, "Presidential Popularity and Presidential Support in Congress: Eisenhower to Carter," *Presidential Studies Quarterly* 10 (Spring 1980): 227.

61. Ibid., 227-230. See also Harvey G. Zeidenstein, "Varying Relationships between Presidents' Popularity and Their Legisla-

tive Success," *Presidential Studies Quarterly* 13 (Fall 1983): 530-548.
62. Quoted in Edelman, *Symbolic Uses of Politics*, 78.
63. Quoted in Ginsberg, *Captive Public*, 237.
64. Ibid., 85.
65. Ibid., 65.

Selected Bibliography

Asher, Herbert. *Polling and the Public*. Washington, D.C.: CQ Press, 1988.

Edelman, Murray. *The Symbolic Uses of Politics* (Urbana: University of Illinois Press, 1985).

Ginsberg, Benjamin. *The Captive Public*. New York: Basic Books, 1986.

King, Gary, and Lyn Ragsdale. *The Elusive Executive: Discovering Statistical Patterns in the Presidency*. Washington, D.C.: CQ Press, 1988.

Lowi, Theodore, J. *The Personal President*. Ithaca, N.Y.: Cornell University Press, 1985.

Mueller, John E. *War, Presidents, and Public Opinion*. New York: Wiley, 1973.

The Presidency and Interest Groups

Balancing the demands of organized interests always has been a major part of the president's job. Observers of U.S. politics have noted Americans' distinctive tendency to form private associations to pursue their political ends, as well as the president's difficulty controlling such groups.

An interest group may be defined as a set of people who form associations to promote ideals or material benefits. Groups usually know in advance what ends they want to pursue, but their goals and tactics evolve according to their relationship with other forces in society. Because interest groups usually seek assistance available only from the public, they often go to the government with their claims.

In U.S. politics, the president has played a greater role in interest group activity in the years following the New Deal and World War II.[1]

Constitutional Debate about "Factions"

Debate over the U.S. Constitution framed the major issues of interest group politics that occupy students of U.S. government today. After the completion of the Constitution in Philadelphia in 1787, Federalists and Anti-Federalists debated about the best way to achieve adequate "energy" in the federal government and the presidency without stifling free debate and competition among social groups, which are central to a democratic society. The debate's basic tension has persisted to the modern day.

James Madison presented what has come to be the main justification for interest group politics.[2] In *Federalist* No. 10, Madison argued that separate, competing interests were inevitable in a free society and that trying to snuff out this competition would require the drastic step of curbing free thought and action. The goal of government should not be to ban interest groups, Madison argued, but to control them by competition. In *Federalist* No. 10, Madison wrote:

> As long as the reason of man continues fallible, and he is at liberty to exercise it, different opinions will be formed.... From the protection of different and unequal faculties of acquiring property, the possession of different

degrees and kinds of property immediately results; and from the influence of these on the sentiments and views of the respective proprietors ensues a division of the society into different interests and parties.[3]

Alexis de Tocqueville, a nineteenth-century French aristocrat, argued in his classic study *Democracy in America* that the "equality of conditions" and the lack of a feudal tradition in the United States gave Americans the freedom to pursue their interests by using large and small associations. Tocqueville wrote:

> Americans of all ages, all conditions, and all dispositions, constantly form associations. They have not only commercial and manufacturing companies, but associations of a thousand other kinds—religious, moral, serious, futile, general or restricted, enormous or diminutive.... Wherever, at the head of some new undertaking, you see the government in France, or a man of rank in England, in the United States you will be sure to find an association.[4]

Tocqueville argued that the American condition was a double-edged sword. He feared that the United States could develop into a "tyranny of the majority" because equality would undermine citizens' willingness to be tolerant of people who express unpopular ideas or have different characteristics. But he said equality and freedom of expression also enabled a variety of institutions—newspapers, the legal profession, and interest groups—to brake the tendency of majorities to impose their will on the entire population.

When Tocqueville published his work in 1835 and 1840, interest groups were established mainly at the local level. State and local governments had control over most matters of public life, including property laws, banking and commerce, morals, education, use of land and resources, and criminal procedures. The states and localities also played an important part in developing "internal improvements," such as roads, canals, railroads, schools, hospitals, and agricultural enterprises.[5]

John C. Calhoun, one of the South's great champions in the nineteenth century, developed another doctrine of interest groups that had a profound effect on U.S. history. Calhoun's theory of "concurrent majorities" asserts that the legitimacy of national government action depends on the acquiescence of the interests affected by the action. The distinct interests of the states, Calhoun said, deserved protection from the larger interests of the nation. Calhoun argued that a state could "nullify," or veto, federal actions

By Charles C. Euchner

that usurp state independence.

Calhoun's home state of South Carolina invoked the doctrine of nullification after enactment of a tariff bill in 1828 that state officials considered to be discriminatory against the South. President Andrew Jackson responded by sending warships to the harbor of Charleston, and, soon after, the state legislature revoked the act of nullification.

Even though Jackson defeated the most extreme form of concurrent majorities, the theory remained a part of U.S. politics. The notion that states' rights have priority over the national interest led to the Civil War. After the war, the states' rights view held considerable sway in national political debate. In the compromise over the 1876 presidential election, the national government ceded considerable autonomy to the states over issues of basic civil rights and commerce.

When the states' rights view crumbled as the national government's rise gained strength in the twentieth century, a doctrine similar in many ways to Calhoun's theory arose. Especially since the Great Society of the 1960s, a practice that might be called "representational democracy" has guided policy making in national politics. This practice encourages or requires the government to gain the consent of groups affected by legislation or regulations before it implements such policies.

The "Two Republics" of U.S. History

As political scientist Theodore J. Lowi has argued, the United States has progressed into two distinct styles of government which he calls the first and second "republics." The national government in the early years of the United States was a "patronage state" based on the demands for internal improvements by governments and businesses at the state and local level.[6] The national party system, with the president at

its apex, played an important role in the process of internal development. That process remained fundamentally parochial—congressional and party leaders from the states merely vied for a fair share of patronage—until Franklin D. Roosevelt's New Deal programs of the 1930s.

National politics developed cohesion in the nineteenth century at least partly because of the development of presidential leadership. Regional politics have always been important because the different demands for internal improvements stem from the needs of the distinctive geographic, economic, and social makeups of different areas. But since national party alliances developed around presidential elections, the president has always been an important part of the system of development.

Starting with the administrations of Theodore Roosevelt and Woodrow Wilson, and developing full strength during Franklin Roosevelt's New Deal, the federal government took on more and more general regulation of the economy. Rather than simply dole out resources to discrete states and constituencies, the government began to play an important role in the management of almost all aspects of political and economic life.

In time, the federal government regulated the everyday activities of a wide range of enterprises, such as banking, labor relations, transportation systems, the media, mining and development of natural resources, manufacturing, product safety, farming, the environment, and civil rights. These enterprises therefore saw a greater need for a regular presence in Washington. Rather than simply seeking direct material rewards from the government—and then using those rewards as they saw fit—a wide variety of enterprises saw even the most mundane business practices regulated by the government. The government continued to offer material rewards, but those rewards had strings attached. Enterprises therefore saw a greater need to establish a permanent presence in Washington to influence the federal agencies and committees that controlled those strings. As the government's regulation of all aspects of economic and social life increased, interest groups sprung up to influence the way the government controlled their affairs.

Library of Congress

President Calvin Coolidge meets with members of the Sioux Indian Republican Club in March 1925.

Modern Interest Group Politics

Interest group politics boomed with the New Deal of Franklin Roosevelt. Today, interest groups are one of the most important parts of national politics. Estimates of the number of interest groups in operation are not entirely reliable, but they are suggestive. A 1929 study estimated that five hundred interest groups were at work in Washington at the time. A 1977 study estimated thirteen hundred interest groups in the nation's capital, and a 1980 study found seventeen hundred. Another indication of the interest group explosion is a survey that found that 30 percent of all groups active in 1980 organized in the previous twenty years. Of 200 groups surveyed in 1980, two-fifths had offices in Washington just since 1970 and three-fifths since 1960.[7]

Those figures underestimate the amount of interest group activity because of the even more extensive activity of national organizations at the state and local level. For example, the Chamber of Commerce and the American Federation of Labor-Congress of Industrial Organizations (AFL-CIO) each count as one interest group in the Washington surveys, but they have many subdivisions across the nation. The chamber, for example, has seventy thousand firms and individuals as members, along with twenty-five hundred state and local chapters. The AFL-CIO includes some fourteen million dues-paying members in more than one hundred affiliates.[8]

Political action committees (PACs) boomed in the 1970s and 1980s after election finance laws were changed in 1974.[9] PACs are essentially checkbook organizations that depend on sophisticated direct mail techniques to raise money for election campaigns, lobbying, and research. They do not have the active membership programs and tangible benefits that other groups like the AFL-CIO have. PACs have become a major contributor to federal and statewide campaigns. In November 1975, just 722 PACs were in business; by 1982, the figure was 3,400.[10]

Interest groups have increased their role in national politics partly because of the decline of political parties, the fragmentation of Congress, the rise of regulatory politics, the greater complexity of many government issues, and changes in the style of campaigning. Interest groups represent the politics of specialization, whereas the political style in the United States previously was generalist.

Modern Theories of Interest Groups

Since the rise of the modern bureaucratic state, scholars have developed theories to justify or explain the place of interest groups in politics. One of the predominant theories of U.S politics uses a market model to justify the role of interest groups in policy making. Sociologist Arthur Bentley argued in 1908 that pursuit of the public interest is misguided; the sum total of government, he argued, was the result of groups competing for position and favor.[11] Interest groups, Bentley maintained, had a "representative quality" that ensured a degree of democratic activity as groups competed for influence.

Political scientist David Truman argued in 1951 that the result of interest group competition and bargaining was a consensus on the public interest.[12] Truman's model resembles the economic model of Adam Smith, which holds that an "invisible hand" guides self-interested competition among firms toward the public interest. According to Truman, the interaction of groups enables a variety of viewpoints and material interests to get a public hearing. The result is a democratic contest over policy at all levels. Political scientist Robert A. Dahl reached similar conclusions in a 1961 study of community power.[13]

Later students of interest groups have disputed the cheery view of pluralists such as Bentley, Truman, and Dahl. Political scientist E. E. Schattschneider and sociologists C. Wright Mills and Floyd Hunter have argued that the interests of economically disadvantaged groups do not receive adequate representation simply because they do not have the resources to press their causes.[14] These scholars maintain that the makeup of the interest group "universe" has an elite bias.[15]

In perhaps the most influential work to question the assumption that citizens easily form groups to represent their interests, economist Mancur Olson argued that many groups with a definite stake in government actions have difficulty organizing because of limited resources and limited incentives for individuals to join the cause.[16] Group formation is most likely when groups can offer material incentives or even can coerce prospective members. Labor unions with automatic deduction of dues from workers' checks are a form of membership coercion. Because the less advantaged groups in society have a smaller "surplus" to spend on political action, they lose out in the competition for influence over the government.

Another critique of interest group politics stresses the "overload" of modern bureaucratic politics. Sociologist Daniel Bell has argued that economic forces have displaced their conflicts to the federal government, asking it to provide entitlements to paper over fundamental contradictions, such as the management—labor and business—environmentalist schisms. "One large question that the American system now confronts is whether it can find a way to resolve these conflicts. Lacking rules to mediate claims, the system will be under severe strains."[17]

A growing danger is erosion of government authority and legitimacy. Rather than integrating citizens into a process of mutual accommodation with a goal of the public interest, interest groups often isolate citizens from one another. The common purpose that is the hallmark of republican theory is lost to self-interested competition that does not recognize common social destiny.[18]

The autonomy given to many interest groups removes many policies from democratic deliberation and reduces the maneuvering room on issues that are on the public agenda. For example, the control given farmers over prices and land cultivation removes agriculture policy from the general debate about how society should allocate resources. Because they are often non-negotiable, policies on agriculture, Social Security, Medicare, job training, and military spending reduce the options for the president and Congress on a wide variety of budget and social issues.

In Theodore Lowi's view, by giving groups autonomy over parts of public policy, the public loses control over the wide range of interrelated issues. The system is inflexible; options for policy are closed.[19]

How the President Deals with Interest Groups

Most students of U.S. national politics conclude that interest group activity is concentrated on the specific bureaucratic agencies and congressional committees that address the particular concerns of organized interests—not on the White House. For example, farmers deal with the Department of Agriculture and the congressional committees that allocate money to farm programs.

Interest groups do not concentrate on the White House for a number of reasons. First, the schedule of the president and top presidential aides is tight, so it is difficult even to get the president's time and attention. It is much easier to get the attention of a member of Congress or of a civil servant. One aide to President Johnson explained: "There are 535 opportunities in Congress and only one in the White House. You get an hour to present your case before each representative, and only fifteen minutes once a year with the president. Where would you put your effort?" [20]

Second, the president's tenure in office is short compared to the terms of key bureaucrats and members of Congress. Postwar presidents have served an average of only five and a half years. Much of the president's time is spent learning the ropes or struggling with "lame duck" status.

Even when presidents are at full strength, they usually devote their time to a few top priorities—and those priorities are shaped by previous alliances. Only occasionally can an interest group alter a president's set agenda. Finally, the president is the nation's most public political figure, and interest groups usually operate best out of the glare of public attention where they can promote their interests through small legislative and regulatory means. Seeking a shift in important duties, for example, is a matter best addressed by Commerce Department bureaucrats, not by the president.

Even if interest groups favor the predictability of agencies and committees, many have a relationship with the presidency. Since World War II, the presidency has developed regular channels for interest groups to make and receive appeals. The size of the White House staff has increased greatly, with many officials assigned in some way to keep track of interest groups. The most formal mechanism for dealing with interest groups is the Office of Public Liaison, created in the administrations of Richard Nixon and Gerald R. Ford. *(See "A Greater White House Role," p. 97, in this chapter.)*

Political scientist Robert Salisbury has noted that interest groups often "tend to gravitate toward the effective centers of power in a given political system." As the White House has become the initiator of national politics, it has become the focus for at least some policy areas such as economic and security policy, and even minor matters such as prayer in schools—even if the bulk of policies are better tended in the bureaucracy and congressional committees. The White House may not be the focus of all interest group activity, but neither is it a place of last resort for groups.[21]

Some authorities maintain that the president has an advantage in dealing with lobbies. The White House "is less likely to be besieged at its most vulnerable points because lobbyists are less likely to know where those points are," according to political scientists Michael Baruch Grossman and Martha Joynt Kumar.[22]

Although interest groups have difficulty finding a point of entry into the White House, they do know their way around the executive bureaucracy. The White House must then struggle to get control over the huge and complex bureaucracy.

The White House and Interest Groups

The ongoing calculations of interest group politics at the White House depend on a number of factors. Perhaps the most important consideration is which interests have supported the president during previous political campaigns and government initiatives. As when dealing with public opinion, the president must maintain the steady backing of a basic core of supporters and bring independents and opposition figures into alliances for different issues. For example, when campaigning for his tax-cutting initiative in 1981, President Reagan could count on the support of large organized business interests. To secure passage of the legislation, Reagan worked to bring other groups such as labor unions and small businesses into his alliance.

Interest group alliances shift from issue to issue. Most groups do not get involved in legislative or regulatory activity outside their direct interests; groups become active when they see a possible gain or threat in government initiatives. Large-scale policy making entails a wider array of competing groups than "incrementalist" policy making. As a result, presidents must consider the extent to which their initiatives will activate interest groups. Business and organized labor often switch sides depending on the issue. The two groups often work together on issues such as construction projects, banking regulation, and other legislation affecting economic "growth." They oppose each other on issues affecting the organization of the workplace, such as "common site" picketing (picketing of a workplace by workers not directly involved in the dispute), "right to work" (restrictions on union organizing), and workplace safety legislation.

Another factor in the shifting interest group calculations is the salience of issues and the timing of events. As economist Anthony Downs has noted, issues have a cycle of attention.[23] After a period of high publicity, most issues tend to fade from public consciousness. The president can bring attention to issues, but the public and interest groups still react according to their own priorities at the time. The president must respond to issues put on the public agenda by concerted interest group efforts.

The president must take into account—and influence, if possible—just how much attention the public is giving an issue and how groups are responding to that attention. Ronald Reagan, long a critic of federal coercion of states, signed legislation in 1984 to penalize states that did not increase the mandatory drinking age to twenty-one after a lengthy campaign by Mothers Against Drunk Driving (MADD) and other citizen's groups produced high public awareness of the problem. At a different time, Reagan probably would have resisted such legislation.

A final factor in the calculations is the relative strength of different interest groups. The membership, wealth, and status of various advocacy organizations varies greatly. Most interest groups have just a few hundred members and budgets in the hundreds of thousands of dollars. Others have multimillion-dollar-budgets, a large membership that can be deployed swiftly on various campaigns, and professional staffs and consultants to advise them. Many are connected with corporations that they can use for overhead expenses, expert advise, technology, and membership lists.

The White House examines the balance of power

Pete Souza, The White House

During his presidency, Ronald Reagan frequently criticized federal coercion of states. In 1984, however, he signed legislation to penalize states that did not increase the mandatory drinking age to twenty-one after a lengthy campaign by Mothers Against Drunk Driving.

among interest groups on specific issues before it plans strategy. That is not to say that the president decides which side of the issue to take based on this balance of power, only whether to attempt to influence the issue and if so, what tactics to use. Jimmy Carter decided to withdraw the second Strategic Arms Limitation Talks (SALT) treaty from the Senate in 1980 after the Soviet Union's invasion of Afghanistan dramatically altered public opinion and the alignment of interest groups.[24] President Reagan decided to pursue "omnibus" budget-cutting reconciliation legislation in 1981 when a wide range of interest groups appeared ready to defeat the administration, issue by issue, in congressional committees. The package cut $130.6 billion from the federal budget over four years.[25]

The president's relationship with interest groups usually develops issue by issue. The president can rely on certain groups always to be supportive and others always to offer opposition; the president usually must seek the support of many fence-straddling groups. Groups traditionally aligning with Republican presidents include business, oil companies, conservative social groups, and some farm groups. Traditional Democratic allies include many multinational firms, labor, environmental groups, blacks, and developers.

Sometimes the president is so concerned about the appearance of interest group activity that the White House will ask supporters to lobby discreetly or not at all. The Reagan administration kept a distance from Teamsters officials, for example, when they were under indictment for corruption in the mid-1980s. In the 1980s, responding to criticism that the Democrats are a party of special interests, Democratic leaders have sought to create an image of independence from supporters such as blacks and Hispanics, feminists, gays, and teachers. After the 1984 campaign, Paul Kirk, chairman of the Democratic National Committee, withdrew party recognition of seven party caucuses for specific groups.[26]

Inevitably, interest groups that supported the president during campaigns become disenchanted with the administration's performance. Organized labor, civil rights groups, mayors, social workers, and advocates of a national health system were disappointed with President Carter's policies—particularly after his budget and defense priorities shifted in the second half of his term. This disappoint-

ment led many to urge Sen. Edward M. Kennedy (D-Mass.) to challenge Carter for the 1980 nomination. The "New Right" groups that supported Reagan's candidacy in 1980 later were upset that Reagan was not more vigorous in promoting their agenda, such as prayer in the schools, tuition tax credits for private schools, and an antiabortion constitutional amendment.

Influencing the Interest Group Balance of Power

Even if presidents are limited in their dealings with interest groups on particular issues, they influence the balance of power among competing interest groups. Presidential use of public opinion, budget priorities, and White House staff can enhance some groups and undercut others. In this way, the president can "set the table" for later political conflicts.

Political scientists Martin Shefter and Benjamin Ginsberg have identified three strategies for a president to shape the makeup of the interest group universe.[27] First, the president can try to transform the identities of established and nascent groups. Second, the president can "divide and conquer" existing alliances of groups and attempt to bring fragments of the old alliance under White House influence. Third, the president can attempt to bring estranged groups together on an issue in a movement where they find common interest.

Franklin Roosevelt provides a textbook example of presidential influence over interest group alignment. Roosevelt gave a number of groups—such as the elderly, labor, and the "third of a nation" that was poor—a positive new identity that led to their involvement in Democratic politics. The New Deal offered a wide range of incentives to certain businesses to support the president, thereby chipping them away from a strong business alliance that had been hostile to previous liberal initiatives. Finally, by stressing the common desire for economic security, Roosevelt forged an alliance of ethnic groups in similarly vulnerable economic positions.[28]

Postwar presidencies steadily expanded the number of interest groups involved in national politics. The expansion of federal regulation over civil rights, workplace safety, consumer products, the environment, trade requirements, energy production and prices, air travel, and home building continued through the Carter administration, regardless of the president's party. That regulatory expansion, added to the hundreds of federal programs and studies, increased the stake of interest groups in the federal government.

Lyndon Johnson's Great Society led to the creation of many new interest groups. Domestic initiatives in housing, community development, job training, education, and health care included specific instructions to involve the communities and interests involved in the programs. The most famous example is the Economic Opportunity Act, which requires some urban programs to be "developed, conducted, and administered with the maximum feasible participation of residents of the areas and members of the groups served." The "maximum feasible participation" provision was among the most controversial 1960s programs. Proponents maintained that the provision allowed poor people to develop self-esteem and political skills so they could become self-sufficient members of society. Opponents argued that it simply gave antagonistic groups resources to undermine the government's efforts.[29]

A president's program does not need an explicit demand for participation to promote interest groups. In fact, such provisions have a minor effect compared with the way a president's budget priorities provide the resources and incentives for interest groups. Robert Reischauer, an official of the Urban League, has explained:

> In each area of federal involvement a powerful network of interest groups developed. First there were the representatives of the recipient governments. These included not only interest groups representing governors, mayors, city managers, county executives, state legislators, and the like, but also recipient agency organizations such as chief state school officers, public welfare directors, and highway commissioners. All told, some seventy-two groups of this sort existed. A second element of the network consisted of the general providers of the services provided by the grants—organized teachers, builders of public housing, and so forth. The recipients of the services also formed an element in this network—ranging from welfare recipients to P.T.A. organizations to automobile clubs. Private-sector suppliers of the inputs needed to provide the services also joined the effort. These organizations might represent the producers of library shelves, manufacturers of school buses, book publishers, or asphalt suppliers. The academics and private-sector consulting firms that made a living evaluating existing programs and planning and designing new programs also formed an element in the support group for the grants strategy.[30]

The Reagan administration skillfully transformed the interest group balance of power.[31] First, the president gave greater visibility to many groups. Reagan attracted the support of southern white conservative groups by appealing not to past racial issues but to the moral concerns of their evangelical churches and organizations. The network of churches throughout the South served as a base for organizing on issues ranging from school prayer to nuclear arms policy. Reagan also helped shift the focus of many blue-collar workers to stress their patriotism and devotion to family issues such as opposition to abortion. The president appealed to middle-class voters not on the basis of federal programs—which they favored and he wanted to cut—but as overburdened taxpayers.

Reagan's policies also unified many groups long at odds. Protestants and Catholics came together with common concerns about abortion and other "moral" issues

pertaining to personal values. Corporations and small domestic businesses—long antagonistic on tariff, trade, and tax issues—united on environmental, consumer, and other regulatory concerns. Middle-class professionals, who often had sided with Democrats and liberals on social issues, were drawn to the Reagan camp with tax cuts.

Many alliances split over Reagan administration initiatives—business and labor on issues of regulation, college-educated professionals over taxes, and beneficiaries of federal programs over tax and budget cuts. Business and labor, which previously allied on many regulatory issues, for example, split in the late 1970s and early 1980s as deregulation led to the rise of nonunion firms that undersold unionized firms. Consumer groups also opposed former allies in business and labor.

Reagan's approach to interest groups extended beyond the federal government. With the budget cuts of 1981 and with his celebration of voluntarism and state and local government Reagan shifted the focus of interest group activity. Reagan's emphasis on nonfederal programs for addressing social problems increased the work of interest groups at the state level. The increased reliance on "public-private partnerships" and voluntarism limited the notion of public responsibility for social problems. The president's task force on private sector initiatives was dominated by business people. Even though Reagan's tax policies reduced incentives for corporate giving, and even though Reagan argued that he was not seeking to replace vital services with private action, his celebration of voluntary action took some of the political pressure off the administration for its budget cuts.[32]

Reagan came to Washington determined to "defund" what he considered to be irresponsible liberal interest groups. Many groups such as environmentalists and legal advocates depended on the federal government for some support, but Reagan cut that support in 1981.

Any president's policies are bound to rouse interest groups that oppose the administration. Many groups develop or improve their organization in response to threats they perceive from the White House. President Nixon's grain export policies led to the creation of the American Agriculture Movement.[33] Independent oil companies organized on a large scale for the first time when President Carter pushed a windfall profits tax.[34] Labor, environmental, women's rights, Social Security, civil rights, and public interest groups improved their membership and fund-raising efforts in response to Reagan policies. Those groups used the negative images of officials such as Interior Secretary James G. Watt, Attorney General Edwin Meese III, and Judge Robert H. Bork as part of their direct mail fundraising appeals and rallies. The Sierra Club's membership almost doubled from 180,000 to 300,000 during Watt's tenure at the Department of Interior.[35]

A number of grass-roots organizations developed sophisticated operations and national bases in their campaigns against Reagan's policies on Central America, nuclear arms, South Africa, and the environment. Some fifty thousand canvassers knocked on doors every night in the early 1980s with petitions and requests for donations.[36]

The President's Staff and Interest Groups

Since the nation's earliest years, the president has assigned staff members to monitor important interest groups. Andrew Jackson's aides, for example, carefully gauged the activities and strength of bankers and businesses opposed to the administration. Franklin Roosevelt's New Deal initiated government growth that gave hundreds of new groups reason to have a regular relationship with Washington politicians, including the president. Today, interest groups are so important to the presidency that the White House has an office devoted exclusively to liaison with them, the Office of Pubic Liaison. *(See "A Greater White House Role," this page.)* The president and top aides continue to play an important role in monitoring and cajoling interest groups.

The president's relations with interest groups have not always been so direct as they are today. Before the expansion of the White House staff in the postwar era, the cabinet served as the main link between interest groups and the administration. Cabinet officials tended to have strong ties to the groups whose affairs their departments oversaw, and over the years they developed an appreciation for the concerns of interest groups. The administration also developed relations with interest groups through political parties and campaign organizations.

Many of the cabinet-level departments were designed to serve the interests of specific groups. The Departments of Agriculture, Commerce, and Labor resulted from years of lobbying by farmers, business leaders, and unions. At first designed to be research centers, the departments later gave their clients authority over a wide range of programs. Other federal agencies created at the urging of interest groups include the Interstate Commerce Commission, the Federal Reserve Board, and Federal Trade Commission. Agencies even helped create organizations for interest groups, as when the Department of Commerce helped to organize the U.S. Chamber of Commerce.

Departments develop strong ties to interest groups even if they were not created specifically to serve those groups. Political scientists have used images of "iron triangles" and "issue networks" to express the common outlooks and interests that develop with agencies and the groups they regulate.[37] Even the most independent administration appointees develop protective views toward their agencies and the interest groups they work with. They "marry the natives," to use the common argot.

To the extent that presidents need advice on issues, they rely on the information provided by the departments as well as the advice of a small staff in the White House and informal advisers. The interest-dominated departments were the incubators of presidential legislative initiatives. Bureaucrats interested in improving the status of their agencies developed programs that enlarged their involvement with interest groups.

Appointing interest group representatives to the administration always has been an important way to gain support. Less than 1 percent of the federal bureaucracy today is filled with presidential appointees, but strategic use of those posts can improve presidential relations with the groups. The president appoints interest group representatives for a number of reasons: to gain insight into constituent groups or leverage in bargaining, to co-opt groups by giving them formal involvement in policy discussions, and simply to establish a common ground for dealing with those groups.

In some agencies, interest groups have almost absolute authority over presidential appointments. The Justice Department must consider the likely rating of judicial appointments by the American Bar Association, for example.

Appointments for the Federal Reserve Board, the Treasury Department, the Central Intelligence Agency (CIA), and the Defense Department must meet the approval of their interest group establishments—bankers, contractors, academic experts, and businesses. President Carter dropped his nomination of Theodore C. Sorensen as CIA director after the intelligence community and conservative activists criticized it strongly.

Democratic presidents must get the blessing of blacks, women's groups, environmental activists, consumer groups, real estate developers, multinationals, social workers, and organized labor for its major appointments, since those groups are an important part of the Democratic coalition. Republican presidents must satisfy developers of natural resources, multinational and small business concerns, financial and insurance interests, conservative social groups, and defense contractors. President Reagan consulted Moral Majority leader Jerry Falwell before appointing Sandra Day O'Connor to the Supreme Court because he was concerned that Falwell might oppose O'Connor over her vote as an Arizona state legislator for funding abortions. President Carter withdrew his nomination of John Dunlop for secretary of labor in 1976 because of opposition from black and women's groups.[38]

Who does not get important cabinet positions is often as revealing as who gets the posts. Some Republican presidents have reached out to groups outside their coalition by appointing moderates to the Environmental Protection Agency and the Labor, Interior, and Energy departments. Reagan, however, rebuffed those agencies' key clients by making appointments antagonistic to their concerns. Reagan's first secretary of interior, James G. Watt, had been a lawyer for a firm strongly opposed to restrictions to development of natural resources. (Watt himself was associated with the Mountain States Legal Foundation, an interest group for developers and oil concerns.) Reagan's first energy chief, James B. Edwards, had no experience in the field and was told to do all he could to close down the department.

A Greater White House Role

As the government extended its reach over more economic and social policy areas, conflicts between departments and agencies developed that required White House arbitration. The sheer size and the inertia of the bureaucracy created difficulties for presidents trying to exert "top-down" control.

In response to a growing feeling that the departments and interest groups were impossible to control without extra help, postwar presidents have increased the size of the White House staff. The staff developed an often antagonistic relationship with the departments as it tried to develop and implement a program consistent with the president's wishes. The president ceased to rely on the departments for key legislative proposals.

Interest groups still had considerable reason to maintain regular contacts with federal departments, but the White House increasingly dominated the formation of legislative proposals and regulatory change. For the White House, contact with important interest groups became an important part of the president's strategy for mobilizing support on specific issues. First lady Eleanor Roosevelt was one of Franklin Roosevelt's most important emissaries to interest groups such as blacks and labor. Roosevelt also appointed White House aides James A. Farley, Harry Hop-

First lady Eleanor Roosevelt was one of Franklin Roosevelt's most important emissaries to interest groups such as blacks and labor. Here she speaks to members of the CIO, AFL, and unaffiliated unions in West Park, New York.

kins, Louis Howe, Adolph Berle, Raymond Moley, and Phillip Nash to stay in contact with interest groups as part of their jobs. Both Roosevelt and his successor, Harry S Truman, expressed discomfort with assigning aides strictly to work with interest groups. Roosevelt informed his advisers that he did not want a formal White House apparatus "on the theory that it brought in people with vested interests," according to political scientist Richard Neustadt.[39]

Roosevelt and Truman recognized the need to deal with interest groups but wanted to work through the Democratic National Committee. Interest groups were considered parts of the electoral coalition rather than a governing coalition.

Despite the lack of a large or formal White House apparatus, presidents have always constructed ad hoc coalitions of interest groups to pursue policies on specific issues. The Truman administration formed a coalition of business, labor, religious, and charitable groups to promote the Marshall Plan. Representatives of these interest groups met with administration officials to help develop the plan and to sell the plan to Congress and the public.

Interest groups also are represented on a major scale on advisory committees, ad hoc groups formed to advise the president on specific policies. The New Deal expanded the ad hoc use of commissions; by 1939, eighty-two advisory committees advised the government. During World War II, some one thousand committees advised the Office of Price Administration. Three thousand committees were in operation in the late 1960s according to one survey.[40]

Recent presidential lobbying includes many examples of building coalitions of interest groups. John F. Kennedy assembled a coalition of interest groups to promote the Trade Expansion Act. Nixon assigned aide Charles Colson to head a campaign to enlist interest group support for the 1969 antiballistic missile treaty with the Soviet Union. Nixon also put together coalitions for his "New Federalism" system of intergovernmental relations, for his economic programs, and for his two doomed Supreme Court nominations.

Nixon planned to create a White House office to oversee contacts with interest groups, but the Watergate scandal distracted him. Nixon's successor, Gerald R. Ford, created the Office of Public Liaison (OPL) in 1976. The new office supplemented the ad hoc efforts of the rest of the White House to stay in regular contact with key groups.

OPL has had an uneven history. The first full-time director was the Carter administration's Margaret Costanza. Costanza made public her differences with the president as she courted "outsider" groups such as blacks, women, and gays. Her most publicized differences with Carter concerned abortion: Carter opposed the use of federal funds for abortion, and Costanza openly favored federal support. Under Costanza, the office was more oriented toward advocacy than toward building coalitions for the president's policies.

After Carter replaced Costanza with Anne Wexler, the office became an effective instrument for White House lobbying. Costanza had complained that the office was strictly an outlet for meaningless public relations, but Wexler involved OPL in the policy formation and lobbying operations of the rest of the White House. The office participated in drafting legislation from the beginning.

One member of Carter's legislative liaison staff said of Wexler's OPL: "The public liaison folks have a pretty sophisticated operation for pinpointing potential interest group allies. When they pulled together a coalition, it could be pretty valuable on the Hill. I guess they had about 30,000 names and contacts on their computer for mobilization." [41]

Even with a sophisticated public liaison office, the president still usually entrusts the most important interest group assignments to specific staff members. Late in the Carter administration, even as OPL gained stature, the president called on Chief of Staff Hamilton Jordan to set up task forces to promote the administration's policy. Those task forces gradually won the administration praise from political professionals, but they came too late to promote much of Carter's agenda. White House attention shifted to the 1980 election just as it developed an effective way to build coalitions.

In addition to OPL and Jordan's task forces, the Carter administration relied on a number of interest group representatives on the White House staff and in agencies to reach out to interest groups. Carter appointed people affiliated with teachers' unions, Ralph Nader advocacy groups, Jewish groups, alternate energy developers, environmentalists, and social work veterans to the administration. Women's groups, blacks, Hispanics, and labor leaders were consulted and given greater representation on courts and agencies.

Good interest group relations give the White House a public relations machine that reaches into every corner of the country. "The realtors can send out half a million Mailgrams within 24 hours," one observer noted. "If they have a hundred target congressmen, they can get out 100,000 Mailgrams targeted by district." [42] The Chamber of Commerce, Moral Majority, AFL-CIO, American Federation of State, County, and Municipal Employees, National Education Association, and American Medical Association all can mobilize their many chapters and members within days. In many ways, the interest groups can be considered the new political machines of U.S. politics.

Carter both wooed and excoriated interest groups throughout his presidency, which created public confusion about his competence. For example, in 1979 Carter created a cabinet-level Department of Education to fulfill a promise to the National Education Association, the teachers' union that endorsed him in 1976 and 1980. Carter also made well-publicized efforts to promote groups such as evangelicals, organized labor, banks, some energy producers, and blacks.

As a result, Carter was criticized for "pandering" to interest groups. But Carter himself expressed frustration with interest group politics. In his 1979 "crisis of confidence" speech and in his farewell address, Carter decried the effects of interest groups on national policy development. In his farewell address, he said:

We are increasingly drawn to single-issue groups and special-interest organizations to ensure that whatever else happens our own personal views and our own personal interests are protected. This is a disturbing factor in American political life. It tends to distort our purposes. Because of the fragmented pressures of these special interests, it's very important that the office of the president be a strong one. [43]

Interest Groups in the 1980s

Interest group politics have continued to grow and change with the inclusion of new groups in the political process. In the 1980s a proliferation of groups on both the right and left presented a new challenge to leaders of both parties. Especially pronounced was the challenge from the right, since its forces were better financed.

Jimmy Carter and Ronald Reagan had no national political experience and won the presidency without much help from the party organizations, so they reached out for interest groups outside the Washington establishment. Their interest group ties did not always bind them to Congress and the bureaucracy. Political scientist Joseph Pika wrote: "In this way, presidents may have weakened political parties just at the time they were most needed as mechanisms to organize effective coalitions to pass legislative initiatives." [44]

An important part of Reagan's electoral strategy in 1980 was the so-called New Right, a wide range of groups that promoted an agenda including tax cuts, reduced federal regulation, an end to legal abortions, a return to prayer in the schools, federal tax breaks for parochial schools, restricted gay rights, and a more rigid interpretation of civil rights. Reagan provided hortatory leadership, submitted legislation on these issues, and involved Christian organizations in drafting tuition-tax credit legislation. But the New Right agenda was a low priority in Reagan's first term. Reagan held on to the groups' support, however, because they had nowhere else to go.

Presidents Carter and Reagan found themselves fighting large and small interest groups when their administrations tried to cut the budget. Social Security recipients, western water interests, military contractors, farmers, hospitals, and state and local governments all resisted the two administrations' budget axe. Carter expended great political capital early in his fights with western water interests, the nuclear power industry, oil companies, and many liberal groups who found his programs on welfare and health care stingy.

Reagan's budget-cutters were forced to look for relatively small savings—but were frustrated even there. The administration once proposed that the Coast Guard charge commercial vessels and pleasure yachts for the $1 billion worth of services they receive at sea. The administration plan would have brought in $400 million. The proposal was roundly criticized and, whittled down, produced only $8 million in new revenues. When Secretary of Education William J. Bennett proposed restrictions on college loans to prevent fraud, a wide range of university and student groups protested. [45]

The size of the White House staff increased from a few dozen under Franklin Roosevelt to 550 under Richard Nixon. After falling to 488 under President Carter, the staff increased again under Reagan to 575. The Executive Office of the President was at its largest—five thousand—in the 1970s. [46]

Tasks of the White House Staff

Political scientists Martha Joynt Kumar and Michael Baruch Grossman have argued that the presidency's relationship with interest groups involves four basic roles. [47] Many of the roles overlap, but they represent distinct tasks for the administration. The administration usually must deal with all four tasks at the same time to enact its policies.

The "marker" keeps track of the president's debts to particular groups and attempts to help those groups. The "communicant" gathers information about current interest group concerns. The "constructor" builds coalitions for specific policy initiatives. The "broker" helps the administration and groups with different interests negotiate their differences to give the president broad enough backing for policy initiatives.

The Reagan administration's action on its tax cuts in 1981 illustrates all four roles. Partly to repay the business community for its support in the 1980 election, the administration proposed and shepherded legislation in Congress that would reduce the marginal tax rates on individuals by 30 percent over three years. The original decision to push the legislation illustrates the "marker" role.

Before and after taking up the legislation, the White House acted as a communicant, sounding out diverse groups on tax and other issues. The White House gathered information about which groups were likely to support and oppose the legislation, and how strong and reliable they were. White House constructors helped to build a coalition to back the legislation in Congress. A wide variety of groups joined the coalition, including the U.S. Chamber of Commerce, the Business Roundtable, the National Small Business Association, the Moral Majority, and the National Conservative Political Action Committee. Wayne Valis, a special assistant to the president, oversaw the coordination of interest group efforts.

Finally, the administration served as a broker to settle differences between the administration, congressional leaders, and interest groups. One result of the bargaining was a reduction of the cut from 30 to 25 percent and a delay of the legislation's implementation.

Interest group relations with the White House are most routine—and important—on budgetary matters. Interest groups develop relationships with bureaucrats in federal agencies throughout the year, and those agencies develop budget proposals in the last three months of the calendar year. Those proposals work their way up the system to the cabinet secretaries and the president.

As it has grown in size, the White House staff has played a greater role in overseeing budget recommendations. The White House often distrusts department recommendations and wants to create coherent domestic and foreign programs that often are impossible without top-down control. Departments and agencies often conflict over budget and program authorities, and only the president and the White House staff can settle the differences.

In the Reagan administration, the Office of Management and Budget (OMB) played an important role not only in arbitrating budget claims but also in developing new federal regulations. Under a presidential order, OMB must study the impact of new regulations before they can go into effect. White House and OMB purview over the budget and regulations means a reduced role for interest groups. Before, the most public action on regulations was publication of comments in the *Federal Register;* under Reagan, regulations must enter the realm of the generalists at OMB. The close relationship that the groups enjoy with specific agencies is not enough for their wishes to prevail.

Criticism of these developments turns on the lack of expertise that the White House staff and OMB officials have on many complex matters under agency jurisdiction. The White House staff is made up of political operatives, and OMB is made up of political professionals and accountants—few of whom know much if anything about the chemical issues involved in environmental regulations, for example, or the complex interrelationship between different components of tax and welfare policy.

The Interest Group Universe Today

The interest groups active in national politics are in many ways the "dead weight of the past." Today's active interest groups are the offspring of past political and economic movements, and their survival and involvement in politics is one of the constraints on the activities of the president, the executive bureaucracy, and Congress. But the interest groups are not just constraints. They offer politicians the means for mobilizing political activity.

Interest groups represent every conceivable group in the United States: big and small business, domestic and multinational manufacturers, banks and insurance companies, real estate developers, teachers, miners, lawyers, blue-collar workers, opponents of unions, the elderly, "peaceniks," military contractors, consumers, evangelicals, Jews, Arabs, guardians of different notions of the "public interest," states and cities, government workers, secretaries, custodians, athletes, actors, environmentalists, developers of natural resources—the list goes on and on.

The interest group universe is so large that it contains innumerable internal contradictions. Within the set of interest groups concerned about military affairs, for example, there is often keen competition. When President Carter signed the SALT II treaty in Moscow in 1978, military-related interest groups lined up on both sides of the issue.

To understand interest groups, it is important to understand their different goals and functions, resources, everyday activities, and long-term strategies.

Goals and Functions

Interest groups form to protect a group's material interests in budget, tax, and regulatory proceedings in Washington, to express a group's ideology and desires, or to provide a forum, services, and standards to a group.

The U.S. Chamber of Commerce is an umbrella organization for seventy thousand firms and individuals, twenty-five hundred state and local chapters, and one thousand trade and professional associations. The chamber's annual $16-million budget allows extensive lobbying of both the federal and state governments. The chamber is dedicated to one overriding goal: improving the conditions for business expansion. It has been active in issues such as tax legislation, labor laws, and regulatory relief. The group has a definite ideology, but it is interested primarily in material concerns.

The chamber is the largest business organization. Other active business groups, designed strictly to produce better conditions for economic activity, include the Business Roundtable, oil lobbies, and the National Small Business Association.

The American Federation of Labor-Congress of Industrial Organizations (AFL-CIO) is also designed to further the material benefits of its members. The AFL-CIO has fourteen million dues-paying members in more than one hundred affiliates, including the Teamsters, the United Auto Workers, the United Mine Workers, and American Federation of Teachers. The AFL-CIO's job is simple: bargain for the best wages, benefits, and working conditions possible, and make organizing workers as easy and efficient as possible.

The Chamber of Commerce and the AFL-CIO are interested mainly in material benefits for their members; other interest groups have a more "expressive" agenda. Rather than simply seeking a share of federal largesse, they exist to promote their ideological or cultural values. Many of the evangelical and conservative groups that fall under the New Right umbrella were founded to promote values rather than material interests.

Frustrated with what they perceive to be a decline in the moral values of the family, groups like the Moral Majority, the National Right to Life Committee, and National Conservative Political Action Committee contributed generously to political campaigns and lobbied hard in the White House and on Capitol Hill. They promoted an anti-abortion amendment to the Constitution, prayer in the schools, and tuition-tax credits for private schools. They also spoke out on foreign policy issues such as the war in Nicaragua and arms control. Other important ideologically oriented organizations include the Americans for Democratic Action, the American Civil Liberties Union, Americans for Constitutional Action, the Eagle Forum, and People for the American Way.

Professional organizations take on both material and expressive functions. The American Bar Association, the American Medical Association (AMA), and the American Association of State Colleges and Universities serve as protectors of professional standards and ideals, but they also want to defend the privileges of their members. The AMA, for example, is among the biggest contributors to political campaigns and actively defends the profession's material interests whenever Congress considers issues such as Medicare or hospital cost-containment legislation.

Many professional organizations, such as the American Political Science Association and the Modern Language Association, are primarily dispensers of information.

Since the 1970s, there has been a boom in "public interest" lobbies. These groups do not promote the interests of any single sector but instead promote their vision of the general interest of all society. The members of these groups themselves do not stand to receive special material benefits if their ideals are realized, but the policies they promote would help some groups at the expense of others.

Prominent public interest groups include Common Cause, People for the American Way, the League of Women Voters, the U.S. Public Interest Research Group and other organizations set up by consumer activist Ralph Nader, the Consumer Federation of America, Americans for Constitutional Action, and the American Civil Liberties Union.

Resources and Everyday Activities

The influence of interest groups differs according to their resources. Money, size of membership, technological sophistication (such as computers, direct mail operations, telephone banks, polling operations), expertise on issues, familiarity with the political process, political reputation and contacts, motivation, and leadership are the important factors defining an organization's strength.[48]

Most lobbies' everyday activities consist of unglamorous work such as monitoring legislation on Capitol Hill and regulatory action in agencies, researching issues, fund raising, surveying and responding to the concerns of membership, and staying in touch with congressional staff members.

Most interest groups have a legislative agenda that they would like to pursue, but they rarely have the opportunity to press specific proposals at the White House or Capitol Hill. Usually they must form alliances with other groups on specific issues that the president, Congress, or federal departments are considering. An interest group's agenda, then, is pursued bit by bit rather than as a whole. This helps explain why interest groups become disenchanted with an administration that considers itself an ally: the interest group considers its program to be the president's program, but presidents also must serve other, often conflicting groups.

Long-term Strategies

Because of the slow pace of legislative action in Washington, lobbies must be content to pursue "incremental" change most of the time. Groups must do what they can to develop a wide range of large and small initiatives, however, so they are able to act when opportunities for exerting influence arise.

Interest groups must decide whether they are going to use "insider" or "outsider" strategies to influence the president and the rest of the Washington establishment.[49] Insiders establish ties with a number of White House, agency, and congressional staffers and, depending on the administration, can play a role in writing legislation and regulations that affect their interests. Outsiders attempt to pressure the administration by putting the public spotlight on the issues they consider important.

Interest groups often move from outsider to insider roles with a change in administration. Before Ronald Reagan was elected president, the Moral Majority and other conservative groups relied on public relations campaigns and insurgent candidates. After Reagan became president, however, the White House consulted these groups on many social initiatives. They actually helped to write tuition-tax credit legislation. Likewise, many consumer protection and environmental protection groups moved from the outside to the inside with the election of Jimmy Carter in 1976. Carter appointed many "Naderites"—disciples of activist Ralph Nader—to top agency positions.

White House Efforts to Rouse Interest Group Support

Presidents' interest group strategies fit somewhere between their attempts to control the huge bureaucracy and to appeal to the public at large. Interest groups have many of the open characteristics involved in public appeals, but groups also become intricately involved with the everyday machinery of hundreds of agencies that develop and execute federal policy.

The president needs to line up interest group support for difficult policy battles to mobilize both the public and the elites who are important players in the complex negotiations of congressional and bureaucratic politics.

Whether a president can persuade Congress to adopt the administration's policy proposals depends on how much pressure interest groups bring to an issue. Interest groups offer the president important tools to prod Congress:

~ Expertise and legitimacy. An organization that includes respected analysts of a political problem not only serves as a school for the president and the White House staff but also puts the reputation of the experts behind the White House.

~ Membership and organization. Most interest groups do not have a large, active membership, but many have access to mailing lists and expertise in mobilizing the important participants in a political battle.

~ Money for media campaigns. Even the most skeletal organizations often have financial resources for a media campaign. Recent battles over issues such as the Panama Canal treaties, the tax cuts of 1981, and the nomination of Robert H. Bork to the Supreme Court have involved extensive broadcast and newspaper advertising to sway public opinion.

~ A system of balancing political concerns. The participation of many interest groups enables the president and members of Congress to engage in extensive bartering that goes far beyond the specific controversy. Votes for highly visible initiatives are won by promising members of Congress support on other, unrelated matters.

~ Leadership. Interest groups include not only many nationally recognized names—such as Lane Kirkland of the AFL-CIO, Phyllis Schlafly of the Eagle Forum, Norman Lear of People for the American Way, and Jerry Falwell of the Moral Majority—but also sophisticated organizational operators. These groups can offer the kind of leadership that mobilizes whole segments of the population on issues important to the president.

Political battles tend to develop into battles between two sets of interest groups and their White House and congressional allies. Interest group activity determines the extent of the propaganda battle and the intricacy and duration of the maneuvering between the president and key members of Congress.

Reagan Confronts Domestic Groups

President Reagan's budget-cutting victory in the summer of 1981 was a classic contest between two sets of interest groups. The outcome of the struggle was determined by bartering, public appeals, strong presidential leadership, and the organizational strength of interest groups.

The prospect of more that $160 billion in budget cuts over Reagan's first term in office activated a wide range of interest groups involved with domestic policy. The usual strategy of such groups is to work with the staff members of congressional committees and the federal agencies to restore proposed cuts, piece by piece, to the budget. This "micro" activity was to be supplemented by a publicity campaign that would show low public support and put both the president and Congress on the defensive. The groups responding to the budget cut proposals included the AFL-CIO, the National Association for the Advancement of Colored People, the Urban League, the U.S. Conference of Mayors, the Children's Defense Fund, the U.S. Public Interest Research Group, the National Organization for Women, Operation PUSH, and the American Association of Retired Persons.

President Reagan and his lieutenants thwarted the two-prong interest group attack, however. First, it reduced the chances for micro response to the cuts by asking Republican Senate leaders for a consideration of the cuts as a single budget package; that is, Congress would have one up-or-down vote on all the cuts. The all-or-nothing legisla-

tion reduced the possibilities for interest groups to appeal to friendly members of congressional committees. One observer noted: "Many hundreds of lobbying groups that had built strong relationships over the years with authorizing with appropriations committee members and aides have found themselves not so much without a sympathetic ear as without a way to leverage that sympathy to get more money." [50]

Second, by including authorizing legislation as well as spending legislation—that is, legislation that allowed funding as well as legislation that actually funded the programs—Reagan forced Congress to deal with otherwise protected entitlement programs. If the authorization for a program were cut, it could not be funded later in that budget year. Third, the administration led supportive interest groups in its own public offensive in favor of the cuts.

The groups Reagan brought into its alliance included the Chamber of Commerce, the National Association of Manufacturers, the National Conservative Political Action Committee, the Moral Majority, the National Jaycees, the National Federation of Small Business, and the American Medical Association. The White House managed the interest groups' campaign. It selected key congressional districts where the administration might find support and instructed the interest groups to pressure House members from those districts. Lee Atwater, the president's assistant political director, explained:

> The way we operate, within forty-eight hours any Congressman will know that he has had a major strike in his district. All of a sudden, Vice President Bush is in your district, Congressman Jack Kemp is in your district. Ten of your top contributors are calling you, the head of the local AMA, the head of the local realtors' group, local officials. Twenty letters come in. Within forty-eight hours, you're hit by paid media, free media, mail, phone, all asking you to support the president. [51]

The interest group politics of the budget cuts had an elaborate system of rewards and punishments. As Reagan sought congressional approval, he co-opted the United Auto Workers union by going along with import relief on Japanese automobiles. The president also punished two of his biggest Democratic foes, House Speaker Thomas P. (Tip) O'Neill, Jr., and Sen. Edward M. Kennedy, by lifting duties on Taiwan and Korea—a move that hurt the shoe-making industry in their home state of Massachusetts. [52]

Under such a system of lobbying, the president depends on interest groups when bartering with reluctant budget-cutters in Congress. The cozy system of back-room bargaining between the White House staff and key congressional figures is not replaced, but it is supplemented by the mobilization of interest groups for the district pressure campaigns.

Reagan was not the only practitioner of interest group politics, just one of the more successful. Carter was considered a failure in congressional relations, but he succeeded in getting Senate approval of the Panama Canal treaties because of his ability to assemble a broad coalition of interest groups and his willingness to barter for the final crucial votes.

Treaty opponents were led by former California governor Ronald Reagan, who had found the issue to be potent in the 1976 presidential campaign. Groups fighting the treaty included the American Conservative Union, the Liberty Lobby, the National States' Rights Party, and the John Birch Society. Some fifteen hundred State Department officials led the fight for the treaty, backed by Common Cause, the National Education Association, the AFL-CIO, the National Jaycees, and business leaders. The interest groups were troops in a battle for public opinion to sway skeptical senators. At the beginning, only 8 percent of the public supported "giving up" the canal; by the time of the Senate vote, a majority favored the treaties. The emotional debate eventually worked to Carter's detriment, however. Leaders of the New Right later said the canal issue was the catalyst for the activism in the 1980 election campaign for Reagan and against Carter. The issue strengthened New Right groups' membership, treasuries, organization, and technological sophistication.

Early Interest Group Politics

Some of the great twentieth-century drives for enactment of legislation resulted from presidential management of interest-group lobbying, including: adoption of the constitutional amendment granting suffrage to women, the amendments for Prohibition and repeal of Prohibition, the Truman administration's aid to Greece and Turkey and the subsequent Marshall Plan for postwar European economic recovery, civil rights legislation of the 1950s and 1960s, Carter's energy package, and Franklin Roosevelt's attempt to gain control of the U.S. Supreme Court by increasing its size.

Even when presidents are at odds with major interest groups, they must at least pay their respects to them, usually with appearances at annual conventions of the organizations. Occasional appearances and meetings are necessary expressions of good faith for the president who wishes to stand as a symbol for the whole nation.

The number of presidential appearances before groups has increased steadily in the postwar era. President Ford attended meetings to deliver "minor" speeches an average of thirty-five times a year; President Carter delivered twenty-one annually; President Reagan twenty. Speeches to interest groups in Washington are far more numerous: Ford, Carter, and Reagan averaged about fifteen each month.[53]

The president often appears before interest groups to appeal for support on specific issues. Johnson appealed to leaders of civil rights organizations to keep the pressure on Congress for passage of the landmark Civil Rights Act of 1964. Reagan asked veterans' and Latin American groups to support the "contra" war against Nicaraguan government.

Presidential appearances before interest groups also can be pure symbolism—the head of state going before unfriendly groups to urge national unity. Reagan's appearances before the NAACP, Carter's speech before the Veterans of Foreign Wars, and Nixon's speech before the AFL-CIO are all examples.

The Use of the "Ad-hocracy"

When the White House faces a crisis or a seemingly intractable problem, the president often appoints representatives of interest groups to a commission to study the problem. Commissions have proved an effective way to use interest group representatives to overcome the difficulties of public wrangling by interest groups.

"Ad-hocracy," as the temporary commission has been called, offers several advantages to a president facing intransigent interest group politics.[54] First, the president can co-opt the interest groups by naming selected representatives to the panel. The president can often ensure favorable policy recommendations by "stacking" the panel. Second, the commission can stifle partisan debate by including members from both parties. Third, the commission can work in almost complete secrecy, thereby bypassing debilitating debate on each major issue that it faces. Fourth, ad-hocracy can offer all-or-nothing proposals that preclude endless public bargaining after the report's release.

President Reagan appointed ad-hocracies for problems including Social Security funding, the deployment strategy of the MX missile, the investigation of the Iran-contra affair, and the health crisis over Acquired Immune Deficiency Syndrome (AIDS). All of these issues proved too difficult for the normal public process of interest group bargaining—or at least the president thought he could defuse public controversy with a panel.

Social Security, for example, was in perilous financial shape, but efforts to trim benefits or raise taxes encountered well-orchestrated opposition campaigns. Democratic candidates campaigned emotionally and effectively against administration reform proposals in 1982. Reagan's 1983 commission helped build support for more taxes.

The debate over the MX missile presented a different problem for the administration. Reagan was committed to the mobile missile program, but Republican supporters in the West were reluctant to see the missiles based in their home states. Commission recommendations skirted the most difficult turf issues.

Even though a commission can cause problems for the president if it recommends actions that antagonize the administration's supporters, a commission's chief virtue is that it is a low-risk venture. President Reagan was pleasantly surprised by the favorable publicity that his National Commission on Excellence in Education created. Reagan initially maintained that the commission was Education Secretary Terrel H. Bell's panel, not his. When the report got rave reviews, Reagan adopted the commission and education issue as his own. Reagan may have been the most successful in his use of commissions, but he was not the first to try them.

John Kennedy, a skeptic of bureaucratic routines, appointed a number of commissions to bypass the usual method of policy development by departments. The Kennedy efforts foundered, however, when the makeup of the commissions received criticism and possible proposals were leaked.

Lyndon Johnson used task forces to develop much of his Great Society domestic legislation. Johnson's panels were more secretive and included fewer intellectuals and more members of the affected groups.

Task forces enabled Johnson and his special assistant, Joseph A. Califano, to maintain tight control of domestic policy. As an official in the U.S. Office of Education acknowledged, "much policy development in education has moved from here to the White House."[55] Johnson's 1964 task forces were ad-hoc efforts to develop a quick legislative package. In later years, the task forces were more entrenched. Fifty task forces worked on domestic programs in 1967. Most of the task forces recommended "incremental," or small-scale, adjustments to already existing policies and programs. But the task forces also proposed major initiatives.

The makeup of the Johnson task forces varied. Some contained a large number of officials from the White House and bureaucracy; others had strong interest group representation.

Public Efforts by Interest Groups

Textbooks of U.S. politics stress the "cozy" behind-the-scenes relationships between interest groups and agencies and committees of government. But many groups are not part of the secure federal establishment and must orchestrate large public demonstrations to influence the president and other parts of the government.

Outstanding examples of interest group efforts to influence the president and the rest of the government by "going public" include: the civil rights movement starting in the 1950s; the protests against the Vietnam War; the movements for and against ratification of the Equal Rights Amendment; the pro- and antiabortion movements; expressions of support and opposition to the Reagan administration's policies in Central America, particularly the activities of Lt. Col. Oliver North; protests by farmers vulnerable to foreclosure; antidrug rallies; protests against Reagan's nuclear weapons policies; and gay rights marches.

The most sustained recent public protests were over civil rights and the Vietnam War. When black organizations confronted the limits of the legal strategies of the NAACP and the state-by-state action to protect rights, a series of protests helped to put the issue on the national agenda. Demonstrations and other "outsider" efforts by civil rights organizations forced Presidents Eisenhower, Kennedy, and Johnson to deal with the issue. The most dramatic demonstration was the 1963 march on Washington, capped by Martin Luther King's "I Have a Dream" speech and civil rights leaders' visit to the White House.

President Johnson first dismissed Vietnam War protests as unrepresentative of public opinion, but the protests drew attention to moral and tactical questions about the war in elite circles such as the media and universities. Extensive war coverage following protests helped to shift public opinion against the war and persuade Johnson to halt bombing in 1968.

Many protests fail to move the president, at least in any direct way. President Reagan stood by his nuclear arms policies—including the decision to base Pershing missiles in Europe—despite massive demonstrations in West Germany, Great Britain, and the United States. Reagan dismissed the protests, including a gathering of several hundred thousand people at New York's Central Park, as inspired and organized in part by Soviet agents. Reagan's aggressive activity on arms control in his second term, however, suggests that the "peace" movement might have had an effect on him after all.

Scholars Frances Fox Piven and Richard Cloward have argued that public protest and disruption have historically been necessary for poor people to obtain benefits from the federal government and the states. Protests develop when economic conditions decline, resulting in government provision of social welfare programs to serve as a "safety net." When the economy improves, and public pressure declines, the government adopts restrictions on benefits.[56]

Public protest opens or narrows the space for political discussion and negotiation. Demonstrations have brought new issues to public debate and thereby opened up debate on matters such as civil rights, the Vietnam War, gay rights, military spending, abortion, and environmental pro-

Frequently, groups not part of the federal establishment feel the need to orchestrate large public demonstrations to influence the president. In August 1976, a group in favor of the Equal Rights Amendment marches in front of the White House.

tection. Debates about Social Security, however, were restricted by the climate created by public lobbying against cuts in benefits.

Protest sometimes blunts the edge of a movement. Groups that mobilize followers for rallies have difficulty translating their activism to sustained research and lobbying on Capitol Hill. Followers mistake their expression of opinion to be adequate political action.

Campaign Promises and Debts

Despite the cynical view that candidates forget campaign promises as soon as they enter public office, studies have found that presidents at least attempt to honor their pledges. Presidents usually target those pledges to specific interest groups, so interest group influence on the White House can be understood to begin before a president even takes office.[57]

An analysis of Carter's 1976 campaign promises and subsequent policies shows that he pursued the policies he promised in seven of ten policy areas. Carter's ambitious and legislative agenda did not lead to success on many major issues, so Carter often was under attack from interest groups even though he pursued many of his promises. The issues in which Carter tried to honor pledges included: creation of a cabinet-level Department of Education (a promise to the National Education Association), creation of a consumer protection agency (Ralph Nader organizations), common-site picketing legislation (AFL-CIO), amnesty for Vietnam War draft dodgers (peace groups), deregulation of businesses such as the airline industry (business and labor groups), expansion of environmental regulations (the Wilderness Society and other environmental groups), and a new public works program (AFL-CIO and big-city mayors).

Other presidents have had similar records honoring campaign pledges. John Kennedy faced a Congress as reluctant to enact his programs as did Carter. Kennedy, however, tried to honor campaign promises and succeeded—most frequently when policy changes did not require legislation to be passed. Kennedy's successes included the Peace Corps, minimum wage legislation, job training, trade expansion, regional development, arms control, the Alliance for Progress, and civil rights protections. Presidents Nixon and Reagan followed up on a number of campaign themes, such as a devolution of power to states and localities, a stronger U.S. military posture, free trade policies, cuts in domestic programs, and reduced federal regulation of business and the environment. Nixon departed from his promises to some interest groups, however, by supporting détente and strict regulation of the economy.

Despite dedication to the campaign agenda, interest groups complain that the president should do better. White House officials complain that interest groups do not understand the limits of political bargaining. One Carter official said of organized labor's impatience:

> The basic issue is not whether we support most of the things labor supports. We do! We had to make decisions about how much of our agenda could be dominated by labor-demanded bills in the first two years. Our decision to go with comprehensive welfare reform meant that health insurance had to wait. Not forever, but just intelli-

gently delayed.... We're using a lot of credit in the Senate on the labor bill. But we get no thanks from them [labor organizations].[58]

Regulation of Lobbying

Lobbying is protected by First Amendment guarantees of the freedom of speech, but Congress has acted several times to monitor and regulate the kinds of contacts that interest groups make with the president and Congress.

Concern about conflicts of interest in the White House and the bureaucracy caused Congress to pass restrictions on the lobbying activities of former administration officials. Under the Ethics in Government Act of 1978, administration officials are not permitted to lobby for a year after they leave the government.

Two top Reagan advisers—Lyn Nofziger and Michael K. Deaver—were indicted for illegally contacting their former Reagan administration colleagues on behalf of clients after the two men had become lobbyists. Nofziger was convicted of illegal lobbying for a military contractor, and Deaver was convicted on three counts of perjury in connection with his lobbying work for the Canadian government.

The history of regulating lobbies has been spotty. Congress and the president have faced intense interest group resistance to any regulation of their activities. The legislation that has passed is either so vaguely defined or restricted that lobbies' activities are barely controlled.

The Revenue Act of 1934 denied tax-exempt status to groups that devote a "substantial part" of their activities to influencing legislation. The provision enumerated vague definitions and no sanctions, and courts applied the law inconsistently. The Foreign Agents Registration Act of 1938 requires representatives of foreign governments and organizations to register with the U.S. government. The act was the source of controversy when President Carter's brother Billy was hired by the Libyan government as a U.S. representative.

The Revenue Acts of 1938 and 1939 deny tax exemptions to corporations devoting a "substantial part" of their activities to propaganda and lobbying. The acts also state that citizens' donations to such corporations are not tax deductible. The Federal Regulation of Lobbying Act of 1946, the most comprehensive legislation at the time, requires registration of anyone who is hired by someone else to lobby Congress. The act requires quarterly reports from registered lobbyists.

Notes

1. For a comparative perspective on interest groups, see Frances Millard, *Pressure Politics in Industrial Societies* (London: Macmillan, 1986).
2. *Federalist* No. 10 was largely ignored by historians and theorists of American democracy until the early twentieth century. See David Rodgers, *Contested Truths* (New York: Basic Books, 1987), 185.
3. Clinton Rossiter, ed., *The Federalist Papers* (New York: New American Library, 1961), 78.
4. Alexis de Tocqueville, *Democracy in America* (New York: New American Library, 1956), 198.
5. Theodore J. Lowi, *The Personal President* (Ithaca, N.Y.: Cornell University Press, 1985), 22-41.

6. Theodore J. Lowi, *The End of Liberalism* (New York: Norton, 1979), 3-63.

7. Jack L. Walker, "The Origins and Maintenance of Interest Groups in America," *American Political Science Review* 77 (June 1983): 394-395; Harold Wolman and Fred Teitelbaum, "Interest Groups and the Reagan Presidency," in *The Reagan Presidency and the Governing of America*, ed. Lester M. Salamon and Michael S. Lund (Washington, D.C.: Urban Institute, 1984), 302.

8. Norman J. Ornstein and Shirley Elder, *Interest Groups, Lobbying, and Policymaking* (Washington, D.C.: CQ Press, 1978), 37, 24.

9. The Federal Election Campaign Act amendments of 1974 limit donations to individual candidates to $1,000 and donations to groups to $5,000. This provision encourages donors to give to PACs rather than candidates. *(See "The Campaign Finance System," p. 182, in The Electoral Process chapter of Part II.)*

10. Jeffrey Berry, *The Interest Group Society* (Boston: Little, Brown, 1984), 160. Congressional PAC spending increased from $23 million in 1976 to $80 million in 1982. See also Martha Joynt Kumar and Michael Baruch Grossman, "The President and Interest Groups," in *The Presidency and the Political System*, ed. Michael Nelson (Washington, D.C.: CQ Press, 1984), 288.

11. Arthur F. Bentley, *The Process of Government* (San Antonio: Principia Press, 1949).

12. David Truman, *The Governmental Process* (New York: Knopf, 1951).

13. Robert A. Dahl, *Who Governs?* (New Haven, Conn.: Yale University Press, 1961).

14. E. E. Schattschneider, *The Semisovereign People* (New York: Holt, Rinehart, and Winston, 1960); C. Wright Mills, *The Power Elite* (New York: Oxford University Press, 1959); Floyd Hunter, *Community Power Structure* (Chapel Hill: University of North Carolina Press, 1953).

15. For a concise examination of the bias of interest group representation, see Kay Lehman Schlozman, "What Accent the Heavenly Chorus? Political Equality and the American Pressure System," in *Journal of Politics* 46 (1984): 1006-1031.

16. Mancur Olson, *The Logic of Collective Action* (Cambridge, Mass.: Harvard University Press, 1965).

17. Daniel Bell, "The Revolution of Rising Entitlements," in *Fortune*, April 1975, 99.

18. For a recent critique of the breakdown of a civic ethic due to individualist and interest-group liberalism, see Benjamin Barber, *Strong Democracy* (Berkeley: University of California Press, 1984), esp. 3-114. For a conservative statement of similar concerns, see Robert Nisbet, *The Twilight of Authority* (New York: Oxford University Press, 1975).

19. Lowi, *End of Liberalism*, 62.

20. Paul Light, *The President's Agenda* (Baltimore: Johns Hopkins University Press, 1982), 94.

21. Joseph A. Pika, "Interest Groups and the Executive: Presidential Intervention," in *Interest Group Politics*, ed. Allen J. Cigler and Burdett A. Loomis (Washington, D.C.: CQ Press, 1983), 312.

22. Grossman and Kumar, "President and Interest Groups," 289.

23. Anthony Downs, "Up and Down with Ecology—The Issue Attention Cycle," *Public Interest* 28 (Summer 1972): 38-50.

24. The Carter and Reagan administrations observed the terms of the arms treaty, but Carter decided that a public battle for ratification would be damaging politically. Carter, therefore, did not reap the usual public relations benefits of a major foreign policy event.

25. Reagan's reconciliation budget-cutting strategy is discussed in Allen Schick, *Reconciliation and the Congressional Budget Process* (Washington, D.C.: American Enterprise Institute, 1981).

26. Larry J. Sabato, *The Party's Just Begun* (Glenview, Ill.: Scott Foresman, 1988).

27. The following discussion relies on Benjamin Ginsberg and Martin Shefter, "The Presidency and the Organization of Interests," in *The Presidency and the Political System*, ed.

Michael Nelson (Washington, D.C.: CQ Press, 1988), 311-330.

28. Ibid., 311-333.

29. Maximum feasible participation never played as important a role as its promoters and detractors argued. Most organizations created by the provision eventually came under the control of local governments and other more conservative groups such as local businesses. But the principles behind the program—that interest groups can be created to promote policies and that interested parties should be consulted before policies affecting them are implemented—have remained part of American politics. Perhaps most important, the provision led to the development of a wide range of interest groups and trained a generation of government and interest group leaders. See Dennis R. Judd, *The Politics of American Cities: Power and Public Policy*, 2d ed. (Boston: Little, Brown, 1984), 311; Daniel Patrick Moynihan, *Maximum Feasible Misunderstanding* (New York: Free Press, 1970).

30. Robert D. Reischauer, "Fiscal Federalism in the 1980's: Dismantling or Rationalizing the Great Society," in *The Great Society and Its Legacy*, ed. Marshall Kaplan and Peggy Cuciti (Durham, N.C.: Duke University Press, 1986), 187-188.

31. Ginsberg and Shefter, "The Presidency and the Organization of Interests," 313-327.

32. Marc Bendick, Jr., and Phyllis M. Levinson, "Private-Sector Initiatives or Public-Private Partnerships," in *The Reagan Presidency*, 455-479.

33. Allan J. Cigler, "From Protest Group to Interest Group: The Making of American Agriculture Movement, Inc.," in *Interest Group Politics*, ed. Allan J. Cigler and Burdett A. Loomis (Washington, D.C.: CQ Press, 1988), 46-69.

34. Thomas Byrne Edsall, *The New Politics of Inequality* (New York: Norton, 1984), 99-103.

35. Jeff Fishel, *Presidents and Promises* (Washington, D.C.: CQ Press, 1985), 168.

36. John Herbers, "Grass-Roots Groups Go National," *New York Times Magazine*, September 4, 1983, 22-23, 42, 46, 48.

37. Thomas Cronin, *The State of the Presidency* (Boston: Little, Brown, 1980), 84.

38. Nelson W. Polsby, "Interest Groups and the Presidency: Trends in Political Intermediation in America," in *American Politics and Public Policy*, ed. Walter Dean Burnham and Martha Wagner Weinberg (Cambridge, Mass.: MIT Press, 1978), 46.

39. Grossman and Kumar, "President and Interest Groups," 284.

40. Joseph A. Pika, "Interest Groups and the Executive," 307-308.

41. Light, *President's Agenda*, 95.

42. Grossman and Kumar, "President and Interest Groups," 309.

43. "President Carter's Farewell Address," *Congressional Quarterly Weekly Report*, January 17, 1981, 156.

44. Pika, "Interest Groups and the Executive," 301.

45. Alfred A. Malabre, Jr., *Beyond Our Means* (New York: Vintage Books, 1987), 111-114.

46. Lowi, *Personal President*, 141-142.

47. See Grossman and Kumar, "President and Interest Groups," 290-307.

48. Ornstein and Elder, *Interest Groups, Lobbying, and Policymaking*, 69-79.

49. Ibid., 82-93.

50. Wolman and Teitelbaum, "Interest Groups and the Reagan Presidency," 308.

51. Hedrick Smith, "The President as Coalition Builder: Reagan's First Year," in *Rethinking the Presidency*, ed. Thomas E. Cronin (Boston: Little, Brown, 1982), 280.

52. Ibid., 281.

53. Gary King and Lyn Ragsdale, *The Elusive Executive: Discovering Statistical Patterns in the Presidency* (Washington, D.C.: CQ Press, 1988), 254-259.

54. Francis E. Rourke, *Bureaucracy, Politics, and Public Policy* (Boston: Little, Brown, 1984), 150.

55. Norman C. Thomas and Harold L. Wolman, "Policy Formulation in the Institutionalized Presidency," in *The Presidential Advisory System*, ed. Thomas E. Cronin and Sanford D. Greenberg (New York: Harper and Row, 1969), 127. See also

Daniel Bell, "Government by Commission," in the same volume, 117-123.

56. Frances Fox Piven and and Richard Cloward, *Regulating the Poor: The Functions of Public Relief* (New York: Random House, 1972).

57. See Fishel, *Presidents and Promises*.

58. Ibid., 93.

Selected Bibliography

Berry, Jeffrey. *The Interest Group Society*. Boston: Little, Brown, 1984.

Cigler, Allan J., and Burdett A. Loomis. *Interest Group Politics*. 2d ed. Washington, D.C.: CQ Press, 1988.

Heclo, Hugh. "Issue Networks and the Executive Establishment." In *The New American Political System*, ed. Anthony King. Washington, D.C.: American Enterprise Institute, 1978.

Lowi, Theodore J. *The End of Liberalism*. New York: Norton, 1979.

Ornstein, Norman J., and Shirley Elder. *Interest Groups, Lobbying, and Policymaking*. Washington, D.C.: CQ Press, 1978.

Schlozman, Kay Lehman. "What Accent the Heavenly Chorus: Political Equality and the American Pressure System." *Journal of Politics* 46 (1984): 1006-1031.

Presidential Appearances

Presidents always work at a distance from the American public. Public opinion polls, interest groups, the media, and relations with Congress and the bureaucracy give presidents indirect access to the public. Speaking directly to the population helps presidents create at least the illusion of a direct relationship, but it does not help them develop the relationships needed to assemble coalitions and to govern. As presidents attempt to build a coalition, they appeal to the many separate groups, or separate publics, within the population as much as to the public at large. Presidents' constant public appeals have made the presidency an extension of electoral campaigns.

The President as Public Figure

The president occupies the most prominent position in American politics, largely because the United States has no other nationally elected leader. One reason for the president's prominence is the ability to use what Theodore Roosevelt called the "bully pulpit." The president's unique ability to promote a national vision and to influence actors in both the public and private spheres has been crucial in disproving the predictions of some observers of early America that the presidency would play a minor role in national government.

In the twentieth century, the president's prominence in American politics has increased not only with a growing involvement in domestic policy and the rise of the United States to international leadership, but also with an expansion of the president's role as the major preacher in American politics.[1] With words and images as well as the actions of the administration, the president plays a major role in setting the terms of debate for the entire political system.

Public speaking is one of the most important ties between the president and the public. For many citizens, the firmest memory of the president is the president delivering a speech.[2] Between 1945 and 1975, public speeches by presidents increased by about 500 percent. A 1972 report estimated that "a half million words annually flow out of the White House in a torrent of paper ink."[3] Not only presidents' words but also their appearances are important in communicating with the public. Academic studies conclude that nonverbal signs, such as appearances, have four

to ten times the effect of verbal signs on "impression formation."[4]

Political scientist Richard E. Neustadt has argued that the president can exert influence only rarely by command. A more important tool of power is the "power to persuade."[5] Neustadt concentrated on the president's power to persuade other members of the Washington establishment, but the breakdown of many stable institutions has moved presidents to use their persuasive abilities more and more on the public. Even when presidents do not speak out, the threat of "going public" is an important tool.[6]

Communications expert Roderick P. Hart has argued that ubiquitous presidential speech has transformed not only the president and the rest of the national government but the way people perceive politics. The president dominates the public sphere. Working within a "matrix of countervailing forces," the president must maneuver with speech. "Virtually every activity in the modern White House is designed to shape or reshape something that the president has said or will say."[7]

Even when urging change, the president's themes are basically conservative. Philip Abbott has written: "President after president, whether advocating reform or retrenchment, attempt[s] to justify policy by calling America back to its origins, restating its basic values, applying them to current problems by seeking to establish an underlying unity amidst current conflict through a call to rededication and sacrifice."[8]

The development of a voluble presidency stems from changes in the U.S. political system as well as from advances in communications and transportation technologies. The president is now the premier figure in American politics and cannot depend on traditional bases of support such as Congress, party organizations, the print media, or the bureaucracy. Without those mediators of public policy, presidents increasingly must rely on their ability to move people with words.

The connection between presidential speech and the absence of institutional bases was underscored by the Nixon administration's handling of the Watergate scandal. As President Nixon lost support in Congress, in public opinion polls, and among interest groups, he depended increasingly on his rhetorical powers. Nixon's last year in office was dominated by behind-the-scenes strategy sessions on how to respond to charges of lawbreaking and the carefully crafted release of information and public statements.[9]

By Charles C. Euchner

The disparate parts of the American federal system—from states and localities to the wide variety of economic and social groups—regularly turn to the president for rhetorical as well as administrative and legislative leadership. As political scientist E. E. Schattschneider has noted, battles that originate in a restricted setting often move to higher and higher levels as the combatants seek to attract powerful allies.[10] The president exerts rhetorical force on almost every possible political and economic issue that Americans face, even if the president plays no direct role in the issue.

The president has a variety of ways to use rhetoric in politics. The chief executive regularly meets with reporters and other media representatives, gives speeches on television and radio, addresses large crowds and groups, holds informal meetings with leaders of interest groups, travels abroad to meet foreign leaders, meets and speaks by telephone with members of Congress and other elected officials, and attends events that feature celebrities. The president also has command of large research and public relations operations in the White House and federal agencies. Presidential appointees also promote the administration's policies.

What presidents say is often less important than how they say it. The potency of presidential remarks lies not in their content but in the ceremonial way they are delivered. Deference to the president is the norm. As Hart has noted: "Precious few of these ten thousand texts [presidential addresses from Eisenhower to Reagan] were remembered by listeners even a day after their delivery. But what was recalled was the speech event itself—the crowds and the color and the dramaturgy and the physical presence of the chief executive."[11]

As theorists of public rhetoric have noted, the setting for speeches can be even more important than the words uttered. Few spectators of all but the most important presidential speeches can remember much of the arguments in the speech, but most retain a memory of the ceremonial or otherwise symbolic backdrop. When the substance of the speech is remembered, it is usually restricted to a few key phrases or ideas.

Political scientist Murray Edelman has argued that the stage on which presidents appear can provide a rhetorical advantage because the stage removes the audience from its daily routine. "Massiveness, ornateness, and formality are the most common notes struck in the design of these scenes, and they are presented upon a scale which focuses constant attention on the difference between everyday life and the special occasion," Edelman writes. Such backgrounds make for heightened sensitivity and easier conviction in onlookers, for the framed actions are taken on their own terms. They are not qualified by inconsistent facts in the environment.[12]

Presidents bask in the regal splendor of the presidency whenever they make a public appearance. The podium usually holds a seal of the president on the front, and flags usually hang somewhere within the audience's frame of vision. Standing alongside the president is usually a line of dignitaries who look on with respect and even reverance. The distance between the president and the audience increases the sense of the president's "untouchable" status.

When presidents give a State of the Union message, they face a rare assemblage of both houses of Congress, the Supreme Court, and the cabinet; the vice president and Speaker of the House are seated behind the president, and a huge flag hangs in the background. When presidents visit military officials, they stand before impressive-looking equipment such as a navy ship, or before highly disciplined officers and troops, or a military band. When they visit a foreign country, they are treated to welcomes from dignitaries and bands as well as formal dinners and presentations. When they welcome the winners of the World Series or Super Bowl, they are surrounded by the team's banners and other trappings of the sport.

Even in the most unceremonial situations, the president evokes strong national sentiment by the setting. After the truck-bombing of marine barracks in Lebanon in 1985, President Reagan stood in the drizzling rain with his wife and somberly read a statement of tribute to the murdered men and a warning to the forces responsible for the attack. After President Kennedy was assassinated in 1963, Lyndon Johnson took the oath of office on an airplane to emphasize the suddenness of the tragedy and the swift assumption of power.

Although the major television networks occasionally refuse to broadcast an address, presidents almost always have the prestige to gain a wide electronic audience for their speeches and informal discussions. Radio stations always will agree to broadcast short speeches and special events, like Jimmy Carter's call-in show. The importance of televised speeches has increased since the 1960s as the number of press conferences has declined. The more formal talks give the president greater control over the agenda and tempo than the give-and-take of press conferences.

Pete Souza, the White House

The setting for a president's speech can be even more important than the words uttered. President Reagan's speech at the Statue of Liberty celebration on July 3, 1986, is a prime example.

Historical Background

Even though the president has always been the preeminent single figure in American politics, it has been only since the rise of an activist national government and vast systems of communications and transportation that the

Mezzotint by H. S. Sadd, 1849 after T. H. Matteson; Library of Congress

George Washington delivers his inaugural address, April 30, 1789, in New York's old City Hall.

president has been at the center of constant, partisan, policy-oriented rhetoric. In the early days of the Republic, presidents usually confined their public appeals to written messages and addressed only matters of broad national interest. Presidential messages, at least until Woodrow Wilson's administration (1913-1921), took on the quality of a national civics lesson in constitutional government rather than open appeals for political support.

The nation's history of presidential rhetoric can be roughly divided into three periods: the age of the Founders, the age of economic expansion and reform, and the age of presidential leadership.

The Age of the Founders and Early Expansion

The president's role in the nation's rhetoric was set by George Washington (1789-1797) and the rest of the "Virginia Dynasty" that ruled the young nation from 1789 to 1829. Everything Washington did was a conscious precedent for later presidents. Washington's successors—John Adams, Thomas Jefferson, James Madison, James Monroe, and John Quincy Adams—all had direct ties to the nation's founding. They all experienced the same fears about the dangers of democratic or "mob" rule and the importance for national leadership to avoid rhetorical excess. The same impulse that led the Founders to set limits on democratic rule also led the first presidents to set limits on presidential rhetoric to avoid demagogy.

The sense of rhetorical limits that guided presidential rhetoric for its first century began with Washington's first inaugural address. After hearing recommendations from his advisors, Washington discarded plans to include a seventy-three page set of policy recommendations in his inaugural speech. Instead he used the occasion to deliver a more general lecture on virtue and the need for guidance from the Constitution and from God. Washington was the only president to deliver his inaugural address to a select crowd of members of Congress and other dignitaries rather

than the people at large. As was true throughout his presidency, Washington tried to offer leadership by example rather than by argumentation. Washington feared that the regal ceremony might give later presidents dangerous dreams of monarchy, so at his second inaugural he issued a simple two-paragraph address.[13]

With the exception of John Adams (1797-1801), subsequent presidents until Abraham Lincoln (1861-1865) used the inaugural address to explain and extoll the principles of republican government, complete with warnings about the potential excesses of democracy. Discussion of specific policy matters was infrequent and always linked directly to the president's conception of American constitutional values. Of the early presidents, James K. Polk (1845-1849) was the most explicit on policy questions; he pushed for lower tariffs and annexation of Texas and Oregon and opposed creation of a third national bank.

The president also issued a variety of proclamations, mostly written. Those proclamations rarely argued any points; they usually stated government policies, from the institution of Thanksgiving Day to the emancipation of black Southerners from slavery during the Civil War. As political scientist Jeffrey K. Tulis has noted, the proclamations derive their force not from argumentation but from appeals to the Constitution, the nation's sacred document.[14]

The most outstanding example of argumentation in a proclamation was Andrew Jackson's statement denying states the right to "nullify," or declare invalid, laws passed by the national government. Jackson's style was more like that of a Supreme Court decision, explaining the rationale for an irrevocable decision rather than seeking to persuade people to join a coalition.

Perhaps the most ceremonious speech presidents regularly deliver today is the State of the Union address. Until Woodrow Wilson, however, presidents since Thomas Jefferson had met the constitutional requirement to address the nation's affairs with a written report. Congressional leaders followed up the written report with a response to each of the president's points. The State of the Union address, then, was just the beginning of a formal dialogue about government policies based on constitutional and republican principles.

The nation's early years saw some presidential appeals to the people, but the rhetoric was restrained and the audience limited. Below the level of presidential politics, however, debate could be bitter and divisive. As historian Michael E. McGerr has noted, political debate took place as a public spectacle: "Through participation in torchlight parades, mass rallies, and campaign clubs and marching companies, men gave expression to the partisan outlook of the [fiercely partisan] newspaper press." [15] Debates in Congress, for example, often took violent turns. City politics were organized by the gangs and political machines that operated in the streets. Mass demonstrations over slavery, labor, and U.S. involvement in wars were a regular part of the American landscape in the nineteenth century. Political discussions in speeches, pamphlets, and newspapers could be personal and invective. People who worked for presidential campaigns often resorted to caustic language and threats. Through it all, however, the president himself stood above the fray, speaking little publicly about some of the most important issues of the day.

The Founders resisted unbridled democracy, and their rhetoric sought to dampen whatever political passions might exist at the time. The Constitution includes many mechanisms for blocking democratic processes, such as a federalist system, an independent executive, a bicameral legislature, indirect election of presidents and (until 1913) senators, and an independent and tenured judiciary. The ideal political leader was not the man of the people, but rather the statesman who could guide the nation. Alexander Hamilton expressed this ideal in *Federalist* No. 71:

> The republican principle demands that the deliberative sense of the community should guide the conduct of those to whom they entrust the management of their affairs; but it does not require an unqualified complaisance to every sudden breeze of passion, or to every transient impulse which the people may receive from the arts of men, who flatter their prejudices to betray their interests.... [W]hen occasions present themselves in which the interests of the people are at variance with their inclinations, it is the duty of the persons whom they have appointed to be the guardians of those interests to withstand the temporary delusion in order to give them time and opportunity for more sedate reflection. [16]

The president was expected to account for his actions with public, but not necessarily popular, messages. Written messages explaining vetoes and the "state of the union" would be available to Congress and anyone else educated and interested enough to seek them out, but presidents would not aggressively seek public support.

From the administration of George Washington through that of Herbert C. Hoover (1929-1933), the president spent several hours a week at the White House shaking hands with any citizen interested in glimpsing him. The "open house," usually held on Sundays after church services, did not communicate anything of substance, but it conveyed the message that the president would not be monarchical and removed from the people. After the sounding of trumpets and bands and the announcement that the president was on his way to meet the people, single-file queues would move rapidly through the public room of the Executive Mansion. Presidents often tried to calculate just how many hands they would shake in an afternoon, as well as the handshake-per-minute rate. The conversation consisted of little more than greetings and best wishes, although some citizens occasionally tried to convey an opinion about a pressing policy question. [17]

The change in presidential rhetoric is marked by the way biographers have treated presidents before and after 1930. Later biographers express puzzlement that the earlier presidents did not turn to rhetoric as a tool of leadership. But earlier biographers underscore the value of the "custom" of limiting public remarks since such remarks would "sacrifice [the president's] dignity to beg in person for their support." [18]

George G. Bain; Library of Congress

Up through the administration of Herbert Hoover, presidents spent several hours a week at the White House shaking hands with citizens. Left, the general public is admitted for a New Year's Day reception.

Political scientist Jeffrey Tulis found evidence of some one thousand presidential speeches before the twentieth century. Of the twenty-four presidents who served during that period, only four attempted to defend or attack a specific piece of legislation, and only three—Van Buren, Johnson, and Cleveland—made partisan speeches. Only Lincoln addressed the war in which the nation was engaged; Madison and Polk did not. Only nine presidents indicated the general policy directions of the nation in popular speeches. Eighty percent of the speeches were brief.[19]

Throughout this period, presidential rhetoric was circumscribed by the mores that Washington established. Those mores changed—policy issues crept into presidential speeches, even if they were tethered to constitutional principles—but they remained strongly in force. Just how strong those mores remained was underscored by the miserable failure of President Andrew Johnson (1865-1869) in his attempt to rally the public through a national speechmaking tour in the early years of Reconstruction.

Washington was the nation's greatest public figure, a symbol of the new nation's unity. Washington made several public tours in which he put himself on display, but the purpose of the excursions was limited. Washington toured to gather information, ease tensions, and simply show himself to the people. Washington treated the tours "as auxiliary to the president's narrow executive function of carrying out the law and preserving tranquility, rather than his legislative responsibility to initiate new policies." [20]

Washington set an important precedent by insisting on written replies to the remarks of others after speeches.[21] Washington's farewell address was a more scholarly document, open for careful analysis but not grand rhetorical movements.

The second president, John Adams, occasionally met with small groups but did not make public tours. Some historians suggest that Adams lost his chance to improve his public standing on issues, particularly foreign affairs, because of his public reticence. Thomas Jefferson (1801-1805), considered the most democratic theorist of early America, limited his public statements to a few meetings with American Indians and his formal, written messages to Congress. Despite a difficult war with Great Britain, James Madison (1809-1817) continued the practice of presidential communication by proclamation rather than speech.

James Monroe (1817-1825) reinstituted Washington's practice of the national tour, but otherwise stayed within the limits of unity appeals and limited speech. Despite his background as a teacher of rhetoric at Harvard College, John Quincy Adams (1825-1829) refused to do more than put himself "on display" in public gatherings. His public remarks were simple statements of greetings and congratulations. Adams almost never even referred to the public issues of the day before popular audiences.

Following the bitter controversy over the 1824 election of John Quincy Adams over Andrew Jackson (1829-1837), the nation experienced major pushes to expand the idea of democratic rule. Suffrage barriers pertaining to property fell during this period as the nation moved westward and politicians from different regions competed for control over the nation's development. Political parties, which put forth radically different views of development and protection, gained legitimacy for the first time and created a regular public clash of ideas. The sectional tensions finally led to the bloody Civil War of 1861 to 1865.

Jackson rarely gave speeches. He enjoyed popular discourse, but once elected president he limited the number of appearances and contained his argumentation within the limits set by his predecessors. Jackson's most public campaigns—against the National Bank and the doctrine of nullification—were quite limited. His public appeals were mediated—that is to say, he spoke to the public through the formal channels of official documents and proclamations. Jackson's annual messages and the nullification proclamation to Congress were all written appeals.

Jackson's successors were also reluctant to speak. Martin Van Buren faced a boycott of councils in three New York towns after he delivered a slightly partisan remark, then abandoned any more such rhetoric. John Tyler (1841-1845) delivered no public addresses. James Polk took one public tour but considered other public appearances a nuisance and therefore avoided them. Zachary Taylor took one tour but avoided being seen; the journey was a fact-finding tour more than a public relations effort.

Millard Fillmore (1850-1853) was the first president since Washington to discuss policy in public when he defended the Compromise of 1850 in a series of short speeches. But these speeches took place after policy had been determined; they were not intended to sway action during the policy-making process. Franklin Pierce (1853-1857) expanded presidential rhetoric, discussing the role of tariffs and federalism. As a lame-duck president just before the Civil War, James Buchanan (1857-1861) discussed the nominating process of the Democratic party and the role of property and popular rule in the states.

Abraham Lincoln appeared before a number of groups but averred that he could not speak about policy except in a more appropriate place. Tulis has outlined five reasons for Lincoln's infrequent public rhetoric: modesty about his own "wisdom" before his inauguration, a desire to let problems sort themselves out, the need for flexibility, the dramatic effect that his statements might have, and a desire to lend greater authority to the few public pronouncements he eventually would make.[22]

Still, some of Lincoln's addresses were important to his governing. As Abbott has noted, all of Lincoln's speeches were rooted in specific political problems, such as the lynching of an abolitionist journalist and the economic aspects of slavery.[23]

Lincoln's successor, Andrew Johnson, was the exceptional case of the voluble president. As a Southern Democrat who rose to the presidency through assassination, Johnson had no real base of power in Washington. He found himself under attack from all sides and fought back with words. But his rhetorical thrusts further undermined his position.[24]

The Age of Economic Growth and Reform

As the nation recovered from the Civil War, economic growth resumed on a scale previously unimagined. Transportation and communications networks stretched across the nation, and businesses grew in size and geographic importance. The national government played an important role in the expansion but did not address the more negative consequences of rapid industrialization and urbanization. The national government responded to the economy's swings of boom and bust, but its role was limited by the constrained rhetoric and vision of public action. As politicians recognized the need for more concerted national action, both the rhetoric and the vision expanded.

Seeking to build his political strength, President Andrew Johnson made a speaking tour of the country in 1866.

In many ways, the dilemmas that Andrew Johnson faced after succeeding President Lincoln resembled the situation of modern presidents. Bereft of a strong party organization, dealing with an independent-minded Congress, facing deep sectional divisions, and lacking control over patronage, Johnson desperately needed to find a way to build his political strength. Similar to presidents in the late twentieth century, Johnson sought that strength by appealing over the heads of political elites to the power of public opinion. Because the system was not accustomed to such appeals, Johnson's attempt to go public failed. He was the only president in history to be impeached, and one of the counts against him actually concerned the style of his "intemperate" rhetoric. Johnson committed the most important rhetorical "crimes" while trying to rally public support for his policies for the defeated states of the Confederacy. Tulis has described Johnson's rhetorical style:

> Like contemporary electoral campaigns, Johnson had one rough outline, carried in his head, on which he rendered variations for particular audiences. In the typical speech, Johnson would begin by disclaiming any intention to speak, proceed to invoke the spirits of Washington and Jackson, claim his own devotion to the principles of Union, deny that he was a traitor as others alleged, attack some part of the audience (depending on the kind of heckles he received), defend his use of the veto, attack Congress as a body and single out particular congressmen (occasionally denouncing them as traitors for not supporting his policies), compare himself to Christ and offer himself as a martyr, and finally conclude by declaring his closeness to the people and appealing for their support.[25]

Johnson's tour, which received bad notices in the Republican-dominated press, was avoided even by Johnson's cabinet and aides. When on February 24, 1868, the House of Representatives resolved to impeach Johnson, the tenth and last article concerned Johnson's bad rhetoric. The Senate acquitted Johnson (by one vote), but no major political figure disagreed with the notion that

his public appeals were improper. The lessons from Johnson's bitter experience were clear: politics are a dirty game, and presidents who become involved in the nasty rhetoric put themselves in danger of getting tarred in the process.

Ulysses S. Grant (1869-1877) and Rutherford B. Hayes (1877-1881), the two presidents immediately following Andrew Johnson, limited their public speechmaking to official greetings and plaudits to veterans and other groups. Both presidents refused to campaign for the White House and issued written statements to indicate policy preferences. Hayes delivered more than one hundred speeches, but they were limited to greetings to groups. This real but unsubstantive expansion of presidential speech might be attributed to the need to shore up national confidence because of the controversy surrounding Hayes's election by the House. Hayes also took several tours and delivered speeches that addressed policy within the larger philosophical framework of republicanism.

James A. Garfield (1881) campaigned for the White House but did not speak on policy as president. His successor, Chester A. Arthur (1881-1885), also limited his talks to symbolic statements at public ceremonies. Grover Cleveland (1885-1889, 1893-1897) discussed taxes, civil service, and labor during his presidential campaigns but made few public remarks as president. He also wrote extensively on many issues.

Benjamin Harrison (1889-1893) broke with tradition when he discussed policy issues such as the railroads and postal service during his public tours; still, he was reluctant to go too far. He told a Kingston, New York, crowd, for example: "You ask for a speech. It is not very easy to know what one can talk about on such an occasion as this. Those topics that are most familiar to me, because I am in daily contact with them, namely, public affairs, are in some measure prohibited to me." [26]

William McKinley (1897-1901) vowed to talk on a wide range of issues, but his speeches were formal and philosophical in character like those of the nineteenth-century presidents. McKinley did not make any speeches on the Spanish-American War, the sinking of the battleship *Maine*, the Philippines, or southern race laws.

Theodore Roosevelt (1901-1909), the feisty former New York governor who assumed the presidency upon McKinley's assassination, was the first president to go over the head of Congress since Andrew Johnson, but Roosevelt did not overturn the longtime balance of power between the two branches of government. As political scientist Elmer Cornwell has noted, Roosevelt's tours on behalf of specific policies began and ended before Congress took up the matter.[27]

Roosevelt's handpicked successor, William Howard Taft (1909-1913), increased presidential leadership of public opinion. Taft regularly issued lists of legislative initiatives he favored. He was more adept as an administrator than as a rhetorician, however. Although his antitrust and environmental policies were in line with Roosevelt's, his hortatory deficiencies were one of the reasons Roosevelt opposed him in the 1912 election.

Woodrow Wilson (1913-1921) was a crucial figure in the transformation of the national government from a congressional to a presidential system. He argued for a more unified system of government with the president as the leader, overcoming the fragmented, plodding committees in Congress. Moving public policy from the darkness of the committee meeting to the bright light of public debate was central to Wilson's system. He argued that the public could judge the president's character; if the public could find a leader to trust, the president could be entrusted with a wide grant of power. Wilson wrote: "Men can scarcely be orators without the force of character, that readiness of resource, that clearness of vision, that earnestness of purpose and that instinct and capacity for leadership which are the eight horses that draw the triumphal chariot of every leader and ruler of free men. We could not object to being ruled by such men." [28]

Wilson's ambitious domestic programs and involvement in World War I and the Versailles peace conference put the presidency in the middle of the nation's rhetorical battles. As historian David Green has argued, Wilson's public comments on the European war left room open for eventual U.S. involvement in the war. Wilson promised to keep the United States out of war but contrasted American "liberty" with German "authoritarianism." [29]

Once the United States entered the war and the Allied powers won, Wilson took an active public role. Wilson's depiction of the war as the "war to end all wars" helped to overcome many of the deep internal divisions within the United States based on the nationalities of U.S. immigrant citizens. Wilson's 1919 trip to Versailles and his subsequent parade through the streets of Paris was a rare foreign trip. The height of this public role was his U.S. tour to build support for U.S. membership in the League of Nations. Wilson's moralistic campaign ended when he collapsed with a stroke, and the Senate rejected the treaty.

The presidents who succeeded Wilson—Warren G. Harding (1921-1923), Calvin Coolidge (1923-1929), and Herbert C. Hoover (1929-1933)—were less active rhetorically. Harding, elected president because of a back-room bargain at the Republican convention in 1920, limited his public appearances and statements and instituted a written-questions-only policy for questions from the media. He died of a heart attack two years into his term. Coolidge—"Silent Cal"—was best known for his taciturn manner. In his press conferences, Coolidge continued Harding's policy of written press questions. Hoover was the first president to use radio extensively, but the audience was too small and Hoover's speaking style too formal for a strong president-public relationship to develop around his speeches.

The Age of Presidential Leadership

During the Great Depression, which began in 1929, the nation turned to Franklin D. Roosevelt (1933-1945) for presidential leadership. Roosevelt was tireless in his efforts to expand the government's involvement in both domestic and international politics.

Both Roosevelt's programs and rhetoric emphasized the need for strong central direction that only a president could provide. For the first time, the government in Washington moved from its traditional role as patronage state to a regulatory state.[30] As the government became involved in all aspects of everyday life, the need for strong executive direction increased. Sophisticated systems of communication also tightened the bond between the president and the public. From the administration of Franklin Roosevelt through that of Ronald Reagan (1981-1989), the president became more of a rhetorical leader on a wide range of issues rather than an executive on a limited set of fundamentally national concerns.

By the time FDR took office, millions of American homes were tied together by the airwaves of radio broadcasting. Politics moved from the crowds to the smaller units of a radio-listening audience. Political speeches, once bombastic, became more conversational and intimate. As communications expert Kathleen Hall Jamieson has noted, this shift was reflected in the metaphors used to describe human relations. Warlike words such as *armed, forceful, take, hold, yield, marshal, battle, weapons,* and *onslaught* once described political debates; with the dawn of the media age came warm, electrical words like *wavelength, relayed, channeled, transformed, turned on, fused,* and *defused.*[31]

Roosevelt was the perfect president to begin the new style of debate. He delivered a series of "fireside chats" to the nation over the radio that identified him with everyday concerns. Roosevelt's secretary of labor, Frances Perkins, described the talks:

> When he talked on the radio, he saw them gathered in the little parlor, listening with their neighbors. He was conscious of their faces and hands, their clothes and homes. His voice and his facial expression as he spoke were those of an intimate friend. . . . I have seen men and women gathered around the radio, even those who didn't like him or who were opposed to him politically, listening with a pleasant, happy feeling of association and friendship. The exchange between them and him through the medium of the radio was very real. I have seen tears coming to their eyes as he told them of some tragic episode, of the sufferings of the persecuted people in Europe, of the poverty during unemployment, of the sufferings of the homeless, of the sufferings of the people whose sons had died during the war, and they were tears of sincerity and recognition and sympathy.[32]

Since the end of World War II, presidents have spoken in public more than ten thousand times—an average of one speech every working day.[33]

Harry Truman used rhetoric as a tool in his relations with Congress, but it was always directed toward specific policy aims. Truman relied on rhetoric to promote his

Table 1 Level of Public Activities of Presidents, 1949-1984

President	Total activities	Yearly average	Monthly average
Truman	520	130	10.8
Eisenhower, I	330	83	6.9
Eisenhower, II	338	85	7.0
Kennedy	658	219	18.8
Johnson [a]	1,463	293	24.0
Nixon, I	634	159	13.2
Nixon, II	204	113	10.2
Ford	756	344	26.0
Carter	1,047	262	22.0
Reagan [b]	1,194	299	24.9

Source: Gary King and Lyn Ragsdale, *The Elusive Executive: Discovering Statistical Patterns in the Presidency* (Washington, D.C.: CQ Press, 1988), 275.

Note: Public activities are defined as including all domestic public appearances by a president, including major speeches, news conferences, minor speeches, Washington appearances, and U.S. appearances but not political appearances.
a. Includes full term from November 1963 to January 1969.
b. Figures for Reagan through first term only.

policies on European redevelopment, relations with the Soviet Union, aid to Greece and Turkey, and civil rights. Truman's 1948 election campaign was a marathon of public speaking, a whistlestop excoriation of Congress and a call for public support. Perhaps the Truman administration's most important legacy was its rhetoric about the Soviet Union. Truman acknowledged overstating the Soviet threat to arouse the public during the Greece-Turkey crisis, after a congressional leader advised him to "scare the hell out of the country."[34] Harsh anti-Soviet rhetoric since the Truman administration may be responsible for the bitterness of U.S.-Soviet relations and the costly nuclear arms race.

Because of improved air transportation, modern presidents have traveled regularly, both within the United States and around the world. Presidents through Dwight D. Eisenhower felt obliged to justify their trips abroad, but international travel has become a regular, expected, and even desired part of the office.

The president's expanded role in national politics has other causes besides advanced systems of transportation and communication, including: the decline of party strength, the development of populist nomination systems, the rise of political consultants, the fragmentation of Congress, and the "nationalization" of politics and policy.

Modern Presidential Appearances and Rhetoric

Presidential rhetoric in the postwar years shifted fundamentally with the ascension of John F. Kennedy to the White House. Harry Truman and Dwight Eisenhower used public speech almost solely in pursuit of a specific policy initiative, but later presidents have spoken out regularly on a wide range of matters. Speech has become a daily fact of life for presidents.

Modern presidents appear willing and even compelled to talk about every possible aspect of political and social issues—even those about which they are ignorant. Presidents also speak before a greater variety of groups.[35]

Presidential speech is more personal today than it ever has been. Whereas previous presidents spoke formally about issues of great national importance, modern presidents talk in a conversational, intimate way.[36] The shift to the informal style was gradual. Eisenhower spoke formally, but, generally, presidents after Roosevelt at least tried to connect with the public in a casual way.

The number of self references a president makes increases throughout the term of office. Typical are the following statements by Jimmy Carter: "I've always been proud of the fact that when I came to Virginia to begin my campaign a couple years ago and didn't have very many friends, I went to Henry Howell's home, and he and Betty were nice enough to. . . ." "I would like very much to tell my grandchildren that I slept in the same bed that was used by the governor of Virginia."[37]

Perhaps the most famous example of intimate discourse—which went beyond the bounds of personal reflection because it tied personal and policy issues too closely—was President Carter's discussion of his daughter Amy's fear of nuclear war during his debate with Ronald Reagan in the 1980 campaign. Personal statements must show the president to be intimate, but citizens expect the president to move from this deep personal concern to tough-minded action.

The Kennedy Style

John Kennedy may be considered the founder of modern presidential speechmaking. Kennedy rose to the presidency partly because of his good television appearance during the 1960 election debates with Richard Nixon. Kennedy took advantage of his ease with television once he occupied the White House. Kennedy used his humor and his ease on camera and in group settings to disarm opponents.

Kennedy was the first president to make regular appearances year-round. Previous presidents and politicians appeared publicly during elections and campaigns for specific policies, but Kennedy stayed in public view even during the slow months of summer. Television—which by the early 1960s was in 90 percent of all American households—presented a powerful new opportunity for speaking directly to Americans.

President Kennedy used the presidential news conference to appear on television more frequently than previous presidents. The conferences usually took place during the day because White House aides worried about overexposure and the effect that mistakes would have on the president's public standing. Despite this reluctance, Kennedy was aware of the way the Oval Office occupant intrigued the public, and he moved to exploit that interest. Kennedy's wit was a central part of the press meetings.

Beyond the development of a personal relationship with the public, speeches were at the center of the most important policy developments of the Kennedy years. The Bay of Pigs invasion, the Cuban missile crisis, the visit to the Berlin Wall, the decision to accelerate the space program, relations with the Soviet Union, and the civil rights movement, all were marked by important addresses. Unlike the addresses of later presidents, the Kennedy speeches remain important events today for their content as much as

John F. Kennedy Library

President John F. Kennedy developed a personal relationship with the public by pioneering the frequent use of televised press conferences.

for the atmosphere in which they were delivered.

The Kennedy inaugural address was one of the most memorable in history because it was a new expression of national purpose and energy. Kennedy won the presidency in 1960 with the narrowest margin of victory ever, and he needed a rallying cry to establish his leadership. Congress was skeptical and moved slowly throughout Kennedy's presidency, making the president's stirring calls to action all the more important.

The speech after the failed invasion of Cuba is a classic statement of presidential responsibility for failed policy. The invasion, planned by the Central Intelligence Agency during the Eisenhower administration and designed to topple Cuban leader Fidel Castro, was one of Kennedy's first tests as a world leader. When it failed, Kennedy pulled American troops out quickly and reported to the nation. The report itself was viewed as an important test of the young president's ability to persevere and learn from mistakes.

In a nationally televised speech, Kennedy told the nation: "There is an old saying that victory has a hundred fathers and defeat is an orphan.... I am the responsible officer of government and that is quite obvious." [38] After the speech, Kennedy's poll support increased by 10 percentage points. Other presidents—most notably, Ronald Reagan—have copied the technique of accepting responsibility for a failed undertaking, thereby diffusing difficult political situations.

President Kennedy used his television address on the Cuban missile crisis as a negotiating tool with the Soviet Union. Kennedy's selective use of information about the stalemate over Soviet placement of nuclear missiles in Cuba gave him flexibility in his private negotiations with Soviet leader Nikita Khrushchev. Later presidents all used dramatic television speeches as levers in their international bargaining. Nixon's speeches on the Vietnam War and Reagan's speeches on arms control are important examples.

The tension over the status of Berlin—a city in the middle of East Germany that was occupied by the four World War II Allied nations—produced two important kinds of public speech. As part of their own strategy of public diplomacy, Soviet leaders had threatened the status of the city's "free" sectors. Kennedy responded with a threatening television speech. The speech was not an ultimatum, but it evoked the possibility of nuclear war and even discussed the advisability of Americans building bomb shelters. One critic called it "one of the most alarming speeches by an American president in the whole, nerve-wracking course of the cold war." [39] The speech was impetus for Congress to mobilize and was a stark warning to the Soviets.

In June 1963, Kennedy visited Berlin. The famous "Ich bin ein Berliner" speech at the Berlin Wall was a classic statement to foreign publics and a warning to U.S. adversaries. The speech spoke through symbols in a very personal way about major world politics. President Kennedy stood at the wall the Soviets constructed to halt the free movement of citizens in the city and declared himself and the rest of the Western world citizens of the troubled city.

President Kennedy's speech at American University the same month helped to establish a framework for the later policy of U.S.-Soviet détente. Few presidential speeches have helped to chart major changes in policy as much as that address at the Washington, D.C., university.

Johnson and Nixon

Lyndon Johnson was a less graceful speaker, but he spoke even more frequently than Kennedy. Johnson's appearance before a joint session of Congress after Kennedy's assassination was crucial in restoring confidence and stability in the government. After winning election as president on his own, Johnson used a State of the Union address to outline his ambitious "Great Society" domestic programs.

Johnson also increased the number of domestic ceremonies, which already had quadrupled from the Eisenhower to the Kennedy administrations. Johnson made a ceremony of the activities of every conceivable group that could be identified with the nation. Like later presidents, Johnson took refuge in ceremony especially when polls

Table 2 Minor Presidential Speeches by Year, 1949-1984

Truman		Nixon, I	
1949	8	1969	5
1950	13	1970	6
1951	9	1971	10
1952	9	1972	4
Total	39	Total	25
Eisenhower, I		Nixon, II	
1953	5	1973	12
1954	2	1974	10
1955	2	Total	22
1956	2		
Total	11		
		Ford	
Eisenhower, II		1974	5
1957	5	1975	36
1958	7	1976	36
1959	2	Total	77
1960	4		
Total	18		
		Carter	
Kennedy		1977	21
1961	6	1978	15
1962	7	1979	22
1963	17	1980	24
Total	30	Total	82
Johnson		Reagan [a]	
1963-64	11	1981	11
1965	9	1982	27
1966	11	1983	19
1967	4	1984	21
1968	14	Total	78
Total	49		

Source: Gary King and Lyn Ragsdale, *The Elusive Executive: Discovering Statistical Patterns in the Presidency* (Washington, D.C.: CQ Press, 1988), 271.

a. Figures for Reagan through first term only.

showed low levels of public support.

Richard Nixon ran his public relations campaign on two tracks—national television, where he gave regular addresses and press conferences, and local communities and White House meetings, where he appeared before groups likely to support him. On the three issues that occupied Nixon the most—foreign policy (especially the Vietnam War), the economy, and Watergate—Nixon's strategy was closely tied to the way he presented himself to the public. From the time of his successful 1968 campaign, Nixon used public relations to bypass the Washington "establishment." Nixon's presidency was plebiscitary in that he sought public approval after acting on important issues.

Nixon was adept at using foreign travels to build public support. His 1972 trips to the Soviet Union and the People's Republic of China attracted unprecedented television and print coverage and established him as an epochmaking world leader.

Toward the end of his presidency, Nixon's public support fell badly—he had the approval of just 23 percent of the public before his resignation—and he tried to revive his fortunes with carefully orchestrated trips to small, friendly communities. Domestic trips to places like Nashville's

Grand Ole Opry gave the president a chance to get away from the insistent questioning of the national press corps. This strategy was lampooned in the newspaper comic strip "Doonesbury," which showed a fictional town called Critters, Alabama, awaiting a presidential motorcade.

Despite his reputation as a cold and even devious politician, Nixon often showed an emotional side to the public and to his staff. The emotional displays were at least partly responsible for many citizens' intense loyalty to the president. In his farewell talk to White House staff after his resignation, Nixon recalled his mother's guidance—he called her a "saint"—and his own setbacks as a politician. With tears streaming down his face, he spoke of how Theodore Roosevelt fought to rebuild his life after the death of his first wife, implying that he would do the same. Nixon's staff—and the television audience—were profoundly moved by the speech.

Ford and Carter

When Gerald R. Ford inherited the presidency after Nixon and Vice President Spiro Agnew resigned, his main job was to restore faith in the badly bruised presidency. In his first address to the nation, Ford declared that "our long national nightmare is over." Ford's relaxed style won him broad public support, but his popularity fell badly when he pardoned former president Nixon. Ford was unable to recover because of a lack of support in Congress and an inability to stir the nation with his words.

Ford was the nation's most voluble president, even if his speaking did not win him public support. Ford made public remarks on 1,236 occasions in less than two and a half years in office.[40] None of his speeches (except his first) was considered memorable, but that was not very important for Ford's immediate purpose of wrapping himself in the prestige of the presidency. The most memorable Ford statements were "gaffes," such as his declaration that Eastern Europeans did not consider themselves to be dominated by the Soviet Union. Ford's aborted public campaign to "Whip Inflation Now" also met with derision.

Jimmy Carter's rise to the presidency stemmed in part from his intimate statements during the 1976 campaign. Carter's presidency was filled with symbolic events and addresses to the nation; for example, he wore a cardigan sweater in his televised address asking the nation to make energy sacrifices. The crucial moment of the Carter term occurred when, after a ten-day consultation with leaders in various fields at Camp David, the president spoke on television about a "crisis of confidence" in the nation.

Carter was a tireless public performer and was sometimes very effective. Especially in small groups, Carter's grasp of facts and quiet manner were rhetorically impressive, but his halting speech and southern drawl did not serve him well on television and before larger groups. Moreover, the public did not always receive well his often gloomy assessments of world affairs, such as his descriptions of American moral decay, environmental dangers, human rights abuses, the Vietnam War's legacy, and nuclear war.

The Reagan Approach

Ronald Reagan presented a rosier picture of the future than Carter. Reagan's training as a movie actor, host of a

Table 3 President Carter's Minor Addresses, October 1977

Date	Location	Audience	Subject
October 4	United Nations	General Assembly	Controlling nuclear proliferation
October 4	United Nations	U.S. delegation	Thanks for fine job, importance of the U.N.
October 5	United Nations	not stated	Remarks on signing international covenants on human rights
October 5	United Nations	Foreign ministers, heads of delegations	Changing international relationships
October 7	Washington Hilton Hotel	Democratic National Committee	Political support for Panama Canal treaties
October 19	State Department	Conference for International Nuclear Fuel Cycle Evaluation	Provisions for adequate power sources
October 21	Des Moines, Iowa	not stated	Importance of Iowa farm bill
October 21	Des Moines, Iowa	Democratic party dinner	New farm legislation, energy issues
October 22	Denver, Colorado	Western states governors	Western water policy
October 22	Denver, Colorado	Citizens from Rocky Mountain West	Panama Canal
October 22	Los Angeles, California	Democratic National Committee dinner	Human rights, peace in the Middle East, energy issues

Source: Samuel Kernell, *Going Public: New Strategies of Presidential Leadership* (Washington, D.C.: CQ Press, 1986), 92.

television show, and speaker on the "mashed potato circuit" for General Electric served him well as a speaker both on television and before large and small crowds. Reagan's optimism gained credibility with his jovial reaction to events such as the attempt on his life. After the 1981 shooting, Reagan told his wife, "Honey, I forgot to duck"— a line from an old Hollywood boxing movie.

President Reagan's reputation as the "Great Communicator" underscored a growing separation between the president and the message. All of Reagan's addresses were drafted by professional speechwriters, and even some of his apparently extemporaneous remarks, such as greetings to specific people and jokes, were scripted. Reagan held the fewest press conferences of any modern president because White House aides questioned his grasp of many policy issues and his ability to make statements that were not written out beforehand.

A number of embarrassing extemporaneous remarks seemed to suggest Reagan was ill-informed about many subjects he addressed, such as the role of Americans in the Spanish Civil War, the effects of budget and tax cuts, weapon systems, the makeup of the nuclear "freeze" movement, American Indians, monetary policy, Central American politics, and Soviet politics.

Still, Reagan succeeded in promoting his policies because of his apparently deep and consistent convictions and his comfort with public speaking. With the possible exception of Kennedy, Reagan was the first president to have a well-developed affinity for the electronic media. That affinity carried over to live events because audiences in the media age are comfortable with public performances that resemble television appearances.

Reagan restored the pomp and ceremony stripped from the presidency in the reaction to Nixon's "imperial" administration. A hallmark of his appearances was the grand celebration of American icons, from the Statue of Liberty to ordinary citizens whom Reagan hailed as "heroes" during State of the Union addresses. Reagan basked unabashedly in hearing "Hail to the Chief" before his speeches, and his rhetoric about liberty and opportunity in America and the need to confront the Soviet Union in world politics was inspirational to many Americans weary of the apparent decline the United States suffered in the 1970s.

As Kathleen Hall Jamieson has argued, Reagan's speech was in line with the more intimate manner of public addresses of the media age.[41] His discussions of first-hand experiences and concrete events were lucid, while his remarks about more abstract policy matters often was disjointed. Previous presidents used first-person accounts, but Reagan's personal remarks were effective because they used humor and modesty to portray him as a likable, stable figure. After brief periods in the hospital, Johnson and Nixon used personal anecdotes to attempt to connect with the public. Johnson's words were cold, Nixon's competitive.

United Press International Photo

Jimmy Carter's presidency was filled with symbolic addresses to the nation. Here he wears a cardigan sweater in his televised address asking the nation to make energy sacrifices.

Reagan's presidency, by contrast, was a string of self-deflating cracks and yarns about his experiences in Hollywood and politics.[42]

Kinds of Presidential Speeches

The president has different ways and reasons to communicate with the public. How widely the president's remarks will be circulated is the main consideration for the tone and content of a speech. The group's role in the president's past and future political battles is another consideration. And still another is the president's present political standing with the public and with various interest groups.

The deadlock of U.S. domestic politics may explain a shift in the content of televised speeches from foreign to domestic affairs. Presidents Carter and Reagan were more likely to devote air time to domestic affairs than were their predecessors. Both sought to overcome interest group alignments on issues like energy, taxes, and budgetary matters with appeals to the public at large.[43]

The effect of presidential speechmaking is complex. In one respect, the greater emphasis on rhetoric centers the whole political system on the presidency; the other parts of the system, such as parties, interest groups, and regions, become subordinate to the White House. But as political scientist Samuel Kernell has argued, presidential speeches are neither a plebiscitary nor a leveling force in U.S. politics. Presidents "go public," in Kernell's words, to assemble temporary coalitions of many different groups on specific policies.[44] Indeed, the explosion in minor addresses supports Kernell's contention that the system remains complex despite the president's primacy.

It is useful to break down presidential communications according to the audience, mode of communication, the purpose of the address, and political situation at the time of the speech. There are six basic categories of presidential addresses: ceremonial speeches, official state speeches, general persuasive speeches, hortatory or moralistic speeches, crisis speeches, and addresses to specific groups. Some of the speeches fit more than one category.

Ceremonial Speeches

As the symbolic embodiment of the nation, the president represents the United States in international affairs and in events designed to underscore the country's unity and progress. The president receives foreign dignitaries at home and abroad. The president also sets the tone for a number of domestic events, such as presentation of awards, space shuttle launchings, and hortatory efforts such as the fight against drug abuse.

As Roderick Hart has noted, the increase in presidential speechmaking since World War II is largely attributable to ceremonial events. The average number of monthly ceremonial speeches has increased from 2.4 under Truman and 3.4 under Eisenhower to 15.2 under Ford and 10.7 under Carter.[45] The number of Reagan ceremonies—7.85—was not so high as that of his predecessors, but it was still significant. Reagan also made ceremonies out of more business-like events, like the State of the Union address and policy and interest group speeches. The pomp surrounding Reagan's addresses restored the ceremony stripped from the presidency in the 1970s.

The chief of state role strengthens the president's ef-

forts to build widespread support for policies and ideas that are part of the president's political program. Hart has noted: "To stand in this spotlight is to risk comparatively little, for in such situations listeners' defenses are down, the press is prohibited by cultural mandate from being excessively cynical, and the institution of the presidency—its traditions and its emotional trappings—insulate the chief executive from partisan attack." [46]

Hart has identified four kinds of presidential ceremonies.[47] *Initiating ceremonies* mark major transitions—signing legislation or treaties and swearing in government officials. *Honorific ceremonies* bestow some formal recognition of achievement. Testimonial dinners, awards of medals, university commencements all fit this category. *Celebrative ceremonies* pay tribute to important national events or values. They include eulogies, dinners for foreign dignitaries, patriotic remembrances, and building dedications. The Statue of Liberty celebration in New York in 1986 was a prime example. *Greeting and departure ceremonies* mark the important travels of presidents and foreign dignitaries.

Inaugural addresses are the premier ceremonies of the presidency. A president sets the tone for the administration at the inauguration. Traditionally delivered at the steps of the Capitol building immediately following the swearing-in, the inaugural address provides the most important hint of the kind of moral leadership the president wants to provide. The president uses the inaugural speech to unite a nation that has just undergone a partisan election campaign. The president asks the opposition for help and asserts that the nation's factions have common purposes despite their disagreements about how to achieve certain goals.

The content of most inaugural addresses is usually forgotten soon after the event. Some addresses are so eloquent or poignant, however, that they have become part of the nation's "civic religion." Thomas Jefferson's first inaugural argued that the nation shared a common purpose despite the bitter battles of the Federalists and the Anti-Federalists. Andrew Jackson asserted the power of the common man in his inaugural. In Abraham Lincoln's second inaugural speech, he made an eloquent appeal for national healing while in the midst of the horrors of the Civil War.

Other famous inaugural addresses include Franklin Roosevelt's 1933 admonition that "there is nothing to fear but fear itself" and John Kennedy's call for national sacrifice in 1961. Kennedy urged: "Ask not what your country can do for you; ask what you can do for your country." Kennedy also pledged to "friend and foe alike" that the United States would be an activist force in international affairs.

Farewell addresses are another important ceremonial speech. What the president says upon leaving office can help set the tone for the next administration and, more likely, help to shape the nation's memory and assessment of the outgoing executive. The farewell can be an emotional time for the president and the public and the president's closest political allies.

When moving from active leader to historical figure, presidents are not subject to the same political pressures as they were while in office, nor are they able to muster the same clout. The farewell address can exert great force over time but is not likely to have much of an effect on immediate politics. The purpose is more to leave the nation with a lasting statement of principles from an elder statesman to which it can refer. George Washington's farewell set substantive policy and etiquette for future presidents. Other important farewell addresses were delivered by Jackson, Cleveland, Eisenhower, Nixon, and Carter.

Official State Speeches

The Constitution requires the president to make a statement on the "state of the nation" every year, and since Woodrow Wilson the president has addressed a joint session of Congress to propose policies and to assess the nation's problems and achievements. (Thomas Jefferson discontinued the practice of personal, oral delivery of State of the Union addresses, which George Washington had begun.)

Once presented in writing, the State of the Union address has become a major event in presidential leadership and congressional relations. Delivered before a joint session of Congress, the Supreme Court, and the cabinet, these addresses survey the range of budgetary and other policies the administration plans to pursue in the coming year. Even if the administration has not completed the design of its programs, presidents announce their major initiatives in the address.

Lyndon Johnson's Great Society and Vietnam initiatives; Richard Nixon's Vietnam, "New Federalism," and economic programs; Jimmy Carter's energy, civil service, welfare and tax reform, and foreign affairs initiatives; and Ronald Reagan's tax, budget, regulatory, and military programs were all outlined in State of the Union addresses.

Because many programs are announced without thorough planning, there is a danger that the State of the Union address could create false expectations and eventual disappointment. Many of Johnson's Great Society programs, for example, were in their nascent stages when announced. The combination of warlike rhetoric and fragmented program designs contributed to the eventual disappointment with many of the programs, such as the Community Action program, which had been designed to "empower" the urban poor.

Other state speeches include addresses to foreign bodies such as the British Parliament and the United Nations General Assembly.

General Persuasive Speeches

Most presidential addresses seek to develop a favorable environment for a wide variety of policies, but less than half of the president's speeches try to persuade the public to adopt specific policies and directions.

Reagan successfully urged passage of his tax and budget packages in 1981. On February 5, Reagan told a national television audience that the nation faced the "worst economic mess since the Great Depression." Less than two weeks later, Reagan told a television audience about his plans to deal with the problem. After an assassination attempt boosted his popularity, Reagan in late April 1981 addressed an enthusiastic joint session of Congress. In July, he returned to national television and asked viewers to pressure Congress to support administration policies. Reagan's appeal generated fifteen million more letters than Congress normally receives in a session.[48]

Woodrow Wilson's national campaign after World War I for Senate acceptance of the Versailles treaty and the League of Nations was perhaps the most dramatic example of persuasive oratory in U.S. history. Unwilling to bargain with the Republican leaders on the treaty, Wilson traveled eight thousand miles over a month starting September 3, 1919. He delivered thirty-seven speeches and attended even more public events during which he urged the treaty's passage. Wilson's tour ended when he collapsed of a stroke. The Senate defeated the treaty.

Recent examples of major persuasive speeches include Reagan's tax and budget speeches; Carter's energy and economic speeches; Ford's addresses on the economy and his pardon of Nixon; Nixon's speeches on Vietnam, the economy, and Watergate; Johnson's addresses on Vietnam, social problems, and domestic disorder; and Kennedy's addresses on civil rights and economics.

Hortatory or Moralistic Speeches

The president attempts to persuade the public to set aside personal, selfish aims and seek a more general public interest. Like a high school football coach, the president also attempts to infuse the public with confidence and zeal for tasks that may seem difficult.

Presidential speechmaking in the nation's first century usually was confined to educational or moralistic messages. On their tours of the expanding nation, presidents discussed constitutional and republican principles, federalism, economic policies, and the place of American values in world politics.

Twentieth-century president Jimmy Carter spoke frequently on the energy crisis—so frequently that he began to worry that Americans were "inured" to the major problems that the issue presented. To confront the public's blasé attitude, Carter delivered—after a ten-day retreat to Camp David—a speech about what he called the nation's "crisis of confidence." That speech—a choppy text—failed to offer a plan of action that matched the spiritual crisis Carter described. Although delivered in an atmosphere of crisis, the address was quickly dismissed. Republican opponents in 1980 revived the speech as evidence of Carter's leadership failures.

Crisis Speeches

The president is the focal point of the nation during times of crisis. The public turns to the president for leadership during difficult times, partly out of normal, practical considerations—the president is the political figure most familiar to most Americans—and partly out of a psychological need for the reassurance that strong leadership can provide.

The president's speech in times of crisis can mobilize the nation almost instantly. Franklin Roosevelt's call for war on the Axis powers in World War II after the bombing of Pearl Harbor, for example, dramatically changed the public's mood and willingness to get involved in a foreign war. Before the dramatic address to a joint session of Congress, the public and Congress were reluctant to enter the war; after the speech, public opinion favored all-out involvement.

John Kennedy's addresses on the failed invasion of the Bay of Pigs, confrontations with the Soviet Union over the status of Berlin, and the Cuban missile crisis were among the most dramatic speeches in modern history. Each suggested the possibility of apocalyptic confrontations. The youthful Kennedy was able to use the speeches to build confidence in his own leadership, even on occasions when his administration had failed, as at the Bay of Pigs.

Lyndon Johnson's first presidential address is another example of a major crisis speech. Both the traumatized Congress and the public watched the address not only for clues of Johnson's policy intentions but also for signs of the stability of the government five days after President Kennedy's assassination. Johnson and his aides worked on the speech almost without interruption throughout those five days and produced an address that reassured the nation of the government's stability and Johnson's own vigor. Johnson was able to outline his own legislative program while paying homage to the martyred Kennedy. "Let us continue," Johnson said, a reference to Kennedy's "Let us begin." [49]

Richard Nixon delivered a number of addresses on the Vietnam War and the Watergate affair, with mixed success. Nixon slowly developed a national consensus on the war and blunted opposition to his bombings of Laos and Cambodia.[50] Nixon was unable to convince the nation of his credibility on the Watergate affair, however. His many television speeches on the campaign scandal in fact produced more questions and criticisms than they answered.

Carter's "crisis of confidence" speech may fit in this category as well as the hortatory category. Other crisis speeches Carter delivered included his address on the Soviet invasion of Afghanistan, on the discovery of Soviet troops in Cuba, and on the American hostages in Iran.

The wide latitude that the public gives presidents during a crisis invites possible abuse of the crisis speech. President Johnson reported that North Vietnam had attacked U.S. ships without provocation in the Gulf of Tonkin and quickly won congressional approval of a resolution that granted him almost unlimited war powers. The evidence for the North Vietnamese attack, however, was questionable at best, as Johnson privately acknowledged. The crisis atmosphere created by Johnson's speech might have been the most important element in the growing U.S. involvement in the war.

The existence of a crisis gives the president an opportunity for rhetorical leadership but does not guarantee it.

Lyndon B. Johnson Library

Just five days after Kennedy's assassination, President Lyndon Johnson delivers a painstakingly worded speech to Congress. The address succeeded in reassuring the nation of its government's stability during a time of crisis.

President Carter's address after the Soviet invasion of Afghanistan eventually fueled the arguments of critics on both the left and the right that Carter was too naive and inexperienced to continue as president. Carter stated that the invasion fundamentally changed his perception of the nature of the Soviet Union.

Failure to give an address during a major crisis can undermine the president's support. Herbert Hoover's unpopularity after the Great Crash of 1929 is attributable not so much to his policies as his inability to convey a sense of national purpose and sympathy for the victims of the economic depression.

Addresses to Specific Groups

As the government has become more complex, and more interest groups have developed permanent ties to the government, the president has spent more time addressing specific groups. The purpose of such addresses often is nothing more than flattery. Whether delivered to faithful supporters or skeptical adversaries, such addresses are designed to create a feeling of awe with the presidency. These addresses often have some kind of appeal that is designed for media coverage.

The advantage of appearing before specific constituency groups is that remarks can be tailored to the group, and the president's words will be transmitted to the larger group membership for weeks after the speech. By merely accepting an invitation to address a particular group, a president tells the group that it is important.

Appearances before constituencies also enable the president to see how the group might behave during the "bargaining" process of budgetary, tax, and other current legislative matters. The president can then fine tune the White House approach on those issues. The National Association for the Advancement of Colored People (NAACP) provided presidents from Franklin Roosevelt on with strong signals about the civil rights initiatives it would find meaningful.

Perhaps more important, the president also can use interest group appearances to line up support for policy initiatives. Presidents frequently appear before business and labor groups to seek backing for their economic programs. Carter tried to build support for his energy program and Panama Canal treaties with appearances before interest groups, but he was opposed by a well-financed cadre of conservatives.[51]

Business organizations are perhaps the most constantly courted in the constellation of interest groups. Presidents of both parties need support from business to pursue their economic and social policies. Some presidents—such as Franklin Roosevelt, Harry Truman, and John Kennedy—have publicly attacked business but eventually had to build support among business people.

Other groups to be courted depend on the president's base of support. Almost half of all presidential speeches by postwar presidents were minor, "targeted" appeals to specific constituencies. Most of these appeals take place in or around Washington, D.C., where national organizations are housed. Groups ranging from the AFL-CIO to the Moral Majority attract the sporadic attention of the president.

Government workers are one of the most important interest groups the president addresses. Especially when morale is low in departments, the president's words can provide a big lift. Speaking before government groups also enables the president to lay out policy positions in the sanctified arena of officialdom. Because the president's words are usually reported widely, the government audience provides an opportunity to talk not just about specific policies but about other issues as well. Jimmy Carter spoke to government workers on the morality of couples living together outside marriage.

As the leader of the national party, the president also delivers a number of partisan addresses. These appeals usually take place during important election campaigns. President Reagan, for example, was tireless in campaigning for Republican congressional and gubernatorial candidates in the 1980s. If a president is not popular, he is not asked to participate in other campaigns. Democratic candidates studiously avoided Carter in the 1980 campaign.

Appearances before groups also can distract them so the administration can pursue other priorities. Reagan used rhetoric to allay the concern of New Right organizations—who wanted immediate action on abortion, school prayer, and other social issues—during his tax and budget initiatives of 1981 and 1982. Reagan promoted state education reforms in a series of speeches in 1983 and 1984, diffusing pressure for national initiatives and spending increases.

Presidents often appear before skeptical groups to co-opt whatever opposition they might present and to portray themselves as leader of all the people. Good examples are Carter's appearances before the Veterans of Foreign Wars, and Reagan's speeches to the NAACP. Presidents sometimes deliberately even antagonize interest groups to solidify the alliances that have developed in opposition to those groups.[52]

The Imperative to Speak

Because the presidency is central to American politics, presidents are expected to offer authoritative opinions even on subjects about which they are ignorant or uncertain about an appropriate position. As presidents move past the first year or so of their term, the imperative to speak grows because they must shore up political standing after an inevitable decline.

Speech is an important strategic weapon for the president. The president usually enjoys a honeymoon period of six months to a year when Congress and the public are inclined to yield to presidential leadership on many important questions. Lyndon Johnson's Great Society legislation of 1965 and Ronald Reagan's budget- and tax-cutting initiatives of 1981 are notable examples.

After the initial period of good will, however, presidents begin to lose their initial appeal. The president is better known and develops disputes with more groups as the term progresses.

The president also must accept responsibility for many of the nation's problems previously blamed on Congress or a former president. Political scientist John E. Mueller has asserted that the longer the president is in office, the more a "coalition of minorities" develops grievances that cut the president's base of support.[53]

Presidents tend to increase their speechmaking considerably from the first to second years in office. For example, Carter delivered 282 speeches in his first year and 323 in his second year; Reagan delivered 211 in his first year and 344 in his second. As the reelection campaign nears, presidents give even more speeches. Ford increased the number of his speeches from 392 to 682 in the year of his reelection bid; the figures for Carter were 272 and 436; for Reagan, 384 and 421.[54]

Because presidents cannnot count on party machinery or congressional leadership for support, they turn to the public. Several presidents have appealed to the public "over the heads of Congress" when Congress has shown reluctance to go along with legislative initiatives. Carter's public statements on western water projects, the Panama Canal treaty, the nation's energy problems, relations with the Soviet Union, and economic problems all were intended to overcome resistance on Capitol Hill to unpopular programs.

The psychological demands of the presidency probably contribute to the tendency to speak often, as political scientist Bruce Buchanan has suggested. The combination of stress, deference from underlings, and the search for clear signs of success combine to push the president toward dramatic rhetoric.

Frustrated presidents search for scapegoats to pummel in public and improve their own relative standing and leverage over the political process.

The imperative to speak is self-generating. "Presidents have developed a rhetorical reflex, a tendency to resort to public suasion as an initial response to a political situation," Hart has written. Carter displayed the built-in push toward presidential speech. "Always he spoke, and the speaking justified its own continuance: if the coverage were favorable, it stood to reason that more speaking would generate even more flattering responses from the media; if the press disparaged him, more speaking would set matters right."[55]

If presidents need to go public to promote their political agendas, that does not mean they speak all the time about important policy issues. Much of the president's time is occupied with noncontroversial, almost trivial appearances, such as presentation of awards and proclamations of special days. Even if these talks appear trivial, they strengthen the president's public standing and symbolic hold on the nation and its different "publics."[56]

One of the reasons the president turns to rhetoric is the institutionalization of speech writing and public relations efforts in the White House. The president has a growing corps of aides who analyze the political situation and develop public campaigns for improving it.

The emergence of a public presidency presents dangers as well as opportunities for the chief executive. If the president is blamed by the media or the voters for problems, making regular appearances can aggravate rather than improve the president's position. The regular presence can serve as a constant reminder of the administration's failings.

Jimmy Carter suffered politically in 1980 because voters associated him with the Iranian hostage crisis, "stagflation," tense relations with the Soviet Union, and divided leadership in Washington. When Carter appeared on television or before groups, he struck many as tired and ineffectual.

The problem of "overexposure" did not begin with Carter. Both John Kennedy and Lyndon Johnson were criticized for speaking too much.

Presidents are in many ways trapped by their public utterances. Because the media record every public word, presidents must carefully weigh the effect of their statements and take care not to get caught in a tangle of contradictory remarks.

Critics of the "Rhetorical Presidency"

Critics of the new rhetorical style argue that it has led to confusion on the part of both the president and the public about the difference between political action and political speech. The president's dominance in politics also "crowds out" other legitimate actors and issues.[57]

When a presidential address or "photo opportunity" is treated as a meaningful political event, attention is diverted from the complicated process of policy making and implementation that is the substance of politics. Not only the public, but also the president, can be deceived about the state of government activity. Media coverage of speeches reinforces the notion that speech is tantamount to substantive action.

As political scientist Bruce Miroff has argued, the president's dominance in U.S. politics starves the political actors and issues not in the president's orbit. The president's "monopolization of public space," as Miroff put it, makes it difficult for citizens interested in an issue to pursue it. The president's public monopoly simplifies issues and distances politics from the average citizen; politics become a spectator sport. The citizen's "vicarious" relationship to important policy issues also reduces important policy decisions to a game. The suspense over Jimmy Carter's decision on whether to produce the B-1 bomber, for example, concerned the game-like political maneuvering and not the merits of the superbomber.[58]

Theodore J. Lowi has argued that the movement toward a rhetorical presidency has led to an "oversell" of specific policies that breeds disappointment. "Such are the president's channels of mass communication that he must simplify and dramatize his appeals, whether the communication deals with foreign policy, domestic policy, or something else again. Almost every initiative is given a public relations name. Every initiative has to be 'new and improved.'"[59] Simplifying and dramatizing policies removes them from their natural state of uncertainty and complexity—and produces frustration and cynicism when major improvements do not result.

Presidents have taken to more frequent speech partly to improve the chances of their legislative and other initiatives, but the link between the two has proved tenuous at best. Legislative success is no greater in the modern age of presidential talk than it was in previous periods of limited speech. Presidents Eisenhower, Kennedy, Johnson, and Nixon won close to three-quarters of their major tests in Congress while giving an average of 150 policy speeches a year between 1957 and 1972. Presidents Nixon, Ford, and Carter won less than 60 percent of the key issues between 1972 and 1979 while speaking more than 200 times a year.[60]

Increased presidential communications—not only speech but also written material—do not appear to have increased the understanding between the leaders and the led. Americans exhibit continued ignorance of most public policy issues despite the ubiquitous media and "teaching" of the president. Even more revealing, Americans tell pollsters that they feel increasingly ignored. Voters sense that politicians talk to them but do not listen.[61]

Presidential speechmaking also reduces the president's control over the job. Because presidents speak so often, they cannot possibly write or even contribute significantly to the drafting of speeches. The White House speech-writing corps drafts all the president's words. If presidents do not have to work on the complex ideas they present to the public, they are less likely to have a thorough and nuanced understanding of issues.

One authority has argued that the "scripted presidency" might have contributed to Reagan's decision to trade arms to Iran in exchange for the release of American hostages in Lebanon. "President Reagan's reliance on speechwriters and before them [movie] scriptwriters played a role in his disposition to accept information about the Iran/Contra dealings uncritically and to trust his aides to act in his best interest."[62]

Proponents of constant presidential talk say it brings the political process into the open. Because presidents are such compelling figures, what they say attracts wide attention and makes politics a more open affair. But presidents must be cautious because their remarks are so thoroughly covered. That caution can drain public politics of any meaningful content. The effect, ironically, is that open, public politics can drive important policy discussions underground. The tendency to "go public" is one result of the decline of party strength in Congress. Since World War II, the president and Congress have been from different parties under Eisenhower, Nixon, Ford, and Reagan. Even when the president's party controls Congress, support for specific policies must be developed issue by issue. Public support has therefore become a crucial tool to prod Congress.

The President and the Foreign Policy Debate

Every president since Theodore Roosevelt has traveled to foreign countries, but only since the Eisenhower administration have such trips become a regular part of the president's routine. Many of the trips have been related to diplomatic events, such as treaty negotiations, but most trips have been more for public relations.

The trips usually give the president a temporary lift in public opinion polls.[63] Longer trips—such as President Nixon's trip to China and President Reagan's trip to the Soviet Union—have a more permanent effect on the president's standing. More important than the brief surge in popularity, however, is the presentation of an image of the president as a statesman in charge of world affairs.

Presidential travel once was considered a risky proposition with the voters. When President Eisenhower embarked on his first foreign trip, he felt obliged to explain the necessity for the trip in almost apologetic terms:

> Now, manifestly, there are many difficulties in the way of a president going abroad for a period, particularly while Congress is in session. He has many constitutional duties; he must be here to perform them. I am able to go on the trip only because of the generous cooperation of the political leaders in Congress of both political parties who have arranged their work so that my absence for a period will not interfere with the business of the government. On my part, I promised them that by a week from Sunday, on July 24th, I shall be back here ready to carry on my accustomed duties.[64]

The surges in public approval that followed Eisenhower's trip led him—and later presidents—to make travel a regular part of the job.[65]

The Importance of Foreign Policy Rhetoric

Control of foreign policy events has always been an important political "card" for the president. Especially since the United States became a world economic and military power at the turn of the century, presidents have been able to increase their prestige with military and diplomatic action. The public often defers to authorities because of its scant knowledge of foreign affairs, so presidents receive a boost in public support even when the action concerns an obscure nation or issue.

Presidents have been able to depend on foreign affairs to enhance their political stock even more than economic or social events because they are able to supersede temporarily the divisions engendered by the domestic struggle over "who gets what, when, and how." On foreign policy issues, the president acts for the nation as a whole, creating a situation in which "we" are acting, but domestic actions always create internal divisions. The president can argue that foreign policy involves outside threats to the security of all of the people and therefore requires a unified response.

The boost that the president gets from foreign policy is usually short-lived. Still, the president can use a series of foreign events and rhetoric about foreign policy to develop a general disposition among the public to defer to presidential leadership.

Foreign policy action can be a double-edged sword, however. If presidents do not appear to assert control over crises after the initial period of emergency, the public might develop suspicions about presidential expertise and control. Presidents also can lose on foreign policy if their actions create or aggravate internal divisions—usually by asking for difficult sacrifices of important domestic constituencies.

Presidents appeal not only to domestic audiences with foreign policy appearances and actions but to foreign audiences as well. By bolstering their prestige with foreign leaders and the foreign public, presidents can develop the kind of leeway necessary to conduct themselves in a wide variety of situations. Federal agencies such as the U.S. Information Agency and the Voice of America can be useful in the long-term propaganda battle with other nations.

Finally, the administration is able to exert a great deal of control over the foreign policy agenda with its control over information held in the federal bureaucracy. The president benefits from the huge operations of the public relations offices of the Pentagon, State Department, and Central Intelligence Agency. Through the power of classification, the president also can exert control over how much information journalists, scholars, and political activists have at their disposal.

Scholars have raised concerns about the effects of the executive's control over information. A constant tension exists between the democratic value of openness and the strategic value of secrecy. As the president speaks more and more in public, the president and government also hold more matters in secrecy. This development may be attributed to the need for different strategies to overcome and control a growing bureaucracy. Political scientist Francis E. Rourke has written:

> To be sure, the bureaucracy did not invent secrecy in American government. The Founding Fathers found it expedient to conduct the deliberations of the Constitutional Convention at Philadelphia in 1787 in private [and] presidents have, through the development of "executive

National Archives

Presidents have often appealed to foreign publics and their leaders to increase their political capital. In December 1918, Woodrow Wilson made a successful European tour to promote his postwar foreign policy agenda.

privilege," contributed a great deal to the secrecy surrounding executive activities.... But it remains true that the growth of bureaucracy in American government has brought about an enormous expansion in the secretiveness with which policy is made.[66]

The erection of a "national security state," critics have argued, gives the president almost dictatorial power over foreign affairs and even many areas of domestic policy. Presidents always can assert that "national security" requires withholding information.

Presidents clearly enjoy an important advantage in deciding what information they want released and how they want to do it. President Nixon's "secret" bombing of Cambodia in 1970 and his handling of the Watergate affair were both justified on the grounds of national-security requirements. The Reagan administration's refusal to allow reporters to witness the invasion of Grenada was based on similar claims. Perhaps more important is the routine information that presidents can keep secret.

Reaching Foreign Publics

American presidents have taken to public speech not only to speak over the heads of their own government, but also to speak directly to foreign publics. Presidents sometimes speak directly to other nations' populations to strengthen their negotiating positions with those nations' leaders. More often, presidents simply try to foster a more general good will abroad with their public appeals.

Some of the boldest appeals to foreign audiences took place during President Reagan's 1988 visit to Moscow. Reagan spoke to Soviet citizens on television during his trip and later met crowds with Soviet leader Mikhail Gorbachev at Red Square, an event televised to millions of homes in both the United States and the Soviet Union. Reagan was most outspoken at the University of Moscow. Standing before a huge Soviet flag and portrait of V. I. Lenin, Reagan challenged the nation to restructure political and economic institutions and praised the U.S. system.

Reagan spoke several times about the protests over the placement of American nuclear missiles on European soil. The U.S. missiles were strongly opposed by peace activists in Great Britain and West Germany, and Reagan alternately sought to win over opponents of the missiles and to undercut their legitimacy.

A speech at Normandy, France, commemorating the fortieth anniversary of the 1945 U.S. invasion was a dramatic statement of solidarity among Western nations and values. President Reagan spoke movingly of the soldiers who died in the invasion and their families and of the need for nations to avoid another world war.

Reagan's foreign appeals sometimes backfired. His trip to Bitburg, West Germany, in 1985 was intended to symbolize the development of ties between former World War II foes the United States and Germany. The visit was controversial from the time of its scheduling, however. The discovery that former officers of an elite Nazi brigade were buried in the Bitburg cemetery insulted Jews and others who had fought the Nazis. Reagan defended the trip by saying that German soldiers "were victims, just as surely as the victims in the concentration camps."[67] Despite calls for him to cancel the trip, Reagan went.

Presidential statements to foreign publics often take the form of threats. Presidents often talk about other nations' weapons buildups, terrorist actions, human rights problems, military actions, and trade policies. Although such statements often are intended for domestic consumption, they also offer flexible ways to communicate with other governments outside the normal channels of diplomacy. The president gives addresses to foreign bodies such as the United Nations (UN) and Organization of American States. These meetings are well-covered by media across the world, so they offer opportunities to address foreign publics. Because many nations practice censorship, presidents often try to embed their true message in larger statements that will be reported.

Even Reagan, who sharply criticized the UN, took advantage of the platform of the international body. His farewell speech in 1988 attempted to promote internal Soviet political reforms and arms control agreements. Reagan and his UN ambassadors used the body to criticize the Soviet Union, Nicaragua, and third world countries.

The president leads the world with words in other ways also. At summit meetings and economic conferences with foreign leaders, the president speaks for the nation on a wide variety of issues. The "news" from most conferences is that the leaders will try to cooperate in pursuit of common goals. But if a president can visibly "take charge," it helps to provide the authority the president needs in world affairs.

Presidents do not speak to other nations only through their own appearances and statements. The U.S. government includes a number of agencies designed to appeal to the "hearts and minds" of foreign peoples. The president's appointments for these agencies can put a distinctive mark on the way the rest of the world sees the United States.

The U.S. Information Agency promotes U.S. foreign policy through a variety of media, libraries, speakers, and programs. With 204 posts in 127 countries, the nation's chief propaganda agency operates a radio service called Voice of America (VOA). The VOA broadcasts 1,003 hours of news and other programs in forty-two languages each week. The State Department and Central Intelligence Agency also disseminate information to foreign nations.

An administration's policy on government information—what documents and information should be classified (that is, made secret) or made public—can have a profound effect on the nation's foreign policy.

Because the president is the commander in chief and controls a huge national security apparatus, the president has access to information about foreign affairs that people outside the government lack.

The president enjoys a huge advantage in the sheer size of the public relations operations of the government. The public information office of the Pentagon, for example, spends more money each year than the major news services. Especially considering that the wire services devote only a small part of their operations to foreign affairs, the Pentagon's public relations work gives the government an awesome advantage in communicating its point of view.

The Terms of Presidential Discourse

Besides dominating the political stage and tilting the balance of many specific public issues, the president's rhetoric has been important in shaping the way political issues are discussed. The president's prominence is crucial in establishing the terms of debate for other participants in the political system.

Many linguistic experts have argued that shaping the political vocabulary is the most important element in gaining public support for a wide range of policies. The president is perhaps the most important political figure in defining and creating a context for widely used terms such as *conservative, progress, liberalism, economic growth, national security,* and *free trade.* The meanings of such terms change over time, sometimes helping and sometimes hurting the presidents' ability to promote their agenda.

Even the most fundamental ideas in American political discourse are constantly changing. The rise and fall of terms like *people* and *interests* closely parallel the historical development of the nation and the evolution of the presidency. The regular public use of the word *interests,* for example, in the nation's early years was tied to the decline of notions of public virtue and the development of more competitive ideals of politics and society. Theodore Roosevelt and Woodrow Wilson, leaders of the national Progressive movement, used the rhetoric of interests both to decry what Roosevelt called "the ferocious, scrambling rush of an unregulated and purely individualistic industrialism" and to propose government remedies. The upshot was the "pluralistic" idea that a clash of interests managed by popular government would redound to the national interest.[68]

Political scientist Murray Edelman has argued that such words always have contradictory meanings. But because people have contradictory interests and beliefs, they need catch-all words that cover up the contradictions. These words help overcome "cognitive dissonance"—the unsettling feeling that comes with the realization that one's thoughts are contradictory. These words also provide enough "signposts," or guides, for people to get along in life without constantly having to assess their situations and alternatives.

An example of a self-contradictory word is *conservative,* which in U.S. politics is used to denote both stability (family, neighborhoods, local control) and turbulence (economic growth, mobility, exploration, and research). President William McKinley described his "Open Door" policy, which reduced trade and cultural barriers among nations, as conservative; although the policy augured unprecedented changes in world trade activities, it also was said to be the surest policy for maintaining traditional American values. President Reagan wove together the contradictory meanings of conservatism. His rhetoric and policies for "unleashing" the dynamic forces of capitalism contradicted his denunciations of the decay of traditional "values" and practices regarding religion, family life, sexual mores, and authority.

The complex and changing definitions of political words mean that presidents have wide latitude in shaping the way people talk about political issues at all levels of society. Presidents not only have a "bully pulpit" from which to promote their choices in important policies, as Theodore Roosevelt asserted, but also the ability to shape the way the population thinks about what those choices are in the first place.

David Green has chronicled the way twentieth-century presidents have used labels to give themselves a privileged position in policy debates. According to Green, presidents have attempted to use words like *progressive, liberal, isolationist,* and *conservative* to give their own actions greater legitimacy and to undercut the legitimacy of their opponents.

Franklin Roosevelt's presidency is a thorough case study of adapting, avoiding, and switching labels. Roosevelt avoided using the label *progressive* because it had connotations of confiscation for many members of the older generation. Roosevelt labeled his policies "liberal" and fended off attacks that his policies were "fascist," "socialist," and "communist." The liberal label connoted openness, generosity, and popular support. Roosevelt branded his opponents "conservative" and "reactionary." When it became apparent that the New Deal policies were not ending the Great Depression, Roosevelt stepped up his attacks on opponents, particularly business interests and the wealthy whom he called "economic royalists." Roosevelt went beyond the debate over domestic and economic policy with a move into international affairs. As the United States inched toward involvement in World War II, Roosevelt branded war opponents "isolationists," "appeaser fifth columnists," and "propagandists of fear" and linked those terms to his broader argument about reactionaries. Critics who questioned the war or specific tactics found themselves undercut.[69]

What goes around usually comes around in rhetoric. By the 1970s and 1980s, the word *liberal* was poison. President Reagan's constant labeling of Democrats as "tax and spend liberals" helped to make *liberal* the scarlet letter of politics in the 1980s. Politicians were so scared to identify themselves as liberal, because of the word's negative connotations, that pundits took to calling it the "L-word" as if it were profanity.

Twentieth-century presidents have tended to use catch-all phrases to describe their policy programs. Among the phrases are Square Deal (Theodore Roosevelt), New Freedom (Wilson), New Deal (Franklin Roosevelt), Fair Deal (Truman), New Frontier (Kennedy), Great Society (Johnson), New Foundation (Carter), and New Federalism (Nixon and Reagan). Such phrases can give the president's program a sense of coherence and completeness but also can create false expectations about what the president's policies can accomplish. Johnson's Great Society, for example, was a collection of relatively small and uncoordinated programs—many of which had no viable support system in the state and local governments where they were to be administered. The policies were prepared hurriedly, and funding was restricted before many of the programs were fully implemented.

David Zarefsky maintains that the potent rhetorical force of the Great Society label left the domestic programs vulnerable to attack: "The very choices of symbolism and argument which had aided the adoption of the program were instrumental in undermining its implementation and in weakening public support for its basic philosophy."[70]

Theodore Lowi has argued that the use of vague slogans and "sentiments" rather than precisely worded programs has corroded the entire U.S. political system.[71] The growth of national involvement in all areas of public life, and the need for the president to lead national efforts, not only breeds constant disappointment with the programs' results but also undermines the president's efforts to gain control of the federal leviathan. According to Lowi, the use of ringing slogans clearly has profound consequences for the government.

Speeches of Departing Presidents

Among the most prominent speeches of any presidency are the addresses delivered at the end of the administration. The farewell addresses of many presidents are remembered long after other speeches have been lost in the bog of presidential rhetoric. Speeches that former presidents deliver also gain prominence because they are so infrequent and because they depict politicians jousting to help determine their place in history.

George Washington delivered the first and most famous farewell address. Washington's most lasting advice to the country was to avoid becoming entangled in European alliances, which he predicted would sap the strength and resources from the young nation. Much of the speech was written by Alexander Hamilton, but Washington himself took an active hand in its drafting. Experts agree that the speech reflects Washington's values and character.

The most influential modern farewell address was Dwight Eisenhower's valedictory of 1961. He warned the nation against a "military-industrial complex" that he argued was starting to dominate the American system and could endanger democratic processes and liberties. Eisenhower said:

> We must never let the weight of this combination endanger our liberties or democratic processes. We should take nothing for granted. Only an alert and knowledgeable citizenry can compel the proper meshing of the huge industrial and military machinery of defense with our peaceful methods and goals, so that security and liberty may prosper together.[72]

Notes

1. Along with the explosion in presidential speechmaking is an explosion of research about the development. See Theodore Otto Windt, Jr., "Presidential Rhetoric: Definition of a Field of Study," *Presidential Studies Quarterly* 16 (Winter 1986): 102-116.
2. Roderick P. Hart, *The Sound of Leadership* (Chicago: University of Chicago Press, 1988), 1.
3. Kathleen Hall Jamieson, *Eloquence in an Electronic Age* (New York: Oxford University Press, 1988), 212-213.
4. Lloyd Grove, "Dukakis: If He Only Had a Heart," *Washington Post*, October 9, 1988, D1.
5. Richard E. Neustadt, *Presidential Power* (New York: Wiley, 1976).
6. Samuel Kernell, *Going Public: New Strategies of Presidential Leadership* (Washington, D.C.: CQ Press, 1986), 37.
7. Hart, *The Sound of Leadership*, 2.
8. Philip Abbott, "Do Presidents Talk Too Much? The Rhetorical Presidency and Its Alternative," *Presidential Studies Quarterly* 18 (Spring 1988): 335.
9. Hart, *The Sound of Leadership*, 5.
10. E. E. Schattschneider, *The Semisovereign People* (Hinsdale, Ill.: Dryden Press, 1975).
11. Hart, *The Sound of Leadership*, xix.
12. Murray Edelman, *The Symbolic Uses of Politics* (Urbana: University of Illinois Press, 1985), 96.
13. Jeffrey K. Tulis, *The Rhetorical Presidency* (Princeton, N.J.: Princeton University Press, 1987), 47-49.
14. Tulis, *The Rhetorical Presidency*, 51-55.
15. Michael E. McGerr, *The Decline of Popular Politics* (New York: Oxford University Press, 1986), 22-23.
16. Alexander Hamilton, *Federalist No. 71*, in *The Federalist Papers*, quoted in Tulis, *The Rhetorical Presidency*, 39.
17. Calvin Coolidge once commented on this practice: "At twelve thirty, the doors were opened and a long line passed by who wished merely to shake hands with the president. On one occasion, I shook hands with nineteen hundred in thirty-four minutes" (quoted in Gary King and Lyn Ragsdale, *The Elusive Executive: Discovering Statistical Patterns in the Presidency* [Washington, D.C.: CQ Press, 1988], 249).
18. Tulis, *The Rhetorical Presidency*, 63.
19. Ibid., 67, 64-65.
20. Ibid., 69.
21. Ibid., 67-68.
22. Ibid., 79-83.
23. Abbott, "Do Presidents Talk Too Much?" 333-334.
24. Tulis, *The Rhetorical Presidency*, 87-93.
25. Ibid., 88.
26. Ibid., 86.
27. Elmer Cornwell, *Presidential Leadership of Public Opinion* (Bloomington: Indiana University Press, 1965), 24-25.
28. Quoted in Tulis, *The Rhetorical Presidency*, 131.
29. David Green, *Shaping Political Consciousness* (Ithaca, N.Y.: Cornell University Press, 1987), 81.
30. Theodore J. Lowi, *The Personal President* (Ithaca, N.Y.: Cornell University Press, 1985), 22-66.
31. Jamieson, *Eloquence in an Electronic Age*, 45-53.
32. Daniel J. Boorstin, *The Americans: The Democratic Experience* (New York: Random House, 1973), 475.
33. Hart, *The Sound of Leadership*, xix.
34. Kernell, *Going Public*, 22.
35. Hart, *The Sound of Leadership*, 11.
36. Ibid., 12-14; see also Jamieson, *Eloquence in an Electronic Age*, 165-201.
37. Hart, *The Sound of Leadership*, 36.
38. Theodore C. Sorensen, *Kennedy* (New York: Harper and Row, 1965), 346.
39. Herbert S. Parmet, *JFK: The Presidency of John F. Kennedy* (New York: Dial Press, 1983), 197.
40. Hart, *The Sound of Leadership*, 8. In calculating the total number of Ford's speeches, Hart counted all public occasions at which the president made remarks, including press conferences, dinners, and welcoming ceremonies.
41. Jamieson, *Eloquence in an Electronic Age*, 182-200.
42. Kathleen Hall Jamieson contrasts the more awkward style of Johnson and Nixon with the casual, modest style of Reagan (ibid., 186-187). The media critic Mark Crispin Miller makes the same point: "Reagan is unfailingly attractive, not at all like a predator, nor, in fact, like anything other than what he seems—'a nice guy,' pure and simple.... We, too, should appreciate the spectacle, after all the bad performances we've suffered through for years: LBJ, abusing his dogs and exposing his belly; Richard Nixon, hunched and glistening like a cornered toad; Jimmy Carter, with his maudlin twang and interminable kin. While each of these men, appallingly, kept lunging at us from behind the mask of power, Reagan's face and mask are as one" (Mark Crispin Miller, *Boxed In* [Evanston, Ill: Northwestern University Press, 1988], 82).
43. Kernell, *Going Public*, 87.
44. Ibid., 91.
45. Hart, *The Sound of Leadership*, 51.
46. Ibid., 50.
47. Ibid., 219-220.
48. Kernell, *Going Public*, 121.
49. Patricia D. Witherspoon, " 'Let Us Continue': The Rhetorical Initiation of Lyndon Johnson's Presidency," *Presidential Studies Quarterly* 17 (Summer 1987): 531-540.
50. Kernell, *Going Public*, 83.
51. Craig Allen Smith, "Leadership, Orientation, and Rhetorical Vision: Jimmy Carter, The 'New Right,' and the Panama Canal," *Presidential Studies Quarterly* 16 (Spring 1986): 317-328.

52. King and Ragsdale, *The Elusive Executive*, 255.
53. John E. Mueller, *War, Presidents, and Public Opinion* (New York: Wiley, 1973); Lowi, *The Personal President*, 11.
54. Hart, *The Sound of Leadership*, 8.
55. Ibid., 33.
56. Ibid., 19.
57. A good overview of the criticism of the trend is James W. Ceaser, Glen E. Thurow, Jeffrey Tulis, and Joseph M. Bessette, "The Rise of the Rhetorical Presidency," *Presidential Studies Quarterly* 11 (Spring 1981): 158-171. For a response, see Abbott, "Do Presidents Talk Too Much?"
58. Bruce Miroff, "Monopolizing the Public Space: The President as a Problem for Democratic Politics," in *Rethinking the Presidency*, ed. Thomas E. Cronin (Boston: Little, Brown, 1982), 226. See also Richard Sennett, *The Fall of Public Man* (New York: Vintage, 1974), 150-194, for an analysis of the way politics dominated by personalities affect discussion of complex issues.
59. Lowi, *The Personal President*, 170.
60. Hart, *The Sound of Leadership*, 32.
61. Ibid., 30.
62. Jamieson, *Eloquence in an Electronic Age*, 220-222.
63. Robert E. Darcy and Alvin Richman, "Presidential Travel and Public Opinion," *Presidential Studies Quarterly* 18 (Winter 1988): 85-90.
64. Hart, *The Sound of Leadership*, 58.
65. Kernell, *Going Public*, 97.
66. Francis E. Rourke, *Bureaucracy, Politics, and Public Policy* (Boston: Little, Brown, 1984), 155.
67. David I. Kertzer, *Ritual, Politics, and Power* (New Haven, Conn.: Yale University Press, 1988), 94.
68. Daniel T. Rodgers, *Contested Truths* (New York: Basic Books, 1987), 182.
69. Green, *Shaping Political Consciousness*, 119-163.
70. Quoted in Tulis, *The Rhetorical Presidency*, 172.
71. Theodore J. Lowi, *The End of Liberalism* (New York: Norton, 1979).
72. Dwight D. Eisenhower, "Farewell Address to the American People," in *Great Issues in American History: From Reconstruction to the Present Day, 1864-1969*, ed. Richard Hofstadter (New York: Vintage, 1969), 451.

Selected Bibliography

Green, David. *Shaping Political Consciousness*. Ithaca, N.Y.: Cornell University Press, 1987.

Hart, Roderick D. *The Sound of Leadership*. Chicago: University of Chicago Press, 1988.

Jamieson, Kathleen Hall. *Eloquence in an Electronic Age*. New York: Oxford University Press, 1988.

Kernell, Samuel. *Going Public: New Strategies of Presidential Leadership*. Washington, D.C.: CQ Press, 1986.

King, Gary, and Lyn Ragsdale. *The Elusive Executive: Discovering Statistical Patterns in the Presidency*. Washington, D.C.: CQ Press, 1988.

Tulis, Jeffrey. *The Rhetorical Presidency*. Princeton, N.J.: Princeton University Press, 1984.

Windt, Theodore Otto, Jr. "Presidential Rhetoric: Definition of a Field of Study." *Presidential Studies Quarterly* 16 (Winter 1986): 102-116.

Index